AMERICAN POLICY TOWARD COMMUNIST CHINA

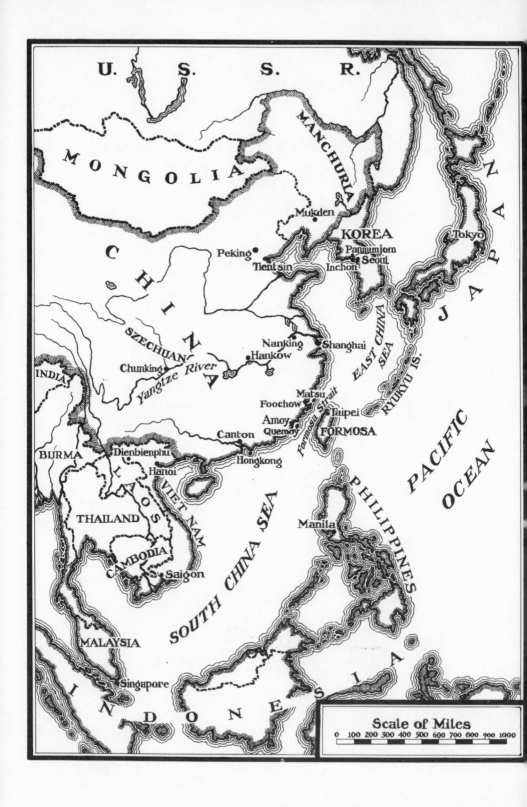

AMERICAN POLICY
TOWARD
COMMUNIST
CHINA
1949–1969

Foster Rhea Dulles

FOREWORD BY
John K. Fairbank

Director, East Asian Research Center, Harvard University

THOMAS Y. CROWELL COMPANY
New York   Established 1834

Map by Frank Dorn

Manufactured in the United States of America

L.C. Card 70-184974

ISBN 0-690-07612-6 (trade)
0-690-07613-4 (text)

2 3 4 5 6 7 8 9 10

Foreword

FOSTER RHEA DULLES made himself an expert on summarizing the evolution of American public attitudes and policies toward China. This book, which he finished before his death in September 1970, is the most succinct and readable account that we yet have of the trends of feeling and opinion that formed our China policy in the era of the Cold War.

In the new climate of opinion after 1971, the Cold War has been left behind, and instead of a Manichean struggle of the good free world against the evil of international Communism we now confront a multipower world in which peace and security seem attainable for mankind, as it seemed in Europe after the French Revolution, only through a concert of powers. The world has turned a corner. We now are seeking contact with the Chinese people and a modus vivendi with their government. This makes it all the more necessary to understand the Cold War climate of opinion from which we have emerged. The younger generation in both China and America have grown up in it, and many vestiges of the Cold War hostility still remain. Indeed, opinion in the United States has probably shifted more than it has abroad. On no subject do we need perspective more than on our recent past of the 1950s and '60s in Sino-American relations.

For the new generation it is of course easy to shrug off the foibles of their predecessors and to castigate fools and knaves among us. Any serious student, however, will try to appreciate the twin forces of Stalinism abroad and McCarthyism at home, which epitomized the Cold War confrontation. Except in China, the crimes of Stalin, who dictated the murder of so many millions of his countrymen, are an old story. But Soviet writers today are still being victimized by his latter-day followers among the secret police. In American annals, the senator from Wisconsin shines evilly in the record

/ v

as a master of demagogic opportunism. But he too has his recent imitators, who may ride again if opportunity allows. This similarity of function may be noted without subscribing to the simplistic relativism that sees Joe McCarthy's brief antics in the United States as somehow equivalent to Joe Stalin's long-term and murderous despotism in the Soviet Union.

One particular merit of Foster Rhea Dulles's survey of the record is his demonstration of how the evil genius of McCarthyism inevitably swayed the policy makers in the State Department. He first distinguishes between the China *lobby*, that group of zealous protagonists of the Nationalist government, mostly private citizens, who were aided by the Chinese embassy in Washington, and the China *bloc*, made up of senators and congressmen, among whom Richard Nixon was an early member. The China bloc were mainly conservative Republicans who were thoroughly frustrated by Truman's unexpected election victory of 1948 and convinced that the Democratic administration was soft on Communism at home and abroad. The China bloc, though generally isolationist toward Europe, were interventionist toward Asia. Asia Firsters, they committed their faith to Chiang Kai-shek, and during the period of the fall of the Kuomintang and the Korean war they led the way in creating the atmosphere of outraged suspicion in which Joe McCarthy found his opportunity. In the end, McCarthy was repudiated as a wild extremist, but the fear of Communist evil that he had exploited remained the prime mover in American policy. With the inauguration of Eisenhower in 1952, the Far Eastern policy constructed by John Foster Dulles and his Assistant Secretary Walter Robertson, a Richmond banker of similarly closed conviction, took on the character of a crusade.

Since Mao Tse-tung's revolution was equally a crusade and aimed to get rid of the American influence in China, Sino-American hostility was mutually reinforced by a whole succession of incidents and statements on either side. We were offered hostility, and we also asked for it. The occasional conciliatory gestures of either party were ineffective. It is no doubt typical of such conflicts, as it is in interpersonal relations, that each side continues to feel for a long time afterward that it was right and the other side wrong. This is the kind of righteousness that historians have to chip away at.

Foster Rhea Dulles, though a cousin of John Foster, presents a record of the latter's pronouncements that clearly portrays his ideological zealotry. Where Truman and Acheson under the prompting of General Marshall had disengaged from the Chinese revolution and made no commitment to Chiang Kai-shek on Taiwan in 1949, their militant confrontation with Stalinism in Europe led them to accept the challenge of the Korean invasion and extend the Cold War to all the western Pacific in 1950. The resumption of relations with the Nationalist government precipitated by the Korean crisis then led to the American military alliance of 1954 and cooperation with the Nationalists in a bellicose confrontation with the People's Republic.

The American posture in the confrontation with China sprang from both ideological and practical assumptions, and of course operated by interaction, each side moving to defend itself against the dangers perceived in the other. Since it would be too much to hope that we can develop foreign policy in the 1970s without ideological and practical assumptions, it behooves us to study those that moved us in the preceding era.

Events have moved rapidly since Foster Rhea Dulles completed his manuscript. The sudden inauguration of people-to-people diplomacy through the visit of the American table-tennis players to Peking in April 1971 and President Nixon's burial of the Cold War era through the secret visit of Henry Kissinger to confer with Chou-En-lai in July 1971 quickly accelerated the trend described in the last chapter of this book. Foster Rhea Dulles's careful account of the trend of American policy through 1969 makes us realize what a long road back it is from Cold War to co-existence and to contact.

The recent disclosures of the Pentagon Papers and the flow of memoirs concerning Vietnam policy serve to underscore the various points in Mr. Dulles's account. Professor Allen S. Whiting has recently brought together the presumptive evidence that the bellicose posture and fulminations of Peking against American imperialism in the late 1950s were in part, and more than we realized at the time, responses to covert operations conducted by the CIA jointly with the Nationalist regime, for example, by air-dropping anti-Communist personnel into Tibet and supporting a secret war in Laos. Studies by Neville Maxwell and others of the Sino-Indian border conflict of 1962 have also made plain that China's posture on the Himalayan frontier was reactive rather than simply aggressive. In the aftermath of the Cultural Revolution of 1967–69, China's potential for waging a foreign war has been downgraded, and historical studies have tended to the view that China's expansionism in the past has been far less than that of European powers and has been confined largely to China's strategic realm in eastern Asia. Most of all, the recognition that the Sino-Soviet split stems from deep-lying national as well as ideological conflicts of interest has provided the sanction for American initiatives toward China in a multi-power world. Americans no longer enjoy the self-image of a super power, and this means they cannot take refuge in the simplicities of the Cold War era.

In Chinese studies also, new motifs have been developed in recent writings of which Mr. Dulles would have taken account. The American analysis of the late 1940s that China needed reform which Chiang Kai-shek refused to provide is now yielding to the recognition that the Chinese revolution had accumulated an urgency and inevitability that probably no reform program could have satisfied. In a way, these recent studies of the deep-seated malaise in Chinese society, of the necessity for mass mobilization and the participation of the farming populace in political life, all lend credence to Chiang Kai-shek's claim that reform would only feed the fire of rebellion. It seems more plain that he represented an old order that could not be remade with the same actors still on the scene; the reforms urged by sundry Americans could not perpetuate his power. It was far too late for reform to stave off revolution, and General Marshall's decision in 1946 to disengage from the Chinese mainland was the only feasible one.

Foster Rhea Dulles's background preparation for this book covered his whole working life. A Princeton graduate of 1921, he spent the next year in Peking for the *Christian Science Monitor* and then had ten years' experience as a journalist for the New York *Herald*, New York *Evening Post,* and other publications. By the time he shifted to a more academic career and took his doctorate at Columbia in 1940, he had already set his style as a writer of informed, usually brief, and always readable books on major public issues, particularly the history of our trans-Pacific relations. His popular account of an earlier era, *The Old China Trade,* was published in 1930 and its successor volume, *China and America,* in 1946. His books on American-Japanese and American-Russian relations summarized the vicissitudes of contact between these peoples. Not a researcher in archives, he was a felicitous and skilled expositor who put the record together for his fellow countrymen in a knowledgable and sophisticated way.

From this long background he came to view the American attitude toward China as peculiarly mind-bound, applying to a new scene the fixations inherited from an earlier time, often unfortunately reinforced by current fears. It is not an inspiring story, but as we go forward in the 1970s it plainly has a lesson for us. Excesses both of hope and of fear can lead us into unhappy conflicts, especially the American penchant to see good in certain protagonists abroad and evil in others. Our crusading zeal may have contributed much to the world, but it is time we saw in it the menace to peace that it also contains. Foster Rhea Dulles's formulations of American and Chinese motivations do not pretend to dig far below the surface, nor does he set himself up as a specialist on the Chinese revolution. His contribution lies rather in the fact that he has surveyed the record with a practiced eye and caught Congressman John F. Kennedy in an early Cold War posture and other American figures such as Robert A. Taft in characteristic pronouncements in favor of virtue and against Communist evil.

The author's warning comes through clear enough: the object of our fear and condemnation may change, but our righteousness is likely to march forward into the brambles and pitfalls of the future.

JOHN K. FAIRBANK

September 1971

Preface

THE PURPOSE of this book in simplest terms is to record the history of the relations between the United States and the People's Republic of China during the past twenty years. The story is an involved, controversial, and often exciting one that has great significance for the further evolution of American policy in the Far East.

I have quite consciously subordinated such other aspects of the Asiatic scene as a rising Japan, the war in Korea, the rivalries between Peking and Moscow, and the conflicts in Indochina to the major problem of Sino-American relations. To develop these related topics more fully was hardly practical within the framework of my narrative. And China remains, as it always has been, the key to the power structure in eastern Asia and a principal determinant of our own policies.

Since the triumph of the Communists in 1949, a militantly awakened China with expansive ambitions has directly challenged the historic position of the United States in eastern Asia. In our obsessive fears of international Communism we failed to realize in the 1950s the strength of nationalism within this new China, and basing our policy on containment, we did not realistically accept the full implications of those forces other than Communism that have been let loose in a revolutionary Asia. The rivalry and antagonism, the potential conflict that has for two decades divided the United States and the People's Republic of China, each accusing the other of a threatened imperialism, have thus given rise to the basic, underlying issues presently agitating the Far East upon whose ultimate solution rests future peace in the Pacific world.

Although drawing as far as possible upon primary source materials, which I have noted wherever feasible in the text and discussed more fully in the bibliographical notes, I have written for the general reader rather than the expert or specialist: my book is a historical narrative rather than a scholarly monograph.

I have incurred heavy debts to previous writers in the field of Sino-American relations, to colleagues and friends. But I have actually worked very independently, and in so doing have been deeply aware of the problems of interpretation and emphasis. Although making no attempt to hide my own views, I have tried to deal with this recent and controversial period with a reasonable objectivity: to let events and the principal actors speak for themselves.

F.R.D.

Dorset, Vermont
September 1970

Note

A LITTLE DIFFICULTY over place names: I have referred throughout the book to Peking rather than Peiping, even though the State Department until quite recently chose the latter designation for the capital of the People's Republic of China. I have generally used Formosa rather than Taiwan. The latter is of course the proper Chinese name for the island over which Chiang Kai-shek holds domain, but old associations have led us in this country, again until very recently, to use Formosa.

Contents

1

The Triumph
of the Chinese Communists

THROUGHOUT 1948 the news from China became every month more ominous. The Communists were all too clearly winning the fateful civil war against the Nationalists, which had broken out following the failure of the United States to avert the conflict by encouraging the formation of a coalition government. At year's end the forces of Mao Tse-tung held all Manchuria and a great part of northern China under their control. On January 1, 1949, Generalissimo Chiang Kai-shek, in a desperate effort to save something from the complete defeat that now appeared to have become inevitable, declared his willingness to open peace negotiations.

The negotiations got nowhere; the war went on. In mid-January, after sixty-five days of fierce fighting in blinding snow and rain, the great battle of Hwai-Hai, on the plains of Hsuchow in central China, ended in a further crushing defeat for the Nationalists and their loss of half a million men. This was the *coup de grâce* for Chiang's military power. During the weekend at the close of the month—in this country President Truman had been inaugurated for his unexpected second term and Dean Acheson was sworn in as his new Secretary of State—the momentum of disaster gathered further headway. The Communists captured Peking, forcing the capitulation of another 250,000 Nationalist troops, and farther to the south they were relentlessly driving ahead toward the Yangtze.

/ I

In the vain hope that his retirement might remove a possible barrier to renewed peace negotiations, Chiang Kai-shek made the gesture of relinquishing the presidency to his second in command, Vice-President Li Tsung-jen, but a scornful Mao Tse-tung derided any idea of ending hostilities short of the unconditional surrender of all the Nationalist forces. "A vast tragedy of unforeseeable consequences for the Western World is now taking place in China," the *New York Times* editorialized on January 24.

The next day a young veteran of the Pacific war whom the Massachusetts Democrats had sent to Congress three years earlier rose on the floor of the House immediately after the opening prayer to ask permission to address the chamber for one minute.

"Mr. Speaker," Representative John F. Kennedy declared, "over this weekend we have learned the extent of the disaster that has befallen China and the United States. The responsibility for the failure of our foreign policy in the Far East rests squarely with the White House and the Department of State. . . . This House must now assume the responsibility of preventing the onrushing tide of communism from engulfing all Asia."

It was Kennedy's thesis in his brief remarks, and in his further elaboration in a speech a few days later in Salem, Massachusetts, that American insistence on a postwar truce and a unified government in China had been a "crippling blow" to the Nationalists and benefited only the Communists. Undue concern over the imperfections of the democratic system in China on the part of our diplomats and their advisers, he said, led the State Department to lose sight of the tremendous American stake in a non-Communist China. Our consequent policy of vacillation, uncertainty, and confusion was reaping the whirlwind. "This is the tragic story of China whose freedom we once fought to preserve," Kennedy somberly concluded. "What our young men had saved, our diplomats and our President have frittered away."

Kennedy's attitude reflected the sense of bewilderment, the pent-up frustrations, and the traumatic shock to which developments in China gave rise among those Americans who in the aftermath of the war against Japan were aware of events in the Far East. Our "loss of China," as it soon was to be called, came as an unbelievable disappointment to all hopes of peace and stability in eastern Asia.

Under the impact of the Cold War, the United States had vigorously built up the defenses against Communism in Europe. It provided economic and military aid to a threatened Greece and Turkey, helped shore up the faltering economy of our Western allies through adoption of the Marshall Plan, took a resolute stand in meeting the challenge of Soviet Russia's blockade of Berlin, and was about to sign the North Atlantic Treaty as a further bulwark against possible Communist aggression in the European theater. But this same Truman Administration, so active in the West, appeared to be standing passively aside in the East while the forces of Communism overran the vast territory of free China. How could this be explained, thought many Americans, other than by the abject failure of the policy makers in Washington to understand what was taking place or the indefensible "softness toward Communism" that in spite of everything being done to combat it in Europe somehow condoned its conquests in Asia.

These feelings were further exacerbated as the Chinese Communists continued to sweep ahead in the spring of 1949 on what became a six-hundred-mile front extending from the China Sea to far-off Szechuan. In mid-April their forces crossed the Yangtze—an American observer said it could have been defended with broomsticks if there had been the will to do so—and the ragged, unpaid, ill-fed Nationalist troops, their spirit wholly broken, melted away into the countryside. The Communists occupied Nanking, and closing in around Shanghai, trapped an additional 300,000 of that city's demoralized defenders.

With Generalissimo Chiang and President Li vying for political power rather than trying to consolidate the shattered Nationalist forces, only desultory fighting marked the summer months. Then, in what was the last phase of the mainland war, the Communists moved south and captured Canton, which according to a *New York Times* correspondent fell "with scarcely more than a sigh." Driving westward into Szechuan, they took Chungking and Chengtu against only sporadic resistance. The Nationalists fled finally to Formosa, where early in December they set up their capital at Taipei. Chiang Kai-shek soon afterward resumed the presidency, and stubbornly insisting that he would continue the anti-Communist struggle, promised to return to the mainland within two years.

In the meantime the victorious Communists had made Peking their capital, and on October 1, after a special Political Consultative Conference had adopted an organic law for their regime, they formally proclaimed the establishment of the People's Republic of China. Its authority theoretically rested on a popular front of all anti-Nationalist elements within China, but the hard core of the new government was Communist and ultimate authority rested securely in Communist hands. Mao Tse-tung was the unquestioned leader. The popular cult of this dedicated, tough-minded, self-willed Communist was already firmly established. His portrait hung everywhere and wall posters throughout Peking proclaimed "Mao Tse-tung! Mao Tse-tung! Mao Tse-tung!" The massed crowds in the capital had a new song:

> The sun is rising red in the East.
> China has brought forth a Mao Tse-tung.
> He labors for the welfare of the people.
> Aiyayo, he is the people's great Savior.

In the new regime Mao was Chairman of the Central People's Government, Chou En-lai was Premier and Foreign Minister, and General Chu Teh was commander of the People's Liberation Army—all veterans of the famous Long March of the mid-1930s and of the determined, persistent, and now successful campaign of the Communists to take over national power.

Peking at once asked for international recognition, which Soviet Russia unhesitatingly extended, but at the same time the Chinese asserted a militant antagonism toward the West. Seeking to consolidate the broadest popular support by appealing to the anti-foreign impulses of the Chinese people, recalling all the injustice China had suffered at the hands of the imperialistic powers throughout the nineteenth century, Chairman Mao stated that never again would China be "an insulted nation." He declared —and nothing more enhanced his status among his countrymen—an inflexible resolve to defend China's interests. The revolutionary propaganda of his regime singled out the United States as "the bastion of all the reactionary forces in the world."

With the implications of the Communist victory underscored by the aggressive attitude of China's new rulers, Americans generally were shocked by what had happened. Ignoring the revolutionary nationalistic movement sweeping over all Asia, which significantly underlay the victory of Communism in China, they could see in these frightening developments only another manifestation of "the international Communist conspiracy," which, they were convinced, was directed and engineered by Soviet Russia. In their immediate reaction to what they interpreted as a further Moscow-inspired challenge to the free world, they could hardly view the Far Eastern scene dispassionately. Moreover, many now felt that this threat to American interests in Asia could not have materialized unless even more sinister forces were at work in Washington than the casual disregard of our stake in a non-Communist China that Representative Kennedy singled out.

"I do not say our State Department is under Communist control," Senator Owen D. Brewster, Republican of Maine, generously conceded in a talk in Sacramento on February 11, 1949. "I do say that if Stalin had been in charge of our State Department, he could not have done a better job to secure the Communist penetration in China."

Senator Joseph McCarthy had not yet discovered China; he had not even discovered Communism. The stage was nevertheless being set for the charges and countercharges, the embittered political controversy, the angry recriminations that were henceforth to bedevil the formulation of a new and effective China policy to meet the harsh actualities of the changed Asian world.

The conflict that has developed between the United States and Communist China since 1949, leading to such dangerous confrontations in Korea, Formosa, and Indochina, has many political, ideological, and emotional ramifications. It has involved all of Asia, our relations with our Western allies, and the whole course of postwar history. Underlying all else, regardless of ideology, has been the rise of a formidable new China determined to restore the power and influence of the Middle Kingdom as the arbiter of Asia's destiny. The United States has found itself faced with a revived challenge to its own historic ambition to play a vital role in the affairs of the Far East.

Our response to this challenge has been governed by a firm resolve to contain any further expansion of Communist China's power and to safeguard American interests at all costs. However, this response has in many ways been shaped by myths and misunderstandings growing out of the past course of Sino-American relations, which have often blinded both the American people and their government to Far Eastern realities.

2

Myth and Reality

"OUR RELATIONSHIP WITH CHINA," John Foster Dulles said in a speech at the United Nations in late 1950 before becoming Secretary of State, "is primarily based upon a long background of religious, cultural and humanitarian association. . . . There is a foundation, and we believe a stable and lasting foundation, of friendship between the people of China and the people of the United States. . . . History will never judge that we have been motivated by anything other than a desire to serve what we honestly believe to be the welfare of the Chinese people."

In these rather complacent statements, the man who was to play such an important role in the further development of our China policy was expressing a point of view shared by most Americans. And in the light of such an interpretation of the past, it was little wonder they could not comprehend how China could possibly have accepted Communism, broken away from the West, and turned so fiercely against the United States. How could the foundations of our historic friendship prove so fragile? How could the reservoir of good will built up over so many years be so suddenly exhausted?

Our policies toward China have not been so highminded, so oblivious of the pragmatic issues of trade and power politics, as the future Secretary of State claimed. They have been based on what has been judged to be the national interest. Although the United States has often shown an appreciation of what might also be in the interests of China, this by no means has invariably been the case, but occurred only when those interests conformed to our own. Moreover, any idea that the Chinese have always accepted American policy as being motivated by generous impulses and consequently felt eternally grateful toward the United States is equally fallacious. They have always been skeptical, and often highly critical. "The Chinese behind their polite exterior," John King Fairbank, director of the East Asian Research Center at Harvard University, has written in notable understatement, "did not always share our national enthusiasm for Sino-American friendship."

The United States has never been exempt from the basic and continuing anti-foreign feelings that have characterized China's attitude toward the outside world down through the long years of the past. Wholly apart from today's conflict between Communism and democracy, the clash of two antithetical economic and political systems, is the traditional Chinese resentment of the West—an anti-imperialism that has always been directed against this country as well as the European powers. This has been a stronger force than the surface ties of friendship. A great deal in the past helps to explain why the Communists were so successful in 1949 in arousing in the Chinese people an almost fanatic hostility toward the United States.

Nor were the Chinese Communists breaking new ground when they turned away from the United States and other Western powers to seek aid from Soviet Russia in the immense task of creating a new China through the modernization of its economy and the strengthening of its military power. The government set up after the first Chinese revolution, which in 1911 overthrew the Manchu dynasty, despaired of help from the West. During the period of warlordism in the 1920s, Sun Yat-sen sought in vain for American or European aid to support his regime in Canton. "We no longer look to the western powers," he finally said in December 1923. "Our faces are turned toward Russia."

When the Kuomintang—the Nationalist Party—came into power five years later under Chiang Kai-shek's leadership, the new government also made no effort to align itself with the West. In seeking to create a sense of national unity, it on the contrary did everything possible to fan the flames of Chinese chauvinism. In writing China's Destiny, Chiang Kai-shek blamed all China's ills on the intrusion of the foreigners who had reduced the country to a semi-colonial status. He made no exception of the United States when he called upon the Chinese to throw off alien bonds and assert their independence. Had the Nationalists remained in power, their antagonistic attitude, for all our protestations of friendship, might well have led them to adopt policies as much in conflict with American interests in eastern Asia as the policies the Communists have pursued.

George F. Kennan testified to this possibility at a hearing of the Senate Foreign Relations Committee in 1966. "There have been very few of the troubles we have been having in the last few years," he said, "which we would not have had with any other Chinese regime."

America's historical interest in China has been primarily in trade and commerce rather than in the welfare of the Chinese people. Ever since a little 260-ton New York privateer, renamed the *Empress of China*, first carried the United States flag to Canton in 1784, the seemingly great potentialities of the China market exercised a magnetic attraction irresistibly drawing American merchants across the Pacific. Our great expectations have never been fully realized, but that has made little difference. The mythical lure of being able to sell vast quantities of American goods to what an enthusiastic writer in the 1930s happily called "four hundred million customers" has never lost its enduring appeal.

"How much of our tobacco," one Congressman declared in the early 1840s, "might be chewed there in place of opium!" A Senate committee a little later reported that by persuading the Chinese to substitute wheat for rice in their national diet, all the riches of the East would pour forth "in exchange for the products of the Mississippi Valley." Sanguine prospects for the development of the China trade were a significant factor in the westward drive to the Pacific Coast and our imperialist advance to the shores of Asia half a century later. Eloquently calling for the acquisition of the Philippines in 1898, Senator Albert J. Beveridge of Indiana emphasized that just beyond those islands were "China's illimitable markets."

At no time during these years did the China market absorb more than five percent of American exports, but no dream has been more persistent than that of its immense potential. This vision carried over into the twentieth century and influenced both our wartime and postwar China policy in the 1940s. Donald Nelson, chairman of the War Production Board, who was sent by President Franklin Roosevelt on a special Far Eastern mission, expressed his conviction that with China becoming the leading industrialized nation in the Orient at the war's end, "a market of enormous size should progressively open up for American export industries." Secretary of State Acheson referred to the possibilities of enhanced trade even in the midst of his difficulties in trying to work out a new

Far Eastern policy after 1949. American business interests, disregarding the political implications in dealing with a Communist state, reverted in the 1960s to the familiar theme that the United States could not afford to neglect the China market and took the lead in urging a normalization of relations with Peking in the interests of trade and commerce.

In its early efforts to develop and protect this trade, the United States, unlike the European powers, never attempted to wrest by force of arms any rights or privileges infringing on Chinese sovereignty. It rigorously insisted, however, that China should extend to this country whatever concessions it granted other nations. Americans were thereby able to enjoy all the commercial benefits and extraterritorial rights that England and France exacted through their military expeditions against the helpless and impotent Manchu rulers. The United States shared in foreign control over the Chinese tariff, maintained consular jurisdiction over its own citizens, and enjoyed the right to station gunboats in the Yangtze.

Granted that some of these extraterritorial rights were at the time justified, the treaties that the United States negotiated with China from the opening of Sino-American relations in 1844 to the close of the nineteenth century were quite as inequitable as those concluded by Great Britain, France, or Russia. We stood in the wings, affirming our desire to respect Chinese sovereignty, and then stepped forward to claim our share of the booty. Thus American policy toward China throughout the nineteenth century has been described as "hitch-hiking imperialism." Our self-serving moral platitudes only thinly disguised our zeal in maintaining our trade with China.

This was graphically illustrated when in 1858 an Anglo-French military expedition advanced on Peking to wrest new concessions from the harassed imperial government. The United States had no part in it, but the American minister, William B. Reed, followed on the heels of the allied forces in order to be in a position to insist on participating in whatever privileges Great Britain and France might obtain. When the allied forces bombarded the Taku forts at the entrance to the Peiho River, the American vessel conveying Reed merely stood aside while the forts were razed. Nor did the United States make any protest when on entering Peking in 1860 the British and French troops wantonly burned down the emperor's summer palace. And once again it shared the plunder in the form of still further extraterritorial concessions.

In reporting on these developments the imperial commissioner wrote the emperor voicing what was becoming a familiar complaint. "The English barbarians," he said, are "full of insidious schemes, uncontrollably fierce and imperious. The American nation does no more than follow in their direction."

Another compelling American interest in China supplementing our political and commercial ambitions was broadly represented by missionary enterprise. The United States very early developed a sense of responsibility to bring the Chinese into the fold of Christianity and to lead them along the paths of democracy. The missionaries first sought only religious converts, but through a multitude of educational activities they soon became equally engaged in trying to guide China in accepting American political ideals and institutions. The sincerity of this purpose admits of no question. John Foster Dulles was thinking primarily of missionary activities when he made the statement already quoted of America's constant desire to serve the welfare of the Chinese people and further affirmed that our relationship with China was "almost unique in its spiritual quality."

The broad sweep of this concern for China was attested by American generosity in supporting Christian missions, medical work, schools and colleges, and famine relief. Thousands upon thousands of Americans, in small towns as well as cities, identified themselves with the Chinese through their churches. Henry Stimson, Secretary of State in the 1930s, was later to bear witness to this in commenting that there was hardly a community in the entire country, especially in the Middle West, where the churches were not contributing to the expenses of a missionary in China. Whatever this may have meant for the Chinese, it created among Americans a sentimental, emotional feeling that has lastingly affected the popular attitude toward China.

And yet, however noble in purpose, this missionary enterprise was flawed, as in our promotion of trade and commerce, by the insistence that the United States should share all the fruits of European imperialism. In their passion to convert the Chinese and spread throughout the land the beneficent influence of Western progress, the missionaries were quite as energetic as the American merchants in demanding for themselves whatever privileges England or France won for their nationals through force of arms. Missionaries frequently played a decisive role in the negotiation of American treaties for the further elaboration of the special rights accorded foreigners living in China.

A case in point was the agreement in 1858. After the Anglo-French war the imperial government was forced to grant special privileges for missionary activity. One of the most prominent American missionaries, S. Wells Williams, played a major part in wringing these concessions from the reluctant Chinese, and he frankly stated in the course of the negotiations that nothing could be obtained "unless we stand in a menacing attitude toward them." Moreover, he subsequently acknowledged that had the imperial government's envoys fully realized the extent to which the so-called toleration clauses constituted a direct intervention in China's internal affairs, "they would never have signed one of them."

The missionaries were both the instigators and the beneficiaries of the Western campaign to open up the interior of China to foreigners. They were strong advocates of the "gunboat policy" whereby the powers enforced these privileges. The treaties embodying guarantees for the special position of missionaries in China had the effect, as Paul Varg has written in his illuminating *Missionaries, Chinese and Diplomats,* "of making the church a partner in Western imperialism."

Another factor in the relationship between the missionaries and the Chinese that militated against a reciprocal feeling of sympathy and friendship was the condescending attitude many of the gospel bearers displayed toward their possible converts. While the more tolerant missionaries liked and admired the Chinese, others, in their own pride of racial, religious, and cultural superiority, looked down disparagingly on "these heathen Chinese" whom they had come to guide toward a higher way of life. Williams had a real empathy for the Chinese, but he could still write that in dealing with the masses he felt exposed to "a kind of moral degradation of which an excessive statement can hardly be made, or an adequate conception hardly formed."

The Chinese gentry and intellectuals were quite aware of such attitudes. They especially resented the tendency of the missionaries to discredit and undermine China's traditional institutions in promoting Christian concepts and Western political ideals. In their basic conservatism they were stubbornly opposed to all alien influences and railed against the pervasive impact of the West on the Chinese way of life. Their position, it hardly need be said, stemmed from the ethnocentrism of a nation that always believed it had a far superior civilization to that of any other part of the world.

The scornful attitude of imperial China found classic expression in a letter the Emperor Ch'ien Lung addressed to King George III in 1793 after the failure of a British mission to open up diplomatic relations. "Now, O King," read this document, "you have again prepared a memorial and offerings. . . . Your reverent submission to Our person is manifest. Our Celestial dynasty which sways the wide world, attaches no value to the costly presents which are offered at Our Court; what we appreciate is the humble spirit of the offerers. We have commanded Our Viceroy to accept your tribute in order that your reverence may be duly recognized."

For all the intrusions of foreigners in later years, the traditions of the Middle Kingdom survived. In their pride and arrogance, the Chinese continued to want nothing from the West. The more progressive-minded might recognize the value of medical and educational contributions from abroad, and even acknowledge that the Americans were well intentioned in some of their other activities, but none of this allayed the historic anti-foreign sentiments of the Chinese people.

A wonderful example of how Americans clung to the comfortable idea of their generosity and allowed themselves to be persuaded that China appreciated such good will and reciprocated their friendship can be found in certain events of 1868. That year Anson Burlingame, who had been the United States minister in Peking for the previous seven years, was about to relinquish his post. Always sympathetic to the aspirations of the Chinese people, he was so zealous in assuring the imperial court of the American desire to safeguard China's political integrity that the Chinese asked him to lead a delegation abroad to seek revision of the unequal treaties. Burlingame undertook this mission with great enthusiasm. In a series of public addresses on his arrival in the United States he eloquently pleaded for closer relations with China and played endlessly on the theme that China was eager to broaden all possible contacts with the United States.

"She tells you that she is willing to trade with you, to buy of you, sell to you, to help you strike off shackles from trade," Burlingame declaimed. "She invites your merchants, she invites your missionaries. She tells the latter to plant the shining cross on every hill and in every valley."

It was a glowing vision; it evoked among Americans an immediate popular response. "What a grand spectacle," one enraptured Congressman declared, "to witness four hundred millions of China men, as it were, stopping in the long tide of centuries, resting on their oars and catching across the ocean the sounds of republican America, the hum of their machinery, the scream of their whistles, the roar of their trains, and all the multitudinous voices of progress, so familiar to us."

Our great mission in China, both commercial and religious, appeared in the light of such fervid oratory as on the eve of being gloriously fulfilled. Ancient China was about to cast off the thralldom of the past, accept a philosophy of progress, and follow American leadership in adapting itself to the modern world—into the hum of machinery and the roar of trains.

But what were the actualities on the far-distant Asian scene? The same year that found the lyrical Burlingame painting such an optimistic picture of conditions in China, his successor in Peking, J. Ross Browne, was candidly warning in his dispatches to Washington against the false idea that the mandarinate was grateful and happy over American commercial and missionary activities. "An impression seems to have gained in the United States," Browne wrote, "that the government of China is peculiarly friendly to our country, and that great advantages to our commerce are to accrue from this preference. . . . I need scarcely say that these anticipations are without foundation. The government of China may have preferences; but it has no regard for any foreign power. The dominant feeling is antipathy and distrust toward all who have come to disturb the administration of its domestic affairs." A short time later he wrote that since the United States had been the recipient of all the favors Great Britain and France had secured by force, the Chinese regarded the Americans as no more than "accomplices in the acts of hostility committed by those powers."

This antagonism toward all foreigners is further confirmed in a number of contemporary Chinese documents. For example, Grand Secretary Wo-jen, recalling the destruction of the emperor's summer palace ("How can we forget this enormity and this humiliation even for a single day?"), felt that the activities of the foreign barbarians were such a menace to the empire that he even opposed a school in foreign languages. "Should we spread further their influence," he asked, "and fan the flames?" And in another memorial to the throne, on which the dowager empress Tzu Hsi, herself the most formidable of anti-Westerners, cast the "sacred glance," the censor Wu K'o-tu wrote with utmost scorn of foreigners who "think only of profit, and with the meretricious hope of profit they beguile the Chinese people."

What later writers have often described as the historic love affair between the United States and China was already marked by a disconcerting gap between myth and reality.

Informed Chinese were also not unaware at the close of the nineteenth century that the American attitude toward the immigration of their countrymen rather contradicted our protestations of enduring friendship.

The United States at first welcomed Chinese immigrants, for the entirely practical reason that they provided an essential labor force in the building of the transcontinental railroads. Anson Burlingame himself concluded a treaty with Secretary of State William Henry Seward for their free entry into this country. When the great task of railroad building was completed, however, popular feeling toward the Chinese abruptly changed. As those living in the Far West, and especially in California, became an increasing drag on the labor market, workingmen and their political spokesmen insisted that in spite of the Burlingame treaty Chinese immigrants should be excluded. Furthering this campaign, the anti-immigration forces not only complained that the Chinese laborers were undercutting the wages of American workingmen, but viciously attacked them as a racially inferior and heathen people who could never be assimilated in American society.

An address that the state senate of California sent to Congress in 1876 declared that the Chinese living in this country "never discovered the differences between right and wrong, never ceased the worship of their idol gods, or advanced a step beyond the traditions of their native hive." Western newspapers constantly assailed them for immorality, gambling, opium smoking, and every other possible vice. Nor were the labor agitators content with such verbal assaults. Irate mobs in the western states frequently chased the Chinese through the streets, pelting them with stones and cutting off their pigtails. Sometimes they burned down their homes. In one tragic incident in Rock Springs, Wyoming, a gang of whites invaded the local Chinese quarter, killed twenty-eight of its residents, and injured another fifteen. These were the days that gave rise to the familiar expression "not a Chinaman's chance."

Responding to the pressures growing out of this anti-Chinese feeling, Congress progressively moved during the last quarter of the century to limit, suspend, and then wholly prohibit Chinese immigration without regard to existing treaty rights. It is a complicated story. Both President Rutherford B. Hayes and President James A. Garfield vetoed this legislation on the ground that it violated the Burlingame treaty, and the whole issue became deeply involved in domestic politics. In the end, however, Congress had its way. The United States followed an indefensible course in ignoring its commitments under international law.

The Peking government bitterly protested this lack of good faith, and its minister in Washington shrewdly pointed out that in bypassing its treaty obligations the United States was doing exactly what it charged against China when that country failed to provide adequate protection for foreigners. He declared that the congressional acts subverting the immigration clauses in the Sino-American treaty were "a violation of every principle of justice, reason and fairness between two friendly powers." The only difference in the situation as between China and the United States appeared to be that the Chinese had no gunboats sailing up the Mississippi or the Potomac to compel redress for their injuries. For a time diplomatic relations were virtually suspended. A violent anti-American campaign swept through the Chinese treaty ports, and trade associations in Shanghai and other cities instituted a widespread boycott of American imports.

The United States did not modify its policy. It continued to exclude the Chinese and to deny citizenship to those already in the country. Not until the exigencies of World War II underscored the importance of Chinese friendship did it finally move (the same year in which it also surrendered extraterritorial rights) to set up an immigration quota governing the admission of Chinese.

President Franklin D. Roosevelt stated that nations, like individuals, must be big enough to acknowledge mistakes and correct them. But this belated recognition of the wrong done China could not erase the past. The injustice of our immigration policy, with all its overtones of racial prejudice, always rankled in the minds of a proud, self-reliant people and left a lasting shadow.

What has more than anything else persuaded the American people that the attitude of the United States toward China has historically been more sympathetic than that of any other Western power is the popular interpretation of the Open Door policy. In his original notes setting forth this doctrine in September 1899, Secretary of State John Hay sought no more than international assurances of that equality in trade that had always been our objective in China. However, his declaration the next year that American policy was "to preserve Chinese territorial and administrative entity" had a broader and more generous significance. The rub lay in how far the United States was actually prepared to go in upholding this policy in its professed concern for China.

Secretary Hay made his famous pronouncements during the feverish anti-foreign upheaval of the Boxer Rebellion, when the legations in Peking were under shot and shell. American and European relief expeditions set out for their rescue. Hay's pledge was an attempt to exert such pressure as he could to prevent a possible partition of China among the European countries that had been scrambling for new concessions. "The various powers," lamented Empress Tzu Hsi, "cast upon us looks of tiger-like voracity, hustling each other in their endeavors to seize upon our innermost territories." For the sake of its own political and commercial stake in the Orient, the United States hoped to block these intrigues.

The American people ingenuously hailed Hay's notes as a magnificent stroke of diplomacy and a wonderful expression of the new-found power of the United States resulting from its victory in the Spanish-American war. Moreover, the Open Door policy helped to salve the national conscience. Deeply involved in our own imperialistic ventures in the Philippines, which found the United States fighting its first Asian war to suppress a nationalistic drive for freedom, this brave stand against European imperialism helped to cover over what we were doing to control our own Pacific colony.

It soon became apparent, however, that in adopting its new policy toward China the United States had no idea of upholding it by any forceful measures. The Open Door was vigorously sustained in theory; it won popular support almost comparable to that accorded the Monroe Doctrine. But in practice we persistently backed away from doing anything about it. As George Kennan has critically written, we were not prepared to admit that our intervention in the affairs of the Far East actually involved any responsibility for maintaining Chinese sovereignty, nor were we willing to use force to compel compliance with the principles underlying our policy.

Following the Boxer Rebellion and the intervention of the foreign powers, a weakened, impoverished, and restless China, in which the tides of change were slowly gathering new force, struggled to assert itself in the face of continued Western encroachments. But the moribund Manchu dynasty was too ineffectual to meet these challenges and institute the reforms that might enable China to build a modern state and win recognition of its independent position among the nations of the world. The possibly inevitable consequence was the revolution that in 1911 overthrew the imperial government and led to the establishment of a precarious republic designed by Sun Yat-sen along democratic lines.

This dramatic development awoke an immediate and enthusiastic response in the United States. President Woodrow Wilson hailed the Chinese revolution as "the most significant, if not the most momentous, event of our generation. With this movement and aspiration the American people are in profound sympathy." Yet in spite of this initial reaction and its own revolutionary traditions, the United States did not rush to recognize the Chinese republic or offer any assistance. It maintained for a time a careful neutrality between the imperial government in Peking and Sun Yat-sen's provisional republican regime in Nanking. Not until effective power was gathered in the hands of the emperor's former first minister, the very conservative Yuan Shih-kai, who replaced Sun as president and pledged himself to maintain order and respect foreign interests, did the United States, in May 1913, finally recognize the new republic. Thus sympathy for the Chinese was significantly tempered by concern for the protection of American loans, investments, and commercial rights.

The Chinese in these circumstances did not feel that the United States had gone out of its way in applying its professed sympathy for their aspirations, and our friendship was soon to be further suspect by events arising out of World War I. When Japan embarked on its initial attempt to establish dominant power over China through the infamous Twenty-One Demands, the Chinese government appealed to the United States for support. The Wilson Administration deplored Japan's action and reasserted its sympathy for Chinese independence, but this was all. "It would be quixotic in the extreme," Acting Secretary of State Robert Lansing stated, "to allow the question of China's territorial integrity to entangle the United States in international difficulties."

At the Paris Peace Conference in 1919 the United States again followed a wholly pragmatic course. In support of its interests China vigorously sought to recover control over Shantung, where Japan had taken over the special rights and privileges formerly asserted by Germany, and it also mounted a determined campaign for revision of the unequal treaties and for abolition of the foreign powers' extraterritorial rights. President Wilson felt unable to back China on these controversial issues because of what he considered the more imperative need to win universal acceptance of the League of Nations. He tried to reassure the Chinese that once the world organization was established, the opportunity would be at hand to redress the wrongs done their country. "Henceforth, for the first time," he said, "we shall have the opportunity to play effective friends to the great Chinese people, and I for one feel my pulses quicken and heart rejoice at the prospect."

This was cold comfort for China, whose leaders believed that the peace conference itself represented a unique opportunity to win recognition of China's independent status. The profoundly discouraged Chinese delegation refused to sign the Treaty of Versailles, and the American minister in Peking shortly reported a feeling among the Chinese of "indignation, discouragement and despair." They were convinced that the United States had let them down badly.

Two years later, at the Washington Conference for the Limitation of Armaments, the United States upheld China's cause by taking the lead for incorporating in a Nine Power Treaty the principle of Chinese territorial integrity, but it was no more willing than the European powers (or Japan) to revise the unequal treaties and surrender extraterritorial rights. For the Chinese a pledge to respect their independence appeared somewhat illusory so long as foreigners still held special privileges directly infringing on China's national sovereignty. The powers agreed to review the whole situation and to take up at a future conference the crucial issue of tariff autonomy, but once again vague promises were substituted for effective action.

The view that for all its protestations of friendship, the United States had again failed China found some expression in this country. Senator William E. Borah declared that the Nine Power Treaty should not be considered as "acquiescence in the wrongs which have already been committed against China." Senator W. H. King criticized our negative attitude toward treaty revision "as an affront to China, a grave wrong committed against a foreign state and the honor and dignity of a great people." The United States, however, continued to drag its feet in helping China extricate itself from the entangling web of special privileges that foreign powers had been weaving around this harassed nation during the past century.

The chaotic conditions prevailing in China during these years following World War I provided some reason for this reluctance to surrender extraterritorial rights. All this was to change, however, with the rise of the Nationalists under the leadership of Chiang Kai-shek and the establishment in the mid-twenties of a new government at Nanking. More unified than it had been since the collapse of the empire, China was now able to insist with greater authority that all special privileges be surrendered. "The time has come," declared Nanking's foreign minister, "to speak to foreign imperialism in the language it understands." Accusing the Western powers of seeking to throttle China's freedom, the Nationalists appealed to anti-foreign sentiments throughout the nation in a hard-hitting campaign.

"Kuomintang political agents," read a contemporary account of these developments in the Boston *Globe*, "tour the country, organize locals, and arouse the whole people against the 'foreign devils' who deprive China of her ports, limit and collect tariffs, run gunboats up and down her rivers at will and live in the country under their own laws, not the laws of China."

This crusade was directed as much against the missionaries as against other foreign elements. Writing a good many years later, Pearl Buck recalled her father, for many years a missionary in China, expressing his deep concern over this steady build-up of anti-Western feelings among the Chinese. When she spoke of how much good the Americans were doing and suggested that they would not suffer from this ill will, he was very skeptical. The American missionaries had come to China without invitation and only from their own sense of duty, he said, and consequently the Chinese did not owe them anything. Moreover, he too pointed out that while the United States had never seized any special concessions, it had kept silent when other nations did so and had profited quite as much from the unequal treaties. "I don't think we shall escape when the day of reckoning comes," he predicted.

Although deeply disturbed over the anti-foreign outbreaks in the 1920s, the United States extended official recognition to the national government, reaffirmed its interest in the unity, independence, and prosperity of China, and stated its willingness to negotiate the explosive issue of extraterritorial rights. Newspaper editorials in this country generally called for restraint and moderation in seeking to safeguard American interests and favored reasonable concessions to the Nationalists' demands. "The friendship of the Chinese people," one spokesman in Congress said, "is more valuable to us than any extraterritorial or jurisdictional rights we now have."

The State Department reflected this desire to come to terms with China. It continued, however, to move with customary conservatism. Agreeing to grant full autonomy in the determination of tariff rates, it was less willing to give up extraterritorial rights. Their surrender was made dependent on the establishment of greater internal security within China and comparable action by the other powers.

This cautious approach did little to distinguish our policy from that of either Japan or the European states (Soviet Russia had already relinquished its extraterritorial rights), and visitors to China reported mounting antagonism toward America. The educator John Dewey wrote of this feeling in 1926 and warned his countrymen of their misconceptions about Chinese attitudes. "The plain truth is," he said, "that while the United States wore with a flourish the mantle of China's guardian-protector, in fact it served China's national interests only when it seemed to serve American national interest to do so." We could expect no gratitude, he implied, for our supposed benevolence.

Lewis Gannett, writer and critic, also stressed at this time the difference between promise and performance in American policy. The United States might be doing many "nice things," he wrote in an article for the *Survey*, but it was not doing the one thing China wanted most—giving up its special privileges. "Thinking men in China," Gannett reported Chiang Kai-shek as telling him, "hate America more than they hate Japan. Japan talks to us in ultimatums; she says frankly she wants special privileges. . . . The Americans come to us with smiling faces and friendly talk, but in the end your government acts just like the Japanese."

When Japan invaded Manchuria in 1931 and set up the puppet state of Manchukuo, the Open Door policy and American friendship for China were put to their most critical test. The United States, however, was no more prepared than in the past to offer direct aid to China. Secretary of State Stimson favored the possible application of economic sanctions against the militaristic Tokyo government for its violation of China's sovereignty, but President Herbert Hoover was unwilling to take a step that might possibly lead to war. He adamantly opposed "the imposition of any kind of sanctions except purely public opinion." While most Americans felt the warmest sympathy for the Chinese, they went along with the President in wishing to avoid direct involvement in the Sino-Japanese conflict. The Nationalist government again saw this country passively standing aside. "The interest, although sympathetic," Madame Chiang Kai-shek wrote bitterly, "was as detached as that of spectators at a college football game cheering from the safety of the stand while taking no personal risk in the game themselves."

Yet in spite of this reluctance to come to China's defense or to become more directly involved in its troubles, Americans generally still felt the old sense of mission in furthering its economic, social, and political development. Pursuing what the Communists in rewriting the history of these days were to call "a sinister policy of cultural invasion," the United States wanted to see China develop along lines that would identify it ever more closely with Western civilization. Senator Kenneth S. Wherry of Nebraska once expressed precisely these feelings. "With God's help," Wherry told a receptive audience, "we will lift Shanghai up and up, ever up, until it is just like Kansas City."

The outbreak of World War II, leading to Japan's military occupation of a great part of China and its alliance with the Axis powers, gave a new complexion to events, which now directly threatened our whole position in the Far East. Then and only then was the United States prepared to intervene actively and make good its historic pledge to uphold the Open Door policy. President Roosevelt extended lend-lease aid to China on the ground that its defense had become vital to that of the United States. "China, through the Generalissimo Chiang Kai-shek," he declared, "asks our help. America has said that China shall have our help." Forgetting his earlier diatribes against this country in his hour of need, Chiang responded in kind. "The people of China," he said, "will be immeasurably heartened by your impressive reaffirmation of the will of the American people to assist them in their struggle for freedom from foreign domination."

When the Japanese attack on Pearl Harbor brought this country directly into the Pacific war, the United States and China became military allies and all the changes were rung on the myth of the historic friendship. Chinese interests now so closely conformed to American interests that we were willing to resort to arms in China's defense; the two countries stood side by side. In a joint statement by Vice-President Wallace and Generalissimo Chiang on the occasion of the former's visit to the Nationalists' wartime capital at Chungking, the two leaders declared that in their countries' common goal for a new era of peace in the Pacific, "it was assumed as axiomatic that essential to such a peace structure would be continuation of the ties of friendship that have characterized Chinese-American relations for over a century."

Evocations of the past increasingly influenced our policy In his ebullient sympathy for China as our new wartime partner, also affected perhaps by the fact that his forebears had played a significant role in the development of our trade with Canton, President Roosevelt was ready to go to almost any length in seeking to build upon the foundations of what was accepted as the long history of Sino-American good will. He not only took those steps that finally led to the surrender of extraterritorial rights and repeal of the old exclusion laws, but he undertook to guarantee China's new independent status by insisting that it should be recognized and accepted as one of the major powers. This was his policy at the Cairo Conference in 1943 when he met with Prime Minister Churchill and Generalissimo Chiang to set forth the Allies' war aims in the Pacific. It was also his purpose at the negotiations at Dumbarton Oaks, which bore significance hardly appreciated at the time, to allot China a permanent seat on the Security Council of the projected United Nations.

"Toward China we had two objectives," Secretary of State Cordell Hull wrote in his *Memoirs*. "The first was an effective joint prosecution of the war. The second was the recognition and building up of China as a major power entitled to rank with the three big Western Allies . . . both for the preparation of a postwar organization and the establishment of stability and prosperity in the Orient."

This was a highly idealistic goal. It clearly stemmed from the conviction that Sino-American friendship would continue as uninterrupted in the future as it was believed to have been in the past. In the romantic glow of our wartime alliance and our common victory over Japan, the United States expressed an abiding trust and confidence in China. It assumed a willingness on China's part to cooperate with the West in maintaining peace that neither the historical background nor existing circumstances really warranted. Completely ignored were the economic and military weakness of the government of Chiang Kai-shek, the incipient struggle between the Nationalists and the Communists, and the inherent hostility the Chinese had for so long harbored against the West.

A skeptical Churchill, forced by the demands of wartime unity to accept the program giving our Far Eastern ally great power status, was later to write that he "found the extraordinary significance of China in American minds, even at the top, strangely out of proportion." He could not accept the grandiose American view of China's future in either war or peace. "I said I would of course always be helpful and polite to the Chinese," the British Prime Minister reported telling President Roosevelt, ". . . but that he must not expect me to adopt what I felt was a wholly unreal standard of values."

Sentiment and emotion growing out of the comfortable beliefs of the past thus characterized to a remarkable extent our attitude toward China as the Pacific war came to an end. And so it was impossible for most Americans to understand how a supposedly friendly people whom they had helped so generously down through the years (all those contributions to saving their souls through the gospel and their bodies through famine relief!) could become almost overnight both Communists and anti-American. We had the embittered feeling, as another British statesman, Anthony Eden, wrote in his *Memoirs*, that "the Chinese had bitten the hand that fed them."

In this atmosphere a realistic understanding of the strength of the nationalistic and anti-imperialist forces within China or an objective approach to the problems raised by the Communist victory was almost impossible. Widespread credence was given to the conspiratorial theory that international Communism as plotted in Moscow, and somehow aided and abetted by leftist forces within our own State Department, was primarily responsible for the unhappy course of Asiatic events. To try to fix individual responsibility for the failure of our China policy rather than to see how we could compensate for this failure became a major preoccupation.

"We are swapping brickbats among ourselves," the Washington *Post* was to comment, "trying to purge and expiate and pass the buck instead of soberly seeking the lesson to American interests and applying it."

3

Background of Failure

No POSTWAR DEVELOPMENT has aroused more controversy, been more argued over and hotly disputed, than the causes and responsibility for the triumph of the Chinese Communists in 1949. Yet three basic factors stand out predominantly. Deeply suffering from the demoralizing effects of a protracted foreign war and intermittent civil strife, the Chinese people were restless and discontented, and deeply stirred by the nationalistic impulses affecting all Asia. The dictatorial Kuomintang regime under Chiang Kai-shek's authoritarian leadership failed to recognize the urgent need for internal reforms that alone could have enabled it to maintain popular support. The Chinese Communists, appealing primarily to the peasants, succeeded in riding the crest of a revolutionary movement not entirely of their own making but of which they skillfully took every advantage.

In the first phase of the earlier revolution that had brought the Chinese Nationalists into power in the mid-1920s, the Communist Party, which was already established in China and a member of the Comintern, cooperated through a Kuomintang-Communist coalition in Chiang Kai-shek's successful campaign against the northern warlords. But the Nationalists and Communists soon split apart. After a confused period of factional infighting, intrigues, and purges, Chiang Kai-shek in April 1927, having placed himself at the head of the right-wing elements, savagely purged the Kuomintang of all leftists and openly attacked the Communist forces.

A period of bloody warfare followed in which the Nationalists sought to cut down and isolate their foes, but the Communists maintained their revolutionary front and built up their forces in the mountainous area of Kiangsi. The Red army now came into being (it numbered some 10,000 in the spring of 1929) under General Chu Teh and with Mao Tse-tung its political commissar.

For the next several years the Nationalists conducted a series of "bandit suppression" campaigns that finally succeeded in reducing the area under Communist control and threatened to entrap the entire Red army. Then in the autumn of 1934 the Communists set out on the Long March, which led them a year later, after an epic fighting progress of six thousand miles, to distant Shensi Province in the far northwest, where they established their own regime with its capital at Yenan.

For a time during the Sino-Japanese war, which broke out in 1937, Nationalists and Communists again cooperated in presenting a united front to the common enemy. But their alliance was always an uneasy one, and could not succeed in reconciling their divergent and rival aims. After the American entry into the Pacific war in 1941, with its assurance of ultimate victory over Japan, both factions began to think of their postwar future. Rather than intensifying their attacks on the Japanese, they jockeyed for position in the prospective renewal of their basically irrepressible political and ideological conflict. Neither side entertained any idea other than establishing complete control over postwar China.

Confronted with this obscure and difficult situation, the United States was hard put to carry through its own wartime purpose of helping to bring about a unified, democratic, peace-loving China. "I have been working with two governments there," President Roosevelt told Edgar Snow, the noted correspondent, in February 1943, "and I intend to go on doing so until we can get them together." This also became President Harry S. Truman's policy after the close of the war against Japan. He continued to recognize and aid the Nationalist government, but he was also ready to deal with the Communists in the hope that the two factions could be brought together to establish a broader-based government that would unite the entire country.

Truman's instructions to the mission under General George C. Marshall that he sent to China in December 1945 were to try to bring about a cease-fire between the already warring Nationalists and Communists and encourage the formation of a coalition government in which all Chinese political parties would be represented. Even though this program was later to be violently criticized, conservatives as well as liberals generally supported it at the time. Even such a reactionary as Senator Brewster, who has already been quoted for a later intemperate attack on the State Department, said in July 1946 that "the Republican Party will go along with General Marshall in the Chinese situation." Nowhere was there any support at this time for attempting a more active intervention than this conciliatory mission in the interests of peace.

Ever since the war period, however, fundamental differences prevailed within official American circles, both in Washington and in China, over the political strength of the Nationalists and the nature and character of the Communists. This first came to the fore when General Patrick Hurley, who went to China as a special emissary of President Roosevelt in 1943 and stayed on as ambassador, became embroiled in a policy dispute with the foreign service officers in the field. Both General Hurley and the diplomatic career men accepted the national government as that of all China, but they differed over its ability to maintain public support. The former had great confidence in the regime under Chiang Kai-shek's strong leadership. The latter were convinced that it was rapidly losing all popular backing and was in effect politically bankrupt.

Even more important was a conflict of views over the position of the Communists. The ambassador and his advisers were very much at odds in their opinions on the Communists' strength on China's political stage. Hurley felt they were not strong enough to exercise a decisive influence; the diplomatic career men were sure they would do so.

From these opposing premises flowed sharp disagreement over how the United States could best promote China's national unity. Hurley believed that if we unconditionally supported Chiang he would be able to bring the Communists under control, while the men in the field maintained that only by making further aid dependent upon Chiang's carrying out an effective program of political, economic, and social rehabilitation would the Nationalists have any chance of maintaining their position. The latter were also further convinced—as Hurley was not—that Communist participation in a reorganized government would not militate against American interests. Such a broadened regime, they persuaded themselves, would gravitate toward the United States, seeking our traditional friendship. America, one of them wrote, would "by virtue of sympathy, position and economic resources . . . enjoy a greater influence in China than any other power."

One of the most prescient wartime analyses of the situation was that of John Paton Davies, the State Department adviser to General Joseph W.

Stilwell, who spoke out with a candor for which he was later to suffer dearly. Davies saw Chiang Kai-shek plunging China into civil war with "his dispirited shambling legions, his decadent corrupt bureaucracy, his political moralisms," and then suffering inevitable defeat at the hands of the Communists. He thought the United States should try to prevent this by peaceful means, encouraging the reform and revitalization of the Kuomintang, but should these efforts fail, it should seek some measure of cooperation with the Communists to induce them to adopt an independent position friendly to the United States. "The Communists are in China to stay," Davies said in a dispatch to Washington dated November 7, 1944. "And China's destiny is not Chiang's but theirs."

The policy makers in Washington in effect adopted one approach urged by the men in the field. A year later, after a series of conferences in Washington, President Truman instructed General Albert Wedemeyer, Commander of the United States Forces in China, to inform Chiang Kai-shek that no further aid would be forthcoming for military action against rebellious elements within Chinese territory. "The degree to which China has obtained political stability and security under a unified government representative of the people," General Wedemeyer told Chiang, "will be regarded as a fundamental condition governing the United States economic, military, and other forms of assistance."

Ambassador Hurley thereupon abruptly resigned. In doing so, on November 27, 1945, he angrily charged that the career officials had sabotaged his policy by deserting the Nationalists and siding with the Communists. "A considerable section of our State Department," he declared, "is endeavoring to support Communism generally as well as specifically in China."

In taking up under these circumstances his task of trying to avert a Chinese civil war by encouraging formation of a broader-based government, General Marshall faced insuperable difficulties. At first his mission appeared to meet with some success. It brought about a cease-fire and negotiations between the Nationalists and the Communists. Further developments, however, soon demonstrated that neither side was ready to make the concessions necessary for a coalition government. Unreasonably confident in the ultimate victory of the forces he commanded, Chiang Kai-shek had no intention of adopting reforms or limiting his own power; no less certain of the ultimate success of his cause, Mao Tse-tung was equally uncompromising. In comparable pride and insolence, neither man would give way in any important particular. By the close of 1946 General

Marshall had no alternative but to accept his mission's complete failure, and on January 6, 1947, President Truman announced his recall from China.

The Truman Administration had failed to take into account Chiang's unbending resolve to maintain the one-party dictatorship of the Kuomintang, Mao's firm determination to establish a Communist dictatorship, and the absence of any effective third force in providing a possible bridge between these contending factions. The assumption that the Nationalists and the Communists could be persuaded solely by diplomatic pressure to accept a democratic-oriented coalition government proved to be wholly illusory.

Truman saw nothing further he could do. Acknowledging the disappointment of earlier hopes, he stated that the United States continued to recognize the national government, that it hoped for a peaceful solution of its problems, and that it was pledged not to interfere in China's internal affairs. "Our position is clear," he said, covering over what still was far from clear. "While avoiding involvement in their civil strife, we will persevere with our policy of helping the Chinese people to bring about peace and economic recovery in their country."

As the civil war that the United States had been unable to prevent now broke out with redoubled fury, the Communists, as we have seen, swept on from victory to victory. Yet initially the forces of Chiang Kai-shek outnumbered those of Mao Tse-tung by perhaps as much as three to one, and they also had far superior military equipment, which had been supplied by the United States. The generalissimo and his commanders in the field were unable to profit from these advantages; they made a succession of strategic blunders that played irrevocably into the enemy's hands. Over and above everything else, however, what contributed most to the Nationalist military defeat was the steady erosion of morale among the troops themselves.

"No battle has been lost since my arrival due to lack of ammunition or equipment," Major General David Barr, who served as chief of the United States Joint Military Advisory Group attached to the Nationalists, reported on November 16, 1948. "Their military debacles in my opinion can be attributed to the world's worst leadership and many other morale destroying factors that lead to a complete loss of will to fight."

His views were supported by many other American observers who were deeply sympathetic with the Nationalist cause and strongly anti-Communist. General Wedemeyer had reported in 1947 on the demoralization within Nationalist ranks. Asked at a later congressional hearing for the reasons for their defeat, he could not have been more emphatic. "My military opinion on that, sir," Wedemeyer answered, "is lack of spirit, primarily lack of spirit." Ambassador John Leighton Stuart, who viewed what was happening in China most unhappily and remained loyal to Chiang, repeatedly stressed in his dispatches to Washington the inability of the Nationalist government to maintain any sort of élan among its troops. On the occasion of Nanking's capture he sadly contrasted the defeatist attitude of the defending forces with the Communists' disciplined behavior and high morale.

The disaffection of the Nationalist forces reflected the growing disillusionment of the Chinese people with the government they were being called upon to support. Its failure to meet the peasant's mounting demand for land distribution; its inability to control a disastrous inflation that reduced the value of the Chinese yuan to the vanishing point and impoverished both the middle classes and the urban poor; its inefficiency, nepotism, and flagrant corruption; and, finally, Chiang Kai-shek's stubborn insistence on personal rule all combined to turn virtually the entire populace against the Nationalist regime.

These feelings were inevitably communicated to the troops in the field. They found no support in the countryside or among the villagers. They accepted defeat. Many of them just faded away; others, carrying with them their guns and ammunition, deserted to the Communists.

The foreign service officers whom Ambassador Hurley charged with want of sympathy for the Nationalists are of course all on record testifying to the appalling failure of the government to sustain public confidence. To get a vivid picture of China's complete disorganization and breakdown under Chiang Kai-shek's rule one does not, however, have to rely on their highly controversial evidence. Other accounts are readily available.

On March 16, 1949, the United States Chamber of Commerce in Shanghai sent a revealing telegram to the State Department. It was a scathing indictment of "the military, civil and economic incompetence, or worse, of the Nationalist government," whose failure to provide adequately for the military forces was responsible for "the disintegration of any will to fight." In supporting this "decadent and ineffectual" regime, the Chamber of Commerce declared, the United States was not without a measure of truth being accused of being a party to the abandonment of a large part of China to the Communists. The Chinese people did not believe in Communism, the telegram continued, but "they are battered, beaten, and helpless—

accepting a fate they hate but feel cannot be worse than that which they have gone through the past four years."

This same month our consul general in Tientsin forwarded to Washington a memorandum from that city's Chamber of Commerce that took very much the same line in condemning the Nationalist regime. The consul general stated that the Americans in Tientsin felt that our global policy of opposing Communism, however warranted in other parts of the world, "should not oblige us to support a hopelessly corrupt government which has lost the support of its people."

The question may perhaps be raised whether the United States could not at some earlier point have exerted more effective pressure to compel Chiang Kai-shek to adopt the reforms that would have strengthened his position in combating Communism. But the situation had by 1949 become hopeless. The collapse in administration and the loss of public confidence were irreversible. As the United States Chamber of Commerce indicated, the Chinese people fatalistically accepted their "liberation" because they felt they had no other alternative. The Communists promised economic and political reforms, the distribution of land, and an end to the notorious corruption in government circles. Basically, however, they were moving into a vacuum created by the virtual disintegration of all government. As had occurred so many times in the history of the successive dynasties that had ruled China in the long past, the Nationalist regime had exhausted the "Mandate of Heaven" through its betrayal of the interests of the people and thereby left the way open to successful rebellion.

Many of those Americans who were later to deplore our failure to back up the Nationalists more actively recognized the inadequacies of Chiang's regime. Their position, however, was that "these imperfections of the democratic system" should not be allowed to influence American policy: reform was not our business. In accordance with what was the prevailing attitude during these years of the Cold War, the sole criterion of any government's eligibility for American support was an anti-Communist posture.

General Wedemeyer expressed this point of view most succinctly in meeting the charge that Chiang headed a reactionary, corrupt, and inefficient government. "If Chiang Kai-shek is a benevolent dictator . . . or whether he is a Democrat or a Republican, that is unimportant," he said. "The relevant and important facts are that the man has opposed Communism throughout his history."

These views were stated even more emphatically, both at the time and in subsequent years, by General Douglas MacArthur, Commander of the United States Forces in the Far East. He was convinced that the State Department had allowed the issue of internal reform to cloud the international aspects of the China problem, and in 1947 he was quoted as saying that this "may prove to be the greatest single blunder in the history of the United States." MacArthur firmly believed that a military victory had to be won over the Chinese Communists before any progress could be expected in domestic rehabilitation. He never contemplated direct American intervention, but he appeared to be certain that in spite of the demoralization within Nationalist ranks further aid on our part would somehow have enabled Chiang Kai-shek to turn the tide. The redoubtable general won many adherents. However, in the light of our later experiences in Vietnam, it may be doubted whether a single-minded concentration on a military victory in China, even if it could have been won, represented the best means for combating Communist penetration in Asia.

In spite of President Truman's statement at the close of 1946 that "our position is clear," American policy actually followed a highly ambiguous course during the civil war. We continued to recognize the national government and extended it substantial assistance. Between 1945 and 1949 this amounted to no less than $2 billion in economic and military aid. But in keeping with our pledge not to interfere in China's internal affairs, we held back from any more active support. General Marshall, who became Secretary of State on his return from China, remained unalterably opposed to any form of direct intervention. As the situation progressively deteriorated, the United States then began to curtail the assistance it was giving the Nationalists until it had almost—but not quite—broken off the close ties formerly maintained with them. Truman turned a deaf ear to the fervid pleas of Madame Chiang Kai-shek, visiting this country at the close of 1948, for a new pledge of $3 billion in aid over the next three years. Shortly afterward, additional cuts were made in the existing assistance program, and in January 1949 the Joint Military Advisory Group was officially withdrawn on orders of the Joint Chiefs of Staff.

It may be recalled that the climax of the strife between the Nationalists and the Communists coincided with the crisis of the Russian blockade in Berlin. In comparison with this threat to the Western allies in Europe, a Communist victory in China did not appear to weigh heavily enough in the scales to warrant the allocation of our limited military resources, resulting from the rapid postwar demobilization, on any all-out effort to try to rescue the Nationalists' failing cause. Washington not only felt it would be beyond our capacity but that more active support might prove disastrous to Chiang Kai-shek by identifying the Nationalists in Chinese eyes as the "running dogs" of imperialism.

As General Marshall explained American policy at the hearings held in 1951 by the Senate Armed Forces and Foreign Relations committees on the recall of General MacArthur from Korea, four factors dictated the decision against active intervention. "In view of our general world situation, our own military weakness, the global reaction to this situation, and my own knowledge out of that brief contact with China," he said, "we could not afford to commit this Government to such a procedure."

General Omar Bradley, chairman of the Joint Chiefs of Staff, held like views. He felt that it would be a great loss for the United States if Asia fell under the influence of the Soviet Union, but that it would not be as important as a comparable development in Europe. Moreover, Bradley specifically stated, he did not see any "apparently effective way that [we] can render assistance in Asia."

This was the situation when Truman's second administration commenced and Dean Acheson became Secretary of State. With the victory of the Chinese Communists seemingly assured, our policy to achieve peace and stability in eastern Asia had completely failed. The United States faced the hard question of how in these untoward circumstances American interests could best be protected.

4

Confusion
and Controversy

DEAN ACHESON accepted the basic approach that the Truman Administration had been following toward China under the guidance of both its diplomatic and military leaders. He was equally persuaded of the primacy of Europe and the undesirability of active intervention in Asia. As a former Undersecretary of State he had played a significant part in formulating earlier China policy. No one could have been more fully convinced in 1949 that any further military assistance to the Nationalists would only prolong a war already lost and arouse among a people desirous for peace a deep resentment against the United States.

The new Secretary of State found himself in a difficult situation. Important elements in Congress and among the general public who still favored continued assistance to the Nationalists were loath to accept a policy that they interpreted as abandoning China to the Communists before Chiang Kai-shek's cause was wholly lost. As the issue became increasingly involved in domestic politics and aroused ever stronger emotional reactions, Acheson came under violent personal attack by members of the Republican right wing. He was unreservedly opposed to Communism. He was a chief architect in the Western allies' successful stand in stemming the Soviet Union's threatened advance in Europe. Yet in spite of this, Acheson's assailants were to charge him with pro-Communist sympathies because he did not believe the United States should intervene in China in support of Chiang Kai-shek.

For all his experience and ability, Acheson was at a great disadvantage in trying to win over these political foes. He did not suffer fools gladly, and at times gave the distinct impression of placing all those who opposed him in this invidious category. His aristocratic and sophisticated bearing, the very way he dressed ("that goddamned floorwalker," as one irate Congressman described him), his air of aloof detachment, and his some-times condescending if not scornful attitude did little to win friends. The Republicans, who found the Democrats' ineffectual record in China a convenient club with which to belabor an administration they generally considered socialistic if not Communist-minded, took a huge delight in concentrating their attacks on the Secretary of State. They singled out his Far Eastern policies as a symbol of everything they opposed in the Truman Administration's conduct of affairs both at home and abroad.

A statement Acheson made only a month after he took charge of the State Department did not help matters. On February 24, 1949, some fifty-one Republican Congressmen sent the President a round-robin letter pro-testing what they called our inaction in China. They declared that a victory for the Communists would be "a monumental and historic de-feat" for the United States and would constitute "a grave threat to our national security." Acheson sought to explain and justify existing policy in an off-the-record meeting with thirty of the letter's signatories. Asked to predict the course of events, he then gave them "a weapon beyond their dreams," as he himself has written in his brilliant memoir, *Present at the Creation*, when he said that the next step the United States might take could not be foretold "until some of the dust and smoke of the disaster clears away."

The Nationalists were still battling the Communists; the war was not yet over. Acheson's seemingly defeatist statement incensed the Congress-men. According to the *New York Times*, Acheson left the meeting, bluntly saying, "We are getting nowhere," and, added the *Times* report, "That was how the Republicans felt about it too." Representative Robert Hale of Maine promptly brought the issue up in the House and roundly condemned the Secretary of State's position. Acheson's unpolitic state-ment continued to rankle. What was abbreviated as "letting the dust settle" became for his foes the label for what they considered his irre-sponsible attitude toward China's fate.

The Truman Administration was clearly anxious at this time to dis-engage itself completely from the civil war. Acheson's statement meant no more than that the United States wanted to maintain complete freedom of action until the course of events in China was further clarified. "Critics may call it 'appeasement,'" an article in *Newsweek* commented. "The State Department calls it 'realism.' The United States, it thinks, has no alternative except to make the best of a bad situation."

Liberal opinion fully approved this policy of standing aside. An editorial in the *New Republic* stridently attacked what it termed the "unparalleled arrogance, incompetence and corruption" of the Nationalist regime, said that Chiang Kai-shek had completely lost the confidence of the Chinese people, and castigated as "monstrous" the idea that he could be saved by more aid. Conservatives, however, were shocked by this attitude at a time —in February 1949—when some hope appeared to exist for fruitful negotiations between China's contending forces. The United States was in their opinion prejudging the outcome of the civil war; by its indifference it was pulling the rug out from under the Nationalists and opening the door still wider to Communist conquest.

Senator Arthur H. Vandenberg, the Republican leader from Michigan and an outstanding advocate of nonpartisan support for foreign policy, was one of the moderates in Congress deeply disturbed by the Truman Administration's program in China. He had few illusions about the Nationalists but even before Acheson's "Wait till the dust settles" statement, he expressed his belief that the United States could not simply retire to the sidelines. At a meeting of congressional leaders summoned by the President to consider a proposal from the National Security Council advocating the suspension of all export licenses for the further shipment of arms to China, he spoke up forcefully.

"If we take *this* step at this *fatefully* inept moment," Vandenburg said, as recorded in his diary on February 5, "we shall never be able to shake off the charge that *we* are the ones who gave poor China the final push into disaster. . . . I beg of you, at the very least, to postpone any such decision for a few more weeks until the China question is settled *by China* and *in China* and not by the *American Government in Washington*. . . . I make it plain that I have little hope for stopping the immediate Communist conquest. That is beside the point. I decline to be responsible for the *last push* which makes it possible."

His argument was persuasive. President Truman took no immediate action to suspend the export licenses.

The harsher critics of the Truman-Acheson policies were hardly content with such a minor concession. Senator Patrick McCarran of Nevada, a Democrat but closely associated with the more conservative Republi-

cans and an inveterate foe of the administration, soon afterward introduced a bill in the Senate to provide a direct loan of $1.5 billion to the
national government. Fifty senators, although they were not all committed to this proposal, joined in calling for its consideration.

With the full support of President Truman, Acheson sent a memorandum to Senator Tom Connally, the Democratic chairman of the Senate
Foreign Relations Committee, energetically rejecting this proposal in its
entirety. Pointing out the extent to which the situation in China had
deteriorated and the demonstrated inability of the Nationalists to with-
stand the further advance of the Communists, he reiterated his view that
conditions had become hopeless. To furnish solely military material and
advice would only prolong hostilities and the suffering of the Chinese
people, Acheson said; yet to furnish the military means for bringing about
a reversal in the situation would require the use of unpredictably large
United States armed forces in actual combat, which would be wholly
contrary to the national interest. "In these circumstances," he concluded
in direct reference to Senator McCarran's proposal, "the extension of as
much as $1.5 billion of credits to the Chinese Government . . . would
embark this Government on an undertaking the eventual cost of which
would be unpredictable but of great magnitude, and the outcome of
which would almost surely be catastrophic."

In the light of such adamant opposition on the part of the Secretary
of State, the Democratic-controlled Foreign Relations Committee held no
hearings on the McCarran bill and it consequently never reached the
Senate floor.

The Truman Administration nevertheless felt it essential to make some
conciliatory gesture toward its political foes because it needed Republican
votes to carry through its major program for European economic recovery. In order to assure passage of its pending mutual aid bill providing
funds for implementation of the Marshall Plan, Acheson consequently
agreed that a limited amount of aid might still be extended to the Nationalists from the unexpended funds of the China Aid Act of 1948. After
considerable political jockeying, Congress adopted on April 14 an amendment to the European recovery bill allocating $54 million to the "non-
Communist areas of China."

Four months later—the Communists had now breached the Yangtze
and were threatening Nanking—the Republicans made still another effort
to provide more assistance to the Nationalists. Senator William F. Knowland of California introduced an amendment to another foreign aid bill

that would have granted an additional $125 million to Chiang Kai-shek and set up a new American military mission to advise his government. The administration strongly opposed this measure, and the issue was fought out along partisan lines. In answering Knowland's fervid plea that the United States should not abandon Chiang, Senator Connally declared that the generalissimo had "already deserted his people in going to Formosa with $138,000,000 in gold in his pocket."

The Senate rejected the Knowland amendment. Once again, however, the administration needed Republican votes for its European program and therefore offered still another compromise in trying to placate the critics of its China policy. It agreed to an appropriation of $75 million for assistance in what was now designated as "the general area of China."

These appropriations, with their careful avoidance of any specific mention of the Nationalist government, were little more than propitiatory political gestures. They had little or no bearing on events in China. Yet the fact that the Truman Administration felt compelled to make such concessions was highly significant. They revealed that while the political opposition could not exert sufficient pressure to force an extension of military aid to the Nationalists, it nevertheless could block any program that might contemplate altogether breaking off our ties with them. A complete disengagement from the Chinese civil war was not politically feasible.

How the American people felt about this in 1949 cannot be accurately determined. However, in one poll conducted in September of that year by the American Institute of Public Opinion, 44 percent of those interviewed favored a hands-off policy in China as compared with only 25 percent who favored additional aid to the Nationalists. Thirty-one percent in this poll reported no opinion.

Throughout this period the controversial question of whether the Chinese Communists were agrarian reformers or authentic Marxists continued to agitate the country. The former concept did not die easily. Liberals clung to it in the belief that the Communists represented progressive forces within China dedicated to the welfare of the people. Conservatives were increasingly certain that the followers of Mao Tse-tung were not only committed Communists, but that in accepting Moscow's dictation were subjecting their country to Soviet Russia's political control.

The actual relationship between Peking and Moscow, whether as cooperating or rival agents in the practice and promotion of Communism, has always—whether in 1949 or in later years—been confusedly obscure. The students of Marxism, the Kremlinologists, and the Sinologues have endlessly disputed each twist and turn in the ideological and political vagaries that have characterized Sino-Russian relations over the past twenty years.

In the first stages of the revolution in China, the available evidence suggests that Stalin viewed with considerable mistrust the policies that Mao Tse-tung was following, and as the Pacific war drew to an end he did not think the time had yet come for the establishment of a Communist state in China. Believing that the immediate future lay with the Nationalists, he was prepared in 1945 not only to recognize their government but to conclude a treaty whereby in return for China's confirmation of the special rights and privileges that the United States had accorded Russia at the Yalta Conference, he agreed to extend both moral support and military aid to Chiang Kai-shek's regime "as the central government of China."

Ambassador Hurley, reporting on a conversation with V. M. Molotov in September 1944, quoted the Soviet foreign minister as saying that his government did not consider the Chinese Communists real Communists and would not support them. Subsequently Hurley said that after a conference with Stalin in April 1945 the Soviet leader told him that Russia subscribed to the policy the United States was following in upholding the national government under Chiang's leadership.

Even though Stalin may have lacked full confidence in the Chinese Communists at this point, these reports of the Soviet government's willingness to go along with American policy are certainly suspect. Molotov and Stalin were playing a more devious game. Averell Harriman, our ambassador at this time in Moscow, was highly critical of what he considered Hurley's over-optimistic account of his conversations with Russia's leaders. George Kennan, the minister-counselor, warned Washington in a special cable of the danger of any undue reliance on Soviet acquiescence in our China program. Whatever the uncertainties of Russian policy at this point (there was perhaps as much confusion in Moscow over what was happening in China as there was in Washington), changing circumstances fully justified Harriman's and Kennan's warnings. When the time came, Russia was more than ready to throw over Chiang Kai-shek and embrace Mao Tse-tung.

Although the Chinese Communists wore the badge of orthodoxy and acknowledged Moscow's socialist leadership, they nevertheless had always followed their own independent line. Mao Tse-tung based the revolution in China on the peasantry rather than the urban proletariat. While this program was so misread abroad as to give rise to the fallacious theory that the Chinese Communists were only agrarian reformers, it nevertheless underscored the extent to which Mao was prepared to go his own way in adapting Communism to China's needs.

He indicated this independent approach in an interview with Edgar Snow as early as 1936. "We are certainly not fighting for an emancipated China," Mao then said, "in order to turn the country over to Moscow." And in a speech nearly thirty years later, he complained that Stalin had tried to prevent the Chinese revolution and had advised Communist cooperation with the Nationalists. Mao Tse-tung was at no time blindly committed to the Kremlin's leadership in his unswerving drive to wrest power from the Nationalists and set up his own Communist dictatorship.

The natural ties between Communist China and Soviet Russia as socialist countries were nevertheless accentuated as the Chinese revolution approached its victorious climax. The Soviet Union gave substantial support to the new regime in Peking; the latter acknowledged this assistance and the importance of close Sino-Russian ties. Mao Tse-tung then gave the final blow to the West's persistent wishful thinking in respect to the Chinese Communists in an important speech on July 1, 1949—some three months before formal establishment of the People's Republic of China—entitled "On The People's Democratic Dictatorship."

In this pronouncement Mao stressed the unity of the socialist movement throughout the world and the interdependent relationship of all Communist parties. In seeking to obtain victory for their own revolution, he now told his countrymen, they had without exception to choose between leaning to the side of imperialism, as represented by Chiang Kai-shek and his Western adherents, or to the side of socialism, as represented by Soviet Russia. Neutrality was a camouflage; no third road was possible.

"In an era when imperialism still exists," Mao concluded, "it is impossible for a genuine people's revolution in any country to achieve victory without various forms of help from the international revolutionary forces. Even when victory is won, it cannot be made secure without such help."

This public affirmation that China had to lean to the side of socialism not only disposed of the myth that the Chinese Communists were agrarian reformers but also dispelled any lingering hopes that they would continue on their own independent course. The idea that Communist China might pursue a policy comparable to that on which Yugoslavia was embarking and develop a form of Asiatic "Titoism" was thrown away in the circumstances of 1949.

"Mao Tse-tung," *Life* magazine declared, reflecting general opinion in this country, "has shattered the illusion cherished by many Americans— the illusion that China's Communists are different."

A public which had harbored the comforting notion that the Chinese would have no part of the world Communist movement now swung over to the opposite extreme, viewing them as the helpless puppets of this international conspiracy centered in Moscow. Communist China was wholly controlled by the Soviet Union, according to this thesis, and Mao Tse-tung was the unwitting dupe of the Kremlin. This theory was accepted in high places as well as low in the fearful atmosphere of the Cold War; Soviet Russia was on the march. Although in some instances the policy makers in Washington were later to place a greater emphasis on China's own revolutionary spirit, almost all of them in 1949 stressed Russian expansionism in Asia. Dean Acheson stated that the Peking government was "serving the interests of a foreign imperialism." George Kennan, recently made head of the Policy Planning Committee of the State Department, said in a public broadcast that what was taking place in China was a catastrophe because the Communists were imposing on the Chinese people a disguised form of alien rule. Echoed in many quarters was Senator Knowland's repeated characterization, "the Soviet regime in China."

In subsequent testimony in his role as Secretary of Defense, General Marshall heavily accented during the MacArthur hearings the extent to which this interpretation of the situation in China was accepted by the Truman Administration. "Do you believe, General Marshall," Senator H. Alexander Smith of New Jersey asked him, "that what has happened in China is a conquest of that country by Soviet Russia, and there is consequently a control of China today by an external power, namely, Russia?" Marshall carefully answered, "I think that is generally a fact."

Although almost all popular commentators, editorial writers, and other contemporary observers accepted this analysis, some few tried to interpret events more objectively. In an important address before the Commonwealth Club in San Francisco, Roger D. Lapham, who had been chief of the Economic Cooperation Administration's mission in China, questioned the prevailing view that the Chinese Communists had sacrificed their independence by accepting Russian aid. He suggested that they might well turn out to be "more Chinese and anti-foreign than tools of Moscow."

Edgar Snow, whose interviews with Mao Tse-tung and other Communist leaders during the days of the Long March (described in his book *Red Star Over China*) gave him a special knowledge of their philosophy, refused to believe that the government they were setting up in Peking would turn China into a Russian satellite. Writing in the *Saturday Evening Post* for April 9, 1949, he emphasized the extreme "nation-consciousness" of the Chinese and predicted that "China will become the first Communist-run major country independent of Moscow's dictation." John Fairbank stressed the uniqueness of Chinese society and soberly warned that the greatest error Americans could make would be "to look at China but think only of Russian expansion."

These dissenting voices were few and far between. A considerable segment of the American people remained wholly ignorant of developments in China and did not even realize that it had accepted a Communist government. But public opinion polls revealed that those who followed the news in eastern Asia agreed with little question that in forswearing democracy and turning against the United States, China had fallen completely under Russian domination. For both policy makers and their congressional critics, this was the accepted approach in interpreting Far Eastern developments.

These misunderstandings were highly unfortunate in their influence on policy making. "We know now and should have known then, that the Chinese Communist movement was not effectively controlled by Moscow," Robert Blum has written in *The United States and China in World Affairs*. In his *Twentieth Century China*, O. Edmund Clubb, the last United States consul general in Peking, says that by no stretch of the imagination "could the new regime be termed a creation of the Kremlin." Yet hindsight is obviously a different thing from trying to assess what was actually happening in Asia in the emotional atmosphere of 1949. The obsession with the threat of international Communism, the feeling of insecurity born of the pressures of the Cold War, made it all too easy to see in events in China no more than a calculated move by the Soviet Union to carry its offensive against the West to another front.

As the Truman Administration, still far more concerned over combating Communism in Europe, waited throughout the spring and summer of 1949 for the dust to settle in China, the White House was flooded with letters and telegrams advising on future policy. Afraid that the United States might find itself on a collision course with the Communist regime in Peking, the Mothers Against War tersely telegraphed the President: "Please stop us." One White House correspondent proposed lending a couple of atomic bombs to Chiang Kai-shek; another suggested that we seek to promote peace by letting loose a barrage of "rice bombs" to feed a hungry people. Trade organizations called for prompt acceptance of the Peking regime and restoration of normal relations whether or not it was Communist-controlled, while patriotic societies condemned any dealings with it whatsoever. These letters and telegrams (which the White House "respectfully referred" to the State Department, as noted in the files of the Truman Library) may not have greatly helped the policy makers in Washington but they reflected a growing popular concern.

In order to clarify its attitude and, it was hoped, win a greater measure of support, the State Department early in August 1949 issued a White Paper relating the course of events in China over the preceding five years. Such a step had been proposed earlier, but General Marshall, while serving as Secretary of State, vetoed it on the ground that exposure of the Nationalist government's inefficiency and corruption might well prove to be the *coup de grâce* for Chiang Kai-shek. Secretary Acheson now decided to move ahead ("A plunge," he was to write later, "that ranks high among those that have caused me immediate, unexpected, and acute trouble"). In the light of the current situation—the Nationalists were everywhere in precipitate retreat and the Communists about to set up their new government in Peking—he felt it essential to explain to the American people why the United States could no longer afford to extend military aid to the Nationalists and had no alternative but to stand on the side lines. The White Paper included a multitude of dispatches in which foreign service officers and other diplomatic officials described and analyzed developments in China. Its most significant section, and that to which the newspapers naturally gave primary attention, was the Secretary of State's letter of transmittal.

Acheson emphasized the historic friendship of the United States and China, our efforts to avert the civil war, and the importance of the $2 billion in supplies and credits we had granted the national government since 1945. He pointed out that such aid had proved ineffectual. A large part of the military equipment furnished Chiang had fallen into Communist hands "through the ineptitude of the Nationalist leaders, their defections and surrenders, and the absence among their forces of the will to fight." Answering the criticism that the United States should nevertheless have provided even more aid, the Secretary of State declared that on the best information available to the government, this would not have saved the day.

One other course was open, he said: full-scale military intervention. But this, he reaffirmed, would have been resented by the masses of the Chinese, would have diametrically reversed our historic policy, and been condemned by the American people. The United States admittedly faced a very difficult situation, Acheson continued. The Communist leaders had forsworn their Chinese heritage and publicly announced their subservience to Russia. Whereas on other occasions we had been able to help the Chinese resist foreign intervention, it was in this instance masked behind the façade of a vast crusading movement and our aid proved unavailing.

"The unfortunate but inescapable fact," the Secretary of State concluded, "is that the ominous result of the civil war in China was beyond the control of the government of the United States. Nothing that this country did or could have done within the reasonable limit of its capabilities could have changed that result; nothing that was left undone by this country has contributed to it. It was the product of internal Chinese forces, forces which this country tried to influence but could not. A decision was arrived at within China, if only a decision by default."

While most students of the Far East would today agree that this is indeed the verdict of history, the tone of the White Paper lent itself to the criticism that its interpretation of events in China was little more than a self-serving justification of American policy; that it sought to gloss over any misjudgments or mistakes on the part of the State Department. The United States had been unable to achieve its postwar objective of restoring peace and stability in eastern Asia, yet Acheson nowhere admitted any possible errors in our dealings with either the Nationalists or the Communists in trying to bring about Chinese unity and preserve Sino-American friendship. The White Paper made out a very strong case, but it more closely resembled a lawyer's brief than a full and objective analysis of why our policy had failed.

It had a very mixed public reception. The *New York Times* warned that the complete disclaimer of any responsibility for what had happened in China obscured the truth and constituted "a gigantic and quite fatalistic blanket approval" of our entire Far Eastern policy. The San Francisco *Chronicle* characterized Acheson's statement as "a funeral sermon preached over the still living body of the Nationalist regime." The Baltimore *Sun* called it "a record of the frustration of good intentions."

Walter Lippmann in his widely published column took a quite different approach. He agreed that nothing in the record suggested that the United States should have given more aid to the Nationalists, but that on the contrary the information now made available raised the question of why the United States had gone as far as it had. The White Paper failed to explain, Lippmann wrote with significant bearing for the future as well as the past, "the causes and remedies for Chiang's stranglehold on American policy." Writing in the *New Republic*, John Fairbank denied that "this stark story of the biggest failure of history's most powerful nation" was self-justifying or face-saving. It was a frank admission, he said, "that we have made the wrong approach to the problem of revolution in Asia."

Whatever the varying tone of newspaper editorials and public commentators, the White Paper completely outraged the Republicans in Congress who thirsted for Acheson's blood. Seizing upon the Secretary of State's assertion that the outcome of the civil war was totally dependent on events within China, Senator H. Styles Bridges, Republican from New Hampshire, declared it quite the opposite: his reading of the State Department document more than ever convinced him "that the Chinese war was lost in Washington, not in China." Representative Walter Judd of Minnesota, the most vocal of Acheson's critics in the House, said that the evidence revealed that while the Nationalist leaders fully understood the grave nature of the worldwide Communist conspiracy as operative in Asia, the White Paper was "a confession that the leaders of our Government possessed no such understanding." In a statement reported in the *New York Times*, Senators Knowland, Wherry, and McCarran joined Bridges in bluntly calling the White Paper "a 1,054 page whitewash of a wishful, do-nothing policy which has succeeded only in placing Asia in danger of Soviet conquest."

So far as the general public was concerned, the polls revealed that the problem of China still seemed very remote to the majority of the American people. They were not as exercised over the failure of our policy as members of Congress. Only 36 percent of those questioned in one sampling of opinion were aware of the State Department publication.

The White Paper most certainly did not clear the air. It confused the administration's supporters, provided new ammunition for its foes, and intensified political controversy over where we should go from there.

In his explicit acceptance of the Nationalist defeat and Communist victory in the civil war, Dean Acheson hardly considered what the United States might try to do in meeting any new challenge to its Far Eastern policy. He went no further than to state that should the Peking regime lend itself to the aims of Russian imperialism and engage in aggression against its neighbors, the United States and other members of the United Nations would be confronted with a situation threatening international peace and security. This was rather obvious, and hardly calculated to provide any specific guidelines for future action.

However, the Secretary of State, some two weeks before publication of the White Paper, had taken a step unknown to the general public that was to prove of immense and far-reaching importance in the further evolution of American policy in eastern Asia. To prepare the way for meeting new circumstances, he had appointed a special State Department advisory committee. It was composed of Philip C. Jessup, an ambassador-at-large who had successfully negotiated the agreement ending the Berlin blockade and was now assigned to Far Eastern affairs; Raymond Fosdick, former head of the Rockefeller Foundation; and Everett Case, the president of Colgate University. What was so highly significant for the long future were the instructions given the committee.

"You will please take as your assumption," Secretary Acheson wrote Ambassador Jessup on July 19, 1949, "that it is a fundamental decision of American policy that the United States does not intend to permit further extension of Communist domination on the continent of Asia or in the Southeast Asia area." The committee was to investigate possible plans, costs, and necessary forces to implement such a policy, and while Acheson intimated that this program might not in fact prove feasible, the committee should explore every possible approach. He wanted to be certain, his instructions concluded, that "we are neglecting no opportunities that would be within our capabilities to achieve the purpose of halting the spread of totalitarian communism in Asia."

When in 1947 President Truman had first proclaimed that it must be the policy of the United States "to support free peoples who are resisting attempted subjugation by armed minorities or outside pressures," he and his advisers were thinking in terms of the immediate Communist threat to Greece and Turkey. Acheson fully recognized the lack of any real parallel between the situation then prevailing in the eastern Mediterranean and conditions on the Asiatic mainland. Nevertheless, acting on the assumption that in both areas the underlying threat was Communism as an expression of Russian imperialism, what he clearly contemplated was the application of the containment policy, as it had evolved in Europe, to the new task of helping to safeguard China's neighbors from Communist attacks or Communist subversion.

This interpretation of Acheson's thinking was confirmed early the next year. Through a resolution adopted in the House, the State Department was called upon to answer a number of questions relating to anti-Communist policy as first applied in Greece and Turkey. Its answer specifically stated that the ideas underlying assistance to countries threatened by Communism "are basic to the policies of this Government with respect to Asia no less than to other parts of the world."

Such assistance was still considered as primarily economic aid, with no thought of active intervention, but nevertheless here was a vital expansion of the idea of containment. The United States would not interfere in China's internal affairs. It was too late. However, we were accepting new responsibilities in preventing the spread of Communist control over any other free country in Asia. In spite of the risks of such an ambitious policy, moving along lines of which the public remained wholly ignorant, the United States reacted to the rise of Communist China by resolving to extend its all-embracing role of global policeman to the Far East.

Here was the genesis of a policy that would lead to our military involvement in Korea, though in this instance the United States nominally acted under the aegis of the United Nations; to our unilateral stand to prevent a Communist takeover of Formosa or the offshore islands of Quemoy and Matsu; to the economic and military aid we progressively extended first to the French colonial authorities and then to the independent states of Southeast Asia; and ultimately to direct intervention in Vietnam.

5

The Problems
of Disengagement

WITH THE COMMUNISTS firmly established in control of the China mainland and the Nationalists reduced to a highly precarious hold on Formosa, the Truman Administration had to deal with more immediate issues in eastern Asia than a long-range policy designed to contain further Communist expansion. How could the United States finally disengage itself from the Chinese civil war? The White Paper as well as other statements by Secretary of State Acheson clearly suggested that the Truman Administration believed that disengagement was the only realistic course the United States could follow. Nevertheless, a number of things stood in the way of implementing any such policy. Divisions of opinion existed within the administration itself, as well as in the country as a whole, with conservatives generally opposed to any retreat before the forces of Communism. In Congress the right-wing Republicans, motivated both by conviction and intense partisanship, continued to combat vehemently any step that might lead to the abandonment of Chiang Kai-shek.

Three practical considerations were inextricably involved in this deepening controversy over China policy: first, the specific question of whether to accord diplomatic recognition to the People's Republic of China; second, our attitude toward its possible admission to the United

Nations; and third, relations with the national government on Formosa. These issues were of course closely related and in some measure interdependent. In attempting to resolve them, a harassed and badgered State Department remained subject to domestic political pressures that further developments in 1949–50 intensified rather than alleviated.

The question of whether the United States should be prepared to recognize the Peking regime arose even before official establishment of the People's Republic of China. Aware of congressional feelings, the State Department knew it had to move very cautiously and let it be known that it was trying to persuade all non-Communist governments to agree on common action. Nonetheless, fearful that the administration might take a step that would mean a final desertion of the Nationalists, twenty-two senators (sixteen Republicans and six Democrats) wrote President Truman as early as June 24, 1949, seeking official reassurance that the United States was not contemplating recognition. The President did not directly answer this senatorial plea, but Dean Acheson wrote Senator Connally that he would consult the Senate Foreign Relations Committee before any decision was made.

This was in itself a concession to congressional critics so far as it affected the State Department's freedom of action. In spite of incessant rivalry between the executive and legislative branches of the government over their respective powers in the formulation of foreign policy, executive responsibility in the matter of recognizing foreign governments had since 1900 been generally accepted. In agreeing to consult with the Senate Foreign Relations Committee, Acheson was thus again seeking to mollify congressional opposition. As in his concessions on continued assistance for Chiang Kai-shek, he was hoping to maintain the political backing so essential in the further evolution of the mutual aid program in Europe.

The possible acceptance of Mao Tse-tung's new government involved the purpose and intent of extending diplomatic recognition to a revolutionary regime. Our traditional policy as first set forth by Thomas Jefferson was to establish relations with any government, however it came into power and whatever its political system, once it was firmly in control and represented, in Jefferson's phrase, "the will of the people substantially declared." Recognition in no sense implied approval. It involved no more than an exchange of diplomatic representatives, which enabled the United States to safeguard its own interests more effectively in dealing with the new foreign government.

On a number of occasions in the past this procedure had not proved to be quite so simple as the Jeffersonian doctrine implied, and on the eve of World War I President Wilson broke sharply with traditional practices. Our troubled relations with a revolutionary Mexico led him to employ recognition—or, more accurately, nonrecognition—as a diplomatic weapon in seeking to discredit the Victoriano Huerta regime. It had come into power through violence rather than the orderly processes of constitutional change, and its denial of the basic principles of democracy outraged the idealistic American President. Wilson was determined on moral grounds to withhold recognition as a means of teaching the Latin American nations to behave properly. "The present policy," Secretary of State Bryan emphatically stated, ". . . is to isolate President Huerta entirely; to cut him off from foreign sympathy and aid and from domestic credit, whether moral or material, and to force him out."

This departure in our policy was again followed when the United States withheld recognition from Soviet Russia from 1917 to 1933. The official grounds were the "uncontestable fact" that the Communists were ruling the country without the consent of the people. However, as in the case of the Huerta regime in Mexico, the United States was expressing its moral disapproval of a government whose political and economic principles were abhorrent to the American people. Nonrecognition was adopted in the hope of undermining the Soviet Union's international position and hastening its ultimate downfall.

Since then American policy had wavered somewhat uncertainly between Jeffersonian practicality and Wilsonian moralism, but the belief was general in 1949 that in its attitude toward the Chinese Communists the United States would approach recognition on a strictly *de facto* basis— as a set of facts, nothing more—and that once the Communists formally set up their government and demonstrated their control over the country, we would be willing to accept them. That the administration was thinking in Jeffersonian rather than Wilsonian terms was indicated in a statement of Secretary Acheson in September. "We maintain diplomatic relations with other countries," he said, "primarily because we are all on the same planet and must do business with each. We do not establish an embassy in a foreign country to show approval of its Government."

However, since the United States still recognized the national government on Formosa and the Republicans insisted that acceptance of the Peking government meant an unconscionable repudiation of Chiang's claims for the legitimacy of his regime, the State Department faced a very real dilemma. When the People's Republic of China made its official bid for international recognition on October 1, 1949, the State Department consequently announced that the United States still recognized the national government and reaffirmed that before making any change in this policy, consultations would be held with the other powers and also with the appropriate congressional committees.

Some few days later, Acheson set forth three broad conditions that he said governed policy on recognition: a new government should control the country over which it claims control; it should accept its international obligations; and it should rule with the acquiescence of its people. He said nothing of approval or disapproval. His statement left open the question of whether the People's Republic of China satisfactorily met these conditions.

Early in October this issue became the major subject of debate at a special round-table conference that the Jessup committee held to advise the State Department on China policy. Its twenty-five participants included General Marshall, John D. Rockefeller, and Harold Stassen, a number of important businessmen, and such recognized China experts from the academic world as John Fairbank, Owen Lattimore, and Edwin O. Reischauer. The sharply divergent views of the conferees reflected popular differences in the controversy and were later to furnish fuel for the bitter disputes over alleged pro-Communist sympathies among State Department consultants.

The conference debate apparently went round and round in endless circles, but the transcript of the proceedings, which was not released until two years later, indicates that "a prevailing group," including many of the best-known Far Eastern authorities, definitely favored recognition of the Peking government. Their point of view, in opposition to those who at least wanted a long delay before taking any such step, was based on the objective fact that the Communists were fully in control of the China mainland. The United States should adopt a realistic attitude, they argued, rather than allow emotion and sentiment to tie us to Chiang Kai-shek. Fearful of a new iron curtain descending in eastern Asia, they insisted not only on the necessity of recognizing the Chinese People's Republic but of doing so "fairly soon."

One of the participants, Ernest R. McNaughton, a banker from Portland, Oregon, who candidly declared at one point that "this talkie-talkie gets me all up in air," introduced a practical note into the discussion that was perhaps more relevant than the theoretical arguments of the academic experts. Accepting the thesis that so far as past policies were concerned "we are all washed up in China" and that the consensus among the experts was that we should recognize the Peking government, McNaughton added this caveat: "General Marshall has been whispering in my ear for the last few days that a lot of the things we were talking about now you cannot get the American people to take right now . . . or the Congress to take."

This was undoubtedly true. Whatever might be said in favor of realistically acknowledging that the Communists and not the Nationalists were the controlling force in China, popular sentiment made it politically impossible to do so. Moreover, at just about this time the Communists greatly aggravated popular hostility in this country by the course they were following in their foreign relations. Far from giving any evidence that they were prepared to respect international obligations, they were conspicuously going out of their way to disregard them. They not only waged their virulent anti-imperialist campaign against the West, but flagrantly violated foreign nations' established treaty rights in China. Their troops invaded the United States embassy in Nanking, molested consular officials in Shanghai and other cities, and callously disregarded the principle of diplomatic immunity.

This campaign, directed particularly against the United States, reached a climax in the notorious Angus Ward affair. After holding the staff of our consulate general in Mukden under house arrest for nearly a year, the local Communist authorities on October 24, 1949, jailed Consul General Ward and four of his associates on charges of having assaulted a Chinese employee. They refused to allow Ward to communicate with his government, and Peking ignored all protests.

The Ward case became a *cause célèbre*. President Truman declared the arrest an outrage, and it aroused the utmost indignation and anger. "We want Angus Ward out alive—or else," said the New York *World-Telegram* in a typical statement, and the American Legion took the lead in demanding direct action, if necessary by armed force, to secure the consul general's release. Yet there was nothing the United States could really do (as would also become evident in a number of comparable incidents in later years) without provoking war. The Communists continued to hold Ward for another month and then summarily deported him. On his return to the United States, something of a hero, Ward denied the charges against him (instead of assaulting the Chinese employee, he said, "I took him by the hand and pacifically led him to the courtyard"), and in his report to the State Department described his experiences in the Chinese jail as "hellish."

In this incident and such later actions as the seizure of our consular properties in Peking, the Chinese Communists appeared to be doing everything possible to humiliate the United States in expressing their defiance of the established conventions of international law. Mao Tse-tung had stated that one of the basic aims of his regime would be "systematically and completely destroying the imperialist domination of China." Instead of smoothing the way toward foreign recognition, he was far more interested in these symbolic acts of retribution for all the indignities China had suffered in the past at the hands of foreigners.

The Ward case made any immediate move toward acceptance of the Peking government out of the question. As the New York Times reported, "there was an obvious hardening of the United States position." Acheson himself said that it seemed apparent that the Chinese Communists did not really want American recognition. Any move he may possibly have contemplated along such lines was at least postponed in these unfavorable circumstances.

The issue could not, however, be completely set aside, and articles in the daily press and news magazines in the late autumn of 1949 pointed to continuing divisions of opinion within the administration. Newsweek said that President Truman believed that the United States should conduct its relations with Communist China as it had those with Soviet Russia between 1917 and 1933, and Time reported that Secretary Acheson was arguing in favor of recognition. In successive articles in the New York Times the usually well-informed James Reston said that the State Department, accepting the Jeffersonian philosophy, believed in principle that the United States should recognize Peking but did not consider such a step feasible until there was a change in the attitude of Congress.

Whatever the validity of these interpretations of what was going on in Washington, Acheson's efforts to preserve some measure of unity among our allies in a delaying action broke down. On December 16 British Foreign Secretary Ernest Bevin informed him that Great Britain—acting, as Churchill phrased it in the House of Commons, "not to confer a compliment but to secure a convenience"—would recognize the Mao Tse-tung regime early in the new year. It did so on January 5, 1950. India had already made such a move, and within the next twelve days eight other nations, including the Scandinavian countries and Switzerland, followed the British example.

These developments had no immediate effect on American policy, but the impression gained headway, as reflected in a number of public statements, that the State Department could not mark time much longer. A story in the New York Times on January 7 said that "informed Senate quarters made it plain that . . . recognition by this country could be regarded as inevitable." Among Democratic spokesmen, Senator Connally was reported as saying that recognition was on its way. Worrying over the issue in his diary, Senator Vandenburg expressed the view that the realities might well force an early abandonment of the position we had so far maintained. An editorial in the *U.S. News and World Report* at the close of the month took the same view. "Soon it will be the painful duty of the United States," wrote David Lawrence, "to extend formal recognition to the Communist-controlled Government of China. . . . As a common sense decision in diplomacy recognition is inevitable."

Such a move was strongly favored by the *New Republic* and the *Nation*, the *Reporter* and the *Christian Century*. Having rejected in its general policies the concept that recognition should be used as a diplomatic weapon, the United States in the opinion of the liberal press had no alternative to accepting the Peking regime as the legal government of all China. The *Nation* maintained that not to do so would be to abandon to Russian leadership "the greatest social revolution of our times," and the *New Republic* argued that we should "keep a hand in the window and a foot in the door, making it clear to as many Chinese as possible that their welfare is important and we support their national ambitions." Somewhat in the same vein was a statement of the American Friends Service Committee published in the *New York Times*. "By treating Communist China as an enemy and refusing to recognize her," the committee said, "we are not isolating China, we are isolating ourselves and throwing away any chance of influencing the course of events in China."

These realistic and predictive comments were echoed in some conservative quarters. The Council on Foreign Relations took a poll of some 720 "leading citizens" throughout the country, largely businessmen, lawyers, and educators. A total of 56 percent replied that if the Peking government afforded reasonable guarantees of American treaty rights in China, the United States should recognize it; 24 percent were uncertain; and only 20 percent took a definite stand in opposition.

But this was not the whole story. Little or no support for recognition existed within Congress, and fearful that Acheson might act without fulfilling his pledge to consult the appropriate committees, the anti-administration forces renewed their offensive against any move that meant abandoning Chiang Kai-shek. In the course of one angry debate in the Senate, Senator Knowland said he did not believe the Secretary of State was prepared to honor his earlier pledges but would one day appear before the Senate Foreign Relations Committee and simply say, "We have determined to recognize the Communist regime in China; we wanted to notify you before the statement was given to the press."

The whole question of whether the Truman Administration was moving toward possible recognition in early 1950 remains very perplexing. It was widely believed at the time that this was Dean Acheson's intent. While a number of his contemporary statements, especially in his correspondence with the British Foreign Secretary, may throw this in some doubt, other evidence suggests that he wanted to withdraw recognition from the national government so as to be free to extend it to the new regime in Peking. "What we must do now," he reputedly told *Time* in December 1949, as that magazine stated two years later in its issue of October 15, 1951, "is shake loose from the Chinese Nationalists." With a clear-sighted prescience that today has a certain irony, he added, "It will be harder to make that necessary break if we go to Formosa."

The Chinese seizure of our consular properties in Peking, following hard upon the Ward case, again postponed any forward move that Acheson might have contemplated. However, such qualifying clauses as "immediately," "at this time," or "in the next few months" in State Department announcements denying any step toward recognition showed that the door to future action was by no means closed.

In later testimony at the MacArthur hearings in 1951, which provide so much information on developments in this earlier period, both Secretary Acheson and Ambassador Jessup very definitely stated that the United States never considered acceptance of the Peking regime. In supporting the Nationalists, Acheson said, "we have never aided, abetted, recognized, made plans to recognize . . . this other government." When Senator Brewster quoted him as having remarked in January 1950 that recognition would depend on future events, the Secretary of State sharply replied that he could not remember ever having made this comment.

Jessup was even more emphatic in declaring that the State Department never considered recognition. In testimony before a Senate Foreign Relations subcommittee questioning him in respect to his confirmation as an American delegate to the United Nations Assembly, he could hardly have gone further. "In my mind . . . the point was never reached at which even under the traditional tests the question of recognition by the United States Government ever arose," Jessup said.

These later statements, however, are suspect. They were made at a time when both Acheson and Jessup were under vicious attack for having supposedly shown irresponsible sympathy for the Chinese Communists and for having been willing to abandon Chiang Kai-shek before the Nationalist cause was wholly lost. Their hostile inquisitors were obviously trying to demonstrate that the two men had personally favored recognition of Mao Tse-tung's regime and had encouraged Communist penetration of eastern Asia. In the prevailing climate of public opinion, the heyday of McCarthyism, Acheson and Jessup were very much on the defensive. In stressing their opposition to Peking's recognition at any time in the winter of 1949–50, they may well have felt driven in 1951 to go much further than their own thinking in the earlier period would really justify.

Acheson throws no light in *Present at the Creation* on this intriguing question. When asked in an interview following his memoir's publication, which appeared in the *New York Times Book Review* for October 12, 1969, whether he thought the United States lost an opportunity in 1949–50 to normalize relations with Communist China, he simply stated that anyone who thought recognition feasible at that time "overlooks the political realities." This was certainly true, in the light both of Peking's recalcitrant attitude and of political pressures at home, but it does not clarify what course Acheson might have liked to choose had conditions taken a more favorable turn. As it was, subsequent developments transformed a wait-and-see attitude into nonrecognition as a fixed and undeviating policy both by the Truman Administration and its successors.

The issue of which government should represent China in the United Nations, especially acute because "the Republic of China" was a permanent member of the Security Council, was at once closely associated with and yet legally distinct from that of diplomatic recognition. It first came up in the Assembly in the autumn of 1949, and then in the Security Council in January 1950. Thereafter at every annual meeting of the Assembly it has been a matter of divisive and acrimonious debate.

The Chinese Nationalist delegation was responsible for indirectly bringing up the whole question when at the close of September 1949, in an effort to stigmatize Peking as a puppet of Moscow, it formally charged the Soviet Union with intervention in Chinese affairs. The Nationalists called upon the Assembly to condemn the Russians for aiding the Chinese Communists, to reaffirm China's political independence, to recommend that member states desist from further military or economic assistance to the Communists, and to agree that no member would accord diplomatic relations with Mao Tse-tung's regime. The Peking government countered this move through a cable to the UN Secretary General, Trygve Lie, denying the right of the Nationalist government to represent the Chinese people in the United Nations. Andrei Vishinsky, the Soviet delegate, promptly came to Peking's support, asserting that since the Chinese complaint against Russian interference was presented by an "ex-government," the Assembly could not legally consider it.

It consequently fell to Lester B. Pearson, the Canadian foreign minister, to make a first ruling on this representation question as chairman of the Assembly's Political and Security Committee. He decided that the Nationalist delegation's right to represent China was valid until successfully challenged. The Assembly was free to debate the anti-Russian charges whether or not the Soviet delegates chose to take part.

A majority of the United Nations members, including the United States,.were generally in favor of the Nationalist resolution, but a number of them were reluctant to commit themselves on withholding recognition from the Chinese People's Republic. The American delegate, Ambassador Jessup, consequently introduced a substitute resolution that sought to assure decisive support for condemning Russian intervention by eliminating the clause pledging member nations not to conclude diplomatic relations with Peking. The new proposal simply called upon the members of the United Nations to uphold China's independence, honor existing treaties, and refrain from establishing any sphere of influence within Chinese territory. It was a reaffirmation of the traditional American policy toward China as originally set forth in John Hay's Open Door notes and then incorporated in the Nine Power Treaty concluded at the Washington Conference in 1922.

In supporting his resolution Ambassador Jessup made every effort to drive a wedge between the Soviet Union and Communist China by depicting the former as an imperialist power seeking domination over North China. He did not attack the Chinese Communists but asserted that Russia was setting up special regimes in Manchuria and Mongolia. The interests of the Chinese people, he declared, were being sacrificed to the demands of Russian expansionism. Soviet Foreign Minister Andrei Vishinsky dismissed these charges as "slander and pettifoggery" but except from other members of the Communist bloc, he won no support. The Assembly referred the original Chinese Nationalist resolution to its interim committee, where no action was ever taken, and then adopted the American resolution by a vote of 47 to 5, with five abstentions.

Although the question of whether the Nationalists or the Communists should properly represent China in the United Nations was only peripheral in this Assembly debate, it came directly to the fore in the Security

Council a month later. On January 8, 1950, Peking's Premier and Foreign Minister, Chou En-lai, cabled Trygve Lie to insist on his government's rights. He demanded the immediate ouster of Dr. T. F. Tsiang, the Nationalist delegate who was serving that month as president of the Security Council, since he represented only "the Chinese Kuomintang remnant reactionary clique." The Russian representative in the council, Yakov Malik, thereupon officially introduced a resolution calling for Nationalist China's expulsion.

The issue was now joined, and the American delegate in the Security Council, Ernest A. Gross, took the floor to argue against expelling the Nationalist delegate. He stated, however, that his government considered the matter a procedural rather than substantive issue. He would vote against the Russian resolution, but the United States would not exercise its veto power; it was willing to accept whatever decision the Security Council reached through an affirmative vote of seven members. The ensuing discussion ranged over all aspects of the representation problem. In spite of his fervid oratory, Malik failed to make his case for expelling the Nationalists. The Soviet resolution failed to muster a majority and went down by a vote of 6 to 3, with two abstentions—Great Britain and Norway.

Immediately after this vote, on January 13, Malik rose to state somberly that the Soviet Union would not remain on the Security Council or accept any of its decisions so long as the Nationalist delegate remained. Thereupon he dramatically walked out of the chamber. The Soviet Union commenced a boycott of the United Nations that in succeeding months created a crisis gravely jeopardizing the organization's very existence.

This drastic move, coming at a time when the trend toward international recognition of the People's Republic of China appeared to be gathering momentum, raised the question of what the Russians were really trying to do. Twenty-six countries had established diplomatic relations with Peking, and among them were fifteen members of the United Nations, including five that were represented on the Security Council. Moreover, two other council members, France and Egypt, were generally expected to recognize the Chinese Communist regime in the near future. Another test in the council might well have shown a majority of seven—the number the United States had agreed to accept—willing to expel the Nationalists and admit the Communists.

Had the Soviet Union been willing to follow a more patient, conciliatory policy, the representation question might have been settled then and there. By arbitrarily rejecting the first Security Council decision and boycotting the United Nations, the Soviet Union antagonized many other UN members, built up resentments against its uncompromising stand, and strengthened the resolve of those nations that opposed expulsion of the Nationalists.

The British delegate on the Security Council, Sir Alexander Cadogan, who abstained on this first vote but whose government recognized the Chinese People's Republic, was among those highly suspicious of Russia's real motives in boycotting the United Nations. He told Secretary Lie, as the latter reported in his memoir, *In the Cause of Peace*, that he believed the Soviet Union was following a calculated policy to discourage further recognition of the Peking government in order that Communist China might "be kept more effectively in isolation from the West and under Russian domination." The UN correspondent of the *New York Times* expressed a similar view. The Soviet government, he wrote, was pursuing a course that, far from promoting Peking's admission to the United Nations, was designed to impede it. Moscow did not want "the Communist representatives exposed to contagious contacts with the democracies in the United Nations."

In spite of its bid for membership, the People's Republic of China itself appeared to be doing everything possible to alienate support among the UN member nations. During this month of January 1950 the Peking government seized American consular properties, recognized the Communist regime of Ho Chi Minh in Vietnam, and intensified its campaign against what its propaganda apparatus described as the imperialistic powers of the West. In this confused situation, with Soviet Russia and Communist China adopting a stance that appeared to run counter to their professed policy on the representation issue, any chance of normalizing relations between Peking and the anti-Communist governments vanished. The trend toward diplomatic recognition, as well as admission to the United Nations, slowed down as France, the British Commonwealth nations, and Egypt took no action. Except for tightening its bonds with Soviet Russia through the Sino-Soviet alliance concluded in February, Communist China became even further isolated from the world community.

Trygve Lie in the meantime remained greatly concerned over the crisis for the United Nations resulting from the Russian boycott. Convinced that it could only be resolved through the admission of Communist China, he continued to exercise all possible influence to bring this about as "a precondition for progress in other directions." In a confidential memorandum to all member nations, supplemented by visits to the capitals of fifty-nine countries, he urged that a distinction be accepted between diplomatic recognition of the Peking government and its representation in the United Nations. A world organization, Lie argued, should be prepared to admit any government, regardless of all other considerations, if it showed itself capable of exercising effective authority and was "habitually obeyed by the bulk of its population."

He carried these arguments to Washington, where they did not prove to be altogether convincing. Truman told him, Lie wrote in his reminiscences, that he opposed admission of the Chinese Communists simply because they could not be trusted. In further talks at the State Department, Lie found Secretary Acheson taking the position that in the light of Russia's boycott of the United Nations, acceptance of the Chinese Communists would be construed as surrender under pressure. Should the Soviet Union win this concession, Acheson said, it would "feel free to indulge in similar blackmail whenever it failed to get its way in the future and the entire machinery of the United Nations would be paralyzed."

Ironically enough in view of his later unrelenting opposition to the admission of the Peking government, John Foster Dulles was one of those who came out strongly in favor of Lie's principle of universalism in United Nations membership. Serving at the time as a Republican adviser in the State Department, Dulles set forth his views so cogently in his book *War or Peace* that on May 18, 1950, the *New York Times* reported the story under the striking headline: "Dulles Wants UN to Admit Red China If It Proves Power."

Dulles's approach, as that of Lie, was that if the People's Republic of China demonstrated its ability to govern without serious domestic resistance, it should be accepted in the United Nations on the ground that the world organization should make no distinction between "good" and "bad" nations. This suggestion, coming from such a source, evoked the greatest alarm among other Republicans, especially the congressional right wing. Already concerned over Lie's campaign, which had inspired a protest memorandum to President Truman signed by thirty-five senators, opponents of any change in China's UN representation redoubled their efforts to keep the administration in line. The prevailing sentiment in Congress was that the United States should not only actively oppose any move to seat the Chinese Communists but should be prepared to exercise its veto power were its objections overruled.

Dean Acheson reiterated that the United States would not be coerced into changing its policy. Whatever his private views as to possible future action, he reaffirmed American support for the Nationalist government as the rightful representative of the Chinese people in the councils of the United Nations. However, he again refused to threaten the use of veto power.

"The present situation in the United Nations," Acheson stated, "does not arise from our position on the question of Chinese representation but from the refusal of the Soviet Union to accept decisions taken by the parliamentary majorities in the various organs of the United Nations. . . . Our position of supporting the Nationalist Government and of opposing the seating of the Chinese Communists continues unchanged. But, we will accept the decision of any organ of the United Nations made by the necessary majority, and we will not walk out."

There, in the spring of 1950, the matter rested.

Our relationship with the national government on Formosa, the third of the immediate issues the United States faced in the winter of 1949–50, was obviously linked to our reluctance to recognize the People's Republic of China or accept its right to membership in the United Nations. For acceptance of the Peking government as that of all China would mean that final abandonment of Chiang Kai-shek which so greatly concerned Congress. Against the desire wholly to disengage from the civil war by accepting the legitimacy of the People's Republic stood all the forces not only of anti-Communism but of tradition, sentiment, and loyalty to a wartime ally. Moreover, a new element soon entered the picture, entirely apart from our obligations to the Nationalists. The critics of a policy of disengagement put forward the powerful argument that in the new circumstances in eastern Asia, keeping Formosa out of Communist hands had become of great strategic importance to the United States and the entire free world.

The Truman Administration nevertheless remained firmly opposed to extending any further military assistance to the Nationalists. Both the State Department and the military establishment were convinced this would be wholly futile. Their attitude moreover took into consideration the very likely contingency that the Chinese Communists would at any time launch an assault on Formosa and that the Nationalists would be unable to repel it. The Joint Chiefs of Staff were not only against any overt action in aiding Chiang but even barred dispatch of a military advisory mission to his headquarters at Taipei.

In late 1949 the People's Liberation Army was assembling troops and landing junks in the Chekiang-Fukien coastal sector opposite Formosa, and by all accounts was preparing for an amphibious assault on the Nationalists' last stronghold. "A Communist conquest eventually—next spring or the following spring—is certain," the *New York Times* reported on December 11. "Formosa alone or even with Hainan cannot fight China." However desperately Chiang Kai-shek might need help, the policy makers in Washington were said to be wholly persuaded that the United States should under no circumstances allow itself to become involved in the final, hopeless stage of a civil war whose outcome was already decided.

If this was the prevailing view in official circles, at least one important member of the administration nonetheless agreed with the Republican opposition that desertion of Chiang meant the loss of an essential anti-Communist foothold off the China coast. Secretary of Defense Louis Johnson not only felt this very strongly, but he was ready to fight for his position. He believed that the Joint Chiefs of Staff were going along with the State Department for political reasons rather than from the conviction that their own strategic ideas were in the national interest.

Johnson put the question squarely to them. Although they did not modify their basic stand against direct American intervention in the civil war, they partially reversed themselves under Johnson's questioning in acknowledging the advisability of continuing some limited military aid to the Nationalists and of sending a fact-finding mission to Formosa. On December 15 the Secretary of Defense forwarded a memorandum outlining these revised views to the President, but Truman stood by the original decision against any further aid. "I had lost my fight on Formosa," Johnson would later testify. "I was told . . . that he wasn't going to argue with me about the military considerations but that on political grounds he would decide with the State Department."

The President's ruling was reaffirmed at an important meeting of the National Security Council on December 29. It approved a policy that, while still allowing Nationalist use of some unexpended funds from former China aid acts, provided that the United States would otherwise give no material support to Chiang Kai-shek, send no mission to Taipei and maintain a hands-off attitude should the Communists actually launch their expected assault on Formosa.

Discussing these matters at the MacArthur hearings in 1951, Dean Acheson gave a somewhat contradictory account of the interplay of diplomatic and military factors in the determination of this policy. "It was the clear unequivocal recommendation of the military services that we could not employ our forces for the defense of Formosa," he said.

Yet he also maintained that short of the employment of force, our policy was "to use all the means that we had . . . to prevent Formosa from falling into enemy hands."

This is hard to reconcile with the veto on any further material support to Chiang's forces and on the fact-finding mission to Taipei. It runs counter to the Secretary of State's own expressed desire to break loose from the Nationalists. Just as in his disclaimers on ever considering recognition of the Peking government, a beleaguered Acheson would again appear in these 1951 senatorial hearings to have been trying to answer his critics' charge that he had been ready to desert the Nationalists. The evidence surely indicates that in saying the United States was ready to use all means short of force in protecting Formosa, he was misrepresenting policy, which, though it might still approve limited financial or technical aid to the Nationalists, was far more significantly seeking our complete disengagement from China's civil war.

A policy information paper the State Department sent to all foreign missions on December 29, 1949, suggests more realistically how far it was prepared to go in writing off Formosa. This paper described the island as "politically, geographically and strategically" a part of China and, anticipating its probable conquest by the Communists, instructed all American representatives overseas to downgrade the importance of its falling under the Peking government's control. All statements issued from embassies or legations were to emphasize that the United States did not feel that Communist occupation of Formosa would seriously damage American interests or those of any other country in the free world. They were further to make plain that in the official view, any move by the United States to establish bases in Formosa or to furnish military aid to the Nationalists would accomplish no particular good for China; would subject this country to charges of militarism, imperialism, and interference; and would play into Soviet Russia's hands.

This information paper was a highly secret document, but its contents were mysteriously leaked from General MacArthur's headquarters in Tokyo. They at once created a popular furor. Acheson valiantly tried to explain that it did not represent policy. The instructions to our foreign missions, he said, were solely to minimize the significance of Formosa so that in the very likely event of Communist conquest, neither our friends nor foes would consider this a serious setback for American policy. Within the context of other contemporary statements emanating from Washington, they were generally interpreted, however, as a final step in completely breaking off relations with Chiang Kai-shek.

The administration's foes were aroused to do everything possible to block what they considered this callous betrayal of the loyally anti-Communist generalissimo. Senator H. Alexander Smith, a moderate and highly respected Republican, had returned from a Far Eastern tour two months earlier and added fresh fuel to the controversy by energetically developing the new theme of Formosa's immense strategic importance. He had talked with MacArthur in Tokyo, and in a memorandum to Dean Acheson, in a report to the Senate Foreign Relations Committee, and then on the floor of the Senate, Smith quoted the general as stating unequivocally that keeping Formosa out of Communist hands had become vital to American security in the western Pacific.

The New Jersey senator advanced his own somewhat bizarre proposal for achieving this objective. Arguing that Formosa's international status was still undetermined pending a peace treaty with Japan, he suggested that in agreement with Chiang Kai-shek the United States should "occupy the island." But he did not mean military occupation. We should merely state our purpose, Smith said, notify the United Nations, and recommend that Formosa ultimately be made a trusteeship area. By following this plan, he contended, the Chinese Communists would be forestalled from an invasion, for under such circumstances an attack on Formosa would be an attack on the United States. In advancing this proposal, he reiterated, reflecting General MacArthur's position, that "under no conditions should we let Formosa fall into the hands of the Chinese Communists or under the domination of Russia."

In defending a policy of disengagement, the administration's supporters in the Senate ridiculed this idea that the United States could occupy Formosa and prevent a Communist assault without the intervention of American military forces. "Does it mean occupation by a few tourists and United States senators?" Senator Connally asked derisively. When Smith repeated that he would not send a single soldier to Formosa, Connally returned to the attack. In an exchange that the *Congressional Record* reported with the parenthetical comment "laughter," the Democratic leader objected that we could hardly hope to occupy Formosa with "two or three senators who . . . at the firing of the first gun, would go into a hole somewhere."

In the meantime several other Republican leaders, equally convinced of the ineptitude of administration policy and of the necessity to protect Formosa, were hardly content with such a dubious scheme of peaceful occupation. They called for more positive action. Senator Knowland urged the immediate dispatch of a military mission to Formosa; Senator

Robert Taft insisted that Formosa should be kept from the Chinese Communists even if it meant employing the Navy; and former President Herbert Hoover proposed naval action to protect not only Formosa but also the Pescadores and possibly Hainan Island. Although other opposition spokesmen were not prepared for such drastic action, congressional and also popular sentiment appeared to be rising in favor of some form of direct intervention.

Confronted with these various proposals for occupying Formosa, dispatching a military mission, and affording the island naval protection, President Truman decided the time was at hand to answer his critics, cut through all ambiguities, and make his position crystal clear. On January 5, 1950, he released to the press a new and decisive policy statement:

"The United States has no desire to obtain special rights or privileges or to establish military bases on Formosa at this time. Nor does it have any intention of utilizing its armed forces to interfere in the present situation. The United States will not pursue a course which will lead to involvement in the civil conflict in China. Similarly the United States will not provide military aid or advice to Chinese forces on Formosa."

Was this indeed the final disengagement it implied, or was there still a loophole in the phrase "at this time"? In a news conference the next day, at which he caustically criticized Taft and Hoover for their "amateur military strategy," Secretary Acheson emphatically affirmed the President's intent to disavow any sort of assistance to the Nationalists. The qualification in Truman's first sentence, Acheson said, applied only to the unlikely event that American forces in the Far East might themselves be attacked. The United States could not furnish the will to resist possible assault, he declared with an oblique reference to Nationalist defeats on the mainland, "to those who must provide for themselves."

Yet congressional critics could not accept this seemingly firm decision. The debate over China policy took on a new intensity. With the Republicans crying "appeasement" and "a Far Eastern Munich," and Democrats upholding the realism and practicality of administration policy, political partisanship ruled the day.

It may be recalled that these early days of 1950, the first two weeks of January, witnessed a series of fast-moving developments that provided a dramatic background for the battle over China policy: Great Britain recognized the People's Republic of China; the Soviet Union initiated its boycott of the United Nations in protesting the Security Council's refusal to eject the Nationalist delegate; the Chinese Communists seized the United States consular properties in Peking; and Mao Tse-tung journeyed to Moscow to commence negotiations for a Sino-Russian treaty. The situation could hardly have been more involved and confusing. Moreover, here at home Madame Chiang Kai-shek, still so popular with the American public, notably contributed to the emotional atmosphere by a moving farewell address to the American people, broadcast over the national radio networks on January 8, in which she skillfully played upon all the old ideas of Sino-American friendship.

"I can ask the American people for nothing more," she eloquently concluded after declaring that no setbacks could stifle the Chinese yearning for freedom. "At such a time no pleading can be made with dignity. It is either in your hearts to love us, or your hearts have turned against us. It is either in your mind and will to aid China in her struggle for liberty, or you have abandoned liberty."

The Republicans responded with renewed insistence that the United States somehow enable the Nationalists to preserve their enclave of liberty from being overrun by the Communists. The Democrats pointedly asked just what they proposed. As the leading spokesman for the administration, Senator Connally repeatedly returned to this key question. "Do you want to send our troops into a Chinese civil war?" he asked. "Do you want to go to war in China?" He accused the Republicans of heedlessly playing politics with the basic issues of national security.

"I want to know who the Senators are, and I shall revive the question from time to time, who want to plunge this country, not directly but possibly, into World War III, in the name of Formosa, but principally in the name of a bitter attack upon the President of the United States and upon the Department of State," Connally said.

The Republicans had in fact overreached themselves; the proposals of Taft and Hoover for naval action awakened apprehension. However critical of a Far Eastern policy that had somehow failed to prevent the loss of mainland China and now seemed ready to allow Formosa to slip into enemy hands, however fearful of still further Communist conquests in other parts of Asia, few Americans wanted to run the risk of the United States becoming involved in an Asiatic war. Little support existed for sending American forces to assist a discredited exile government on a remote Pacific island if such a move might lead to hostilities with Communist China and possibly the Soviet Union.

The Truman Administration held its ground; it made no concessions to the political opposition. When Acheson appeared before the Senate Foreign Relations Committee to explain further the President's statement of January 5, the press reported that he "stood unbending before his Republican critics." The real feelings of the State Department in the face of the senatorial uproar were perhaps reflected in a comment by Ernest Lindley in his column in *Newsweek*. He felt the State Department would be very much relieved "if Formosa fell promptly to the Communists, one way or another, and the Nationalist regime would vanish."

On January 12—with debate in the Senate finally giving way to other matters—Acheson delivered one of his most important speeches on Far Eastern policy, "Crisis in China," before the National Press Club in Washington. He first took up general conditions within China and then turned from this political theme to matters of military security. He declared that the strategic line that the United States should be prepared to defend against Communist aggression in the western Pacific ran from the Aleutian Islands through Japan, down to the Ryukyus, and on to the Philippine Islands. He pointedly excluded Formosa—and also, most significantly in view of later events, Korea—from within this perimeter. So far as the United States was concerned, Acheson declared, the military security of the countries beyond this perimeter "lay beyond the realm of any practical relationship." Should an attack on them occur, "the initial reliance must be on the people attacked to resist it and then upon the commitments of the entire civilized world under the charter of the United Nations."

Acheson was assailed, both at the time and in later years, for encouraging the Communists to believe that if this were indeed American policy, they could attack either Formosa or Korea with impunity. He has consistently defended himself by stating that in drawing this defensive perimeter, he was only expressing what was at the time the well-considered views of the Joint Chiefs of Staff as well as those of the State Department. His earlier statements on the need to contain further Communist aggression in Southeast Asia contemplated no more than possible economic or military aid to China's neighbors. In this policy pronouncement he was not defining the limits for such assistance, Acheson has maintained, but those for American intervention by force of arms.

Moreover, Acheson has always been able to point out that his most severe critic after the event, General MacArthur, laid down the same defensive line a little less than a year earlier in defining American security interests in the western Pacific. "It starts from the Philippines and continues through the Ryukyu Archipelago, which includes its main bastion Okinawa. Then it bends back through Japan and the Aleutian chain to Alaska," MacArthur told a British correspondent, as reported in the *New York Times* on March 2, 1949. He noted that the advance of the Red armies in China placed them on the flank of this position, but nonetheless

maintained that this did not basically alter our military situation. However much MacArthur's views later changed, he originally believed, as did
the Joint Chiefs, that national security did not call for the military defense
of either Formosa or Korea, let alone any other part of Asia.

In his discussion of conditions within China itself, Acheson insisted that
the United States should seek a basis for friendly relations with the Chinese
people by demonstrating our concern for their freedom and independence
in comparison with the dominating goals of Soviet Russia. Trying as had
Ambassador Jessup in his earlier speeches at the United Nations to drive a
wedge between Moscow and Peking, the Secretary of State declared that
the Russians were using Communism as a subtle weapon for their own
aggrandizement and that the single most important fact in the relation of
any foreign power with Asia was the Soviet effort to absorb China's four
northern provinces. He appeared to be certain that sooner or later the
Chinese would come to realize the extent to which they were being
victimized.

"We must not undertake to deflect from the Russians to ourselves the
righteous anger, and the wrath, and the hatred of the Chinese people
which must develop," Acheson said. "It would be folly to deflect it to
ourselves. We must take the position we have always taken—that anyone
who violates the integrity of China is the enemy of China and is acting
contrary to our interests."

In developing this thesis in an effort to persuade the Chinese to throw
off the yoke of Communism and turn to more friendly relations with the
United States, Acheson stressed the "basic revolutionary force which is
loose in Asia." However, in failing to recognize the extent to which the
Communists themselves embodied this nationalistic spirit, he tended to
misconstrue the nature of the movement within China.

In going to Moscow at this time to negotiate a Sino-Soviet treaty, Mao
Tse-tung was not prepared to surrender China's interests or allow Russia
to take over his country's four northern provinces. Acheson was later to
call the resulting pact a "tawdry pretense" and said that Peking again
showed itself "completely subservient to Moscow." But this was not the
case. The Chinese Communists won Soviet acceptance of the principle of
China's territorial integrity, agreement on a military alliance, and the
promise of substantial financial credits and technological aid.

The People's Republic of China was dogmatically Communist; it
initially acknowledged Moscow's leadership in the socialist world. But as
already emphasized, it was never a Russian satellite. Moreover, in turning
against the West and especially the United States, it was neither showing

a supine subserviency to the Soviet Union nor merely parroting the propaganda line of international Communism. Peking's intractable mood, John Fairbank has written, came "out of China's history, not just from Lenin's book."

Dean Acheson's efforts to arouse the resentment of the Chinese people against the Russians by asserting that Moscow called the tune to which their new leaders danced had no perceptible effect on Chinese attitudes. However, his constant emphasis on Peking's subservience to Moscow strengthened the general feeling in this country that this was indeed the case, and it helped to obscure for Americans the inherent strength of Chinese nationalism. Louis Halle has suggested in *The Cold War as History* that the whole approach of the West in stressing the dependence of China on Russia at this time was "something akin to the operation of a self-fulfilling prophecy."

Whatever interpretations or significance may be read into Acheson's address before the National Press Club, the public reaction in this country followed predetermined lines. Liberals welcomed the speech as highly realistic in setting forth the new defensive line supporting our strategic interests in the western Pacific. The *New Republic* characterized it as emphasizing "modesty in place of arrogance, and patience in place of hysteria." Conservatives, on the other hand, interpreted the speech as indicating a still further retreat before the Communist menace that boded no good for the future. The *New York Times* declared that the United States was confronted in China not by "a 'social revolution' or a routine 'civil war,' but by a program of massive aggression."

Within Congress inflamed partisanship marked renewed debate on administration policy. The irrepressible Senator Bridges, whom Acheson has characterized as "my faithful enemy," called for a vote of censure against the administration; Senator Knowland, equally excited, demanded Acheson's resignation. But the Democrats rallied to the administration's support. Meeting in a senatorial party conference, they were reported to be "practically unanimous" in backing President Truman's hands-off-Formosa policy.

In the early spring of 1950, to recapitulate a tangled series of developments, the Truman Administration had not yet succeeded under the impact of domestic political pressure in developing an acceptable approach to the new situation in eastern Asia. But its policy seemed to be gradually taking on some form and substance in seeking complete disengagement from the Chinese civil war and establishing a new line of military defense in the western Pacific for the containment of further Communist expansion.

The United States made no move toward recognition of the People's Republic of China, but nonrecognition had not yet become a policy in and of itself. Our options were still open. We continued to oppose representation of the Peking government in the United Nations, but Secretary of State Acheson had definitely stated that the United States would accept any decision reached by an affirmative vote in the Security Council. And most important, in seeking to avoid any further involvement in China's civil conflict, President Truman had unequivocally stated that the United States would not provide military aid or advice to Chiang Kai-shek's regime on Formosa. Our postwar policy had admittedly failed to create a peaceful, democratic China in close alliance with this country, but there appeared to be some promise of coming to grips with the new problems flowing from failure.

However, the opportunity to win over popular support for an emerging policy that might in time have led to a realistic accommodation with the Chinese Communists, even though it fell far short of re-creating the ancient bonds of Sino-American friendship, was now lost. The forces let loose by Senator Joseph R. McCarthy in his hysterical appeals to passion and prejudice succeeded in identifying in the public mind any move toward a possible rapprochement with the Chinese Communists as a treasonable betrayal of the national interest.

For a time, Richard Rovere wrote on May 13, 1950, in his "Letter from Washington" in the New Yorker, McCarthyism led to "the almost total paralysis of American policy in the Orient."

6

The China Bloc, McCarthyism, and the China Lobby

THE MAIN ASSAULT on the Truman Administration's efforts to develop a viable China policy in the winter of 1949–50 was spearheaded by what has been called the China bloc. What was this China bloc? It was not a cohesive, organized group but a varying number of Congressmen who consistently demanded greater support for the Nationalists and, as a corollary to their unyielding stand on this issue, tenaciously opposed any move toward recognition of the People's Republic of China or its admission to the United Nations. With the notable exception of Senator McCarran, they were for the most part highly conservative Republicans.

Their attitude was compounded of an obsessive dread of international Communism and an almost equal fear of subversion within the United States. On both fronts they felt the administration was failing to protect the interests of the country and, particularly in its China policy, demonstrating a shocking blindness—if not worse—to the Communist threat. Embittered and violent partisanship marked the maneuvers of the China bloc, but its members, however prejudiced and myopic their views, were acting out of convictions that transcended a domestic political quarrel between the outs and the ins.

At home, these Congressmen felt that a socialistic administration was wasting national resources, bankrupting the country, undermining the

American way of life, and leading to inevitable disaster. Looking overseas, they were almost pathologically alarmed over what they saw as a monolithic conspiratorial force directed by Soviet Russia with the single-minded aim of everywhere suppressing liberty, overthrowing free enterprise, and burying America.

In their minds the Chinese revolution was one of the most dangerous manifestations of this evil Communist conspiracy. They were convinced that all-out support for Chiang Kai-shek offered the one hope for the United States in preventing Communism from outflanking the American position in the Pacific and directly threatening our security. In their political campaigning they seized upon the Truman-Acheson Far Eastern policy both for itself and as one of the administration's most vulnerable points of attack. They magnified and distorted the admittedly unsuccessful postwar record in Asia as evidence that the President and his Secretary of State were failing the country.

Many members of the China bloc, over and beyond their fear of Communism and their intense partisanship, were also neo-isolationists. They strongly opposed our deepening involvement in European affairs, but paradoxically favored intervention in Asia. As Republicans had generally in times past, they believed that the Pacific and eastern Asia were more important to the United States than the trans-Atlantic community.

The long association of Republicans with this approach to foreign policy stems back to the days of William H. Seward. As a senator in the 1850s Seward made the often quoted statement that the Pacific rather than the Atlantic "will become the chief theater of events in the world's great hereafter," and after becoming Secretary of State he gave paramount importance to American interests in that part of the world. At the close of the nineteenth century, Republicans carried the flag to Asian shores with the conquest of the Philippines; they initiated the Open Door policy, with our subsequent deep involvement in Far Eastern politics; and then in 1921 they summoned the Washington Conference to implement a more active approach to Pacific problems. When the United States was drawn into World War II twenty years later, a Democratic administration was in office, but Republican isolationists still felt that priority should be given to the Pacific in the conduct of military operations and strongly criticized President Franklin Roosevelt when he insisted that in spite of the Japanese attack at Pearl Harbor, Germany was our number-one enemy.

The rationale behind this historic attitude is found in the repudiation of Europe inherent in the foundation of the American republic and in the westward-looking ambitions of a restless people who refused to accept the

Pacific as a barrier to the further expansion of their influence and power. The mystique of our national mission came particularly to embrace control of the Pacific and unchallenged influence among the countries of eastern Asia. Commercial interests entered very importantly into this Asia-directed ambition—the persistent dream of China's illimitable markets—but many Americans without economic motivation have envisaged an Asia that in transforming its own ancient institutions, entirely apart from trade and commerce, would adopt Christianity, democracy, and the American way of life.

As Asia Firsters, the members of the China bloc were thus heirs to an old tradition. Turning their backs on the Atlantic community, they saw the Pacific holding the key to the future. They had little interest in the Marshall Plan and NATO; they opposed the dispatch of American troops to strengthen Western Europe's defenses against Soviet Russia. But in support of both national security and our long-term goals in the Far East, they militantly demanded a more positive stand in dealing with the threat of Asiatic Communism.

Senator Knowland expressed this attitude in critically comparing American efforts to block Communist aggression in Europe and what he thought was the Truman Administration's passive inactivity in combating its expansion in Asia. "For the life of me," he declared on the floor of the Senate, "I cannot see how we can follow that policy in Europe to keep Western Europe from going behind the iron curtain, and apparently be completely unconcerned whether 400,000,000 Chinese shall be taken behind the iron curtain. This is not consistent policy. We have a foreign policy in Europe. We have had no policy at all in the Far East."

Somewhat later Senator Bridges put the question more bluntly: "Are we men in Europe and mice in Asia?"

President Truman was to complain bitterly in his *Memoirs* of the stand taken by the Asia First advocates. They would have had us, he wrote, seek to impose our way of life on Asia at the cost of letting Europe go. And reporting on their later opposition to his concept of limited war in Korea, he was particularly outspoken: "These were the men who saw nothing wrong in plunging headlong into an Asian war but would raise no finger for the defense of Europe; who thought a British Prime Minister was never to be trusted but Chiang Kai-shek could do no wrong."

Senator Taft was not always associated with the China bloc because as "Mr. Republican" his political interests ranged so broadly, but he fully accepted the Asia First thesis in his concern with foreign policy. During his campaign for the presidency in 1948 he expressed the opinion that "the Far East is ultimately more important to our future peace than is Europe," and two years later his opposition to NATO was countered by his proposal for employing American naval forces in the defense of Formosa. In his little book *A Foreign Policy for Americans*, published in 1951, Taft argued that what we were doing in Europe was far more likely to bring on war with the Soviet Union than anything we were doing in Asia, but that nevertheless we should take a comparably aggressive stand there. "I am only asking," he wrote somewhat petulantly, "for the same policy in the Far East as in Europe."

Taft totally ignored the wholly different circumstances prevailing in the two areas. Accepting the need to combat international Communism, he nevertheless reflected a basic isolationism in dismissing the importance of cooperation with our Western allies. In his generally sympathetic biography, William S. White has admitted that on foreign policy matters Taft was "inconsistent to the point of inconceivability."

The most prominent and vocal spokesman for the China bloc was the heretofore little known Knowland, whom the press called "the Senator from Formosa." In season and out, he called for greater support for Chiang Kai-shek and became the self-appointed champion of the Nationalist cause. Coming from California, he represented a state where in the interest of Far Eastern trade considerable backing existed for establishing at least commercial relations with the Chinese Communists. But nothing could swerve Knowland from his convictions. Receiving on one occasion a resolution from the San Francisco Chamber of Commerce urging recognition of the Peking regime, he severely rebuked its members for being willing to put trade ahead of security in maintaining a resolute anti-Communist front.

The *Nation* once described Knowland as "the noisiest and silliest" member of the China bloc, but he was by no means as irresponsible as this allegation suggests. He was neither as reactionary nor as isolationist as many of his fellow senators in this group, yet throughout his political career he held to his position with undoubted sincerity. No one more consistently stood up for Chiang Kai-shek or resisted more strenuously any move that might strengthen the regime of Mao Tse-tung.

Among his senatorial allies—such Republicans as Styles Bridges of New Hampshire, Kenneth Wherry of Nebraska, Homer Ferguson of Michigan, William Jenner of Indiana, Alexander Wiley of Wisconsin, John Butler of Maryland, and the Democrat Pat McCarran of Nevada—support for the Chinese Nationalists grew more out of a rabid anti-Communism and reactionary opposition to everything about the Truman Administration than from any great concern for China. Again completely disregarding what the administration was doing to combat Communism in Europe, they concentrated on its hesitancies in Asia and took every opportunity to undermine public confidence in Truman and Acheson by accusing them of sabotaging "the valiant attempt of the Chinese Nationalists to keep at least part of China free." In an amazing statement when the President originally appointed as his Secretary of State the man who played such a vital role in building up the defenses of Western Europe, Senator Wherry said: "It is known—somehow it is common knowledge—that Acheson has been an appeaser of Russia."

The two leading members of the China bloc in the House of Representatives were Walter Judd of Minnesota and John Vorys of Ohio. Without being as reactionary as the Senate group, they had generally the same approach to China policy. In their case, however, support for the Nationalists was significantly affected by their own earlier associations with China and the American missionary movement. Judd had been a medical missionary in the 1930s, and Vorys, born of missionary parents, was for a time associated with Yale-in-China. Both men had a sense of personal involvement in the goal of making over China in the image of America and could hardly recover from the shock of seeing the Communist revolution so completely dissipate all their hopes. They maintained their firm faith in Chiang Kai-shek as both an anti-Communist and a Christian convert.

Judd and Vorys repeatedly called for more substantial aid to the Nationalists. In making their support for the European recovery program conditional on such assistance, they played a politically influential role in House action on foreign aid appropriations. Vorys insisted that China should be included in any aid program for "all the reasons that apply to Europe." Judd stressed this same point, stating on one occasion that "we have got to win in Asia, too, or we will ultimately lose in Europe."

Among other public figures closely associated with the China bloc one of the most influential was Henry Luce, the publisher of Life and Time. He too had a China background, being born of missionary parents, and this undoubtedly helped to explain the zeal with which his magazines supported Chiang Kai-shek. William C. Bullitt, former ambassador to the Soviet Union, notably forwarded this campaign. In an article in Life titled "Report on China," appearing as early as 1947, he called for a program of $1,350 million in military and economic aid, which, he believed, could save the day for the Nationalists. The perennial presidential candidate, Harold Stassen, also took up China as a political issue and allied himself with the most conservative critics of the administration. American policy, he said, "has been five years of coddling Chinese Communists . . . and five years of appeasing the arch-Communist, Mao Tse-tung."

The inspiration of the China bloc, the man to whom its members looked for leadership, was General MacArthur. Throughout this whole period he was the first of the Asia Firsters. His background and experience, his long association with the Far East, led him always, in war or peace, to give a high priority to events in the Pacific. He felt that Europe was "a dying system" and, echoing Seward's view almost a century earlier, declared that "the lands touching the Pacific with their billions of inhabitants will determine the course of history in the next ten thousand years." In 1947 he declared that while America's past lay deeply rooted in the lands across the Atlantic, we should look "for the hope of a better life through yet untapped opportunities for trade and commerce in the advance of Asiatic races." As deeply concerned over the threat of Communism as any right-wing senator, MacArthur believed that the triumphs of the Chinese Communists were a greater threat to the United States than anything that might happen in Europe.

Reflecting quite different motives but united in their unrelenting anti-Communism, their acceptance of the overriding importance of the Far East, and their unyielding commitment to the cause of Chiang Kai-shek, members of the congressional China bloc exercised political influence wholly disproportionate to their numbers. One contemporary analysis estimated their numerical strength at about one-fourth the membership of the Senate and one-eighth that of the House, but a considerably smaller number voted consistently for those measures that would have undermined administration policy by providing greater aid to the Nationalists. The China bloc did not succeed in the winter of 1949–50 in compelling the Truman Administration to lend active support to the Nationalists, but as we have seen, its influence did play an important part in preventing that complete disengagement from their cause toward which the administration appeared to be working.

When Senator McCarthy entered the political arena on February 9, 1950, with his notorious charges of Communism in the State Department, he gave both a new direction and a new intensity to the China bloc's attacks on the Truman-Acheson Far Eastern policy. His sensational speech at Wheeling, West Virginia, in which he told the awed members of the local Women's Republican Club that he held in his hand a list of 205 persons in the State Department, known to the Secretary of State as Communists and still helping to shape foreign policy, was to have the most fateful consequences. Earlier charges that the administration was following a program of appeasement in eastern Asia were transmuted under McCarthy's influence to accusations that our policy was the result of a pro-Communist conspiracy in Washington.

In making his intemperate charges, McCarthy discovered a political issue that he would henceforth ride with insensate fervor. A background of more substantial revelations of Communist influence and intrigue in high places strengthened his hand. The Alger Hiss case, the discovery that the British scientist Dr. Karl Fuchs had handed over atomic secrets to a Soviet agent while working in Washington, and other instances of alleged disloyalty unearthed by the House Un-American Activities Committee were very much in the news. They gave a possible credibility to McCarthy's wild and reckless accusations that would not have been possible in a less suspicious and emotionally charged atmosphere. The alarms over Communist influence in Washington were also supplemented at just this time by heightened fears of Soviet Russia's military power resulting from its explosion of an atomic bomb. Senator McCarthy saw an opportunity to build up his own political future by playing upon the public's anxieties, and he did so with callous disregard of truth or consequences.

In the spring of 1950 his major target was the makers of Far Eastern policy. He revived General Patrick Jay Hurley's old charge that there were Communist sympathizers among the foreign service officers in China. Following a shifting, tortuous course as to the exact number of Communists he had found in the State Department, irresponsibly confusing alleged party members, fellow travelers and other security risks, McCarthy gave a new turn to the conspiracy theory that sent shivers of apprehension down the backs of a nervous public.

In a series of speeches in the Senate he repeated that the State Department was "thoroughly infested with Communists" who were plotting to betray the national interest. The more he delved into the matter, the senator from Wisconsin declared, the more he became convinced that two areas of government operations were completely controlled "by individuals who are loyal to the ideals and designs of Communism rather than those of the free, God-fearing half of the world. . . . I refer to the Far Eastern Division of the State Department and the Voice of America."

In other statements he specifically named certain of the foreign service officers in China as security risks, said that Ambassador Jessup was a man with "an affinity for Communist causes," and singled out the distinguished Asian scholar Owen Lattimore as at once "the Soviet's top espionage agent" and "the chief architect of our Far Eastern policy." Becoming overnight an assured expert, Senator McCarthy confidently told the Senate that in the conquest of China, Soviet Russia had an important ally in the "leftwing element in our State Department."

The members of the China bloc did not all approve of McCarthy's methods, but for the most part they succumbed to the spirit of the times and began to echo his thesis of a Communist-directed conspiracy at work in the State Department. They supported his insistence on a thorough housecleaning. "This job," said Senator Bridges, "calls for yellow soap, a scrubbing brush and plenty of elbow grease from the basement to the attic. It should be finished off with a firstclass cyanide fumigation job." Going even further, many of them went along with McCarthy's further demand that Acheson and Jessup, "the Pied Pipers of the Kremlin," should be promptly dismissed.

Taft, who had initially characterized McCarthy's attacks as "a perfectly reckless performance," was soon to follow his lead. He charged that a pro-Communist group in the State Department was "the greatest Kremlin asset in our history" and that through the policies they encouraged, "we have permitted Russia to take over all China." Representative Judd also followed this McCarthyist line. In elaborating on the thesis that our policy "gave China to the Russians," he attributed the debacle to the influence of "the Communists and their stooges, both inside our Government and among writers, lecturers, commentators, professors, and so forth."

President Truman denounced McCarthy's charges, Dean Acheson flatly denied the presence of any Communists in the State Department, and Senator Lucas Scott, the Democratic majority leader, indignantly declared there was "no shred of truth to the senator's false statements." An alarmed and bewildered public hardly knew what to believe. Two editorials in Washington newspapers reflected the sharp division of public opinion. Defending the foreign service officers whom McCarthy accused of having Communist sympathies, the *Post* declared that "the mere fact that they used their eyes and exercised their brains is regarded as circumstantial evidence of guilt," while the *Times-Herald* stated that "the known failure of high officials of the State Department in dealing with subversion, pinkos and Communist agents has destroyed public confidence in this important branch of government."

Acheson soon became the principal target of the McCarthy campaign, all the more vulnerable because of his personal statement that he would not turn his back on Alger Hiss. For those who were determined to pillory him for what they considered a policy designed to appease the

Communists, his attitude on this notorious case confirmed all their worst suspicions. The Secretary of State's manner when called upon to explain his actions at congressional hearings once again served to infuriate his political foes. "Look at that fellow," Senator John Butler, Republican from Maryland, was quoted as saying after one such hearing. "I watch his smart-aleck manner and his British clothes and that New Dealism . . . and I want to shout, Get out, Get out. You stand for everything that has been wrong with the United States for years."

In the face of such violent opposition, at a time when his major preoccupation was building up Western Europe's defenses against possible Soviet aggression, Acheson was compelled to spend an inordinate amount of time trying to win public confidence in his conduct of foreign policy. He traveled about the country, wrote Richard Rovere, "explaining to Elks, Moose, Women Voters, Legionnaires, Steel Workers, and the rest, that he was not corrupt, that he was opposed to Communism and that he did not hire traitors." President Truman never hesitated to give him the fullest support, yet seldom—if ever—in our history has a Secretary of State found himself under more vicious attack than Dean Acheson as Senator McCarthy and the China bloc tried to hound him out of office.

The Senate promptly initiated an investigation in response to McCarthy's free-wheeling charges against the State Department. A special committee under the chairmanship of Senator Millard Tydings of Maryland held hearings throughout April and May 1950. Its report, released in July, completely exonerated the men accused of being Communists or having Communist affiliations. However, the whole issue was so enmeshed in partisan politics that the committee as a whole refused to accept this complete bill of health for the State Department. Where the Democratic majority declared that McCarthy's attack was fraught with falsehood from beginning to end and that "its reprehensible and contemptuous character defies adequate condemnation," the Republican minority countered that in examining his charges the committee's investigation had been superficial and partisan. After violent debate the Senate adopted the majority report by a strictly party vote of 45 to 37, but the dissent to its conclusions left the State Department under a cloud that the administration could not entirely dispel.

Another inconclusive investigation, held the next year, had somewhat the same unsatisfactory consequences. Under the chairmanship of Senator McCarran, a Senate subcommittee held a series of interminable hearings— they continued intermittently from July 1951 to June 1952—into the affairs of the Institute of Pacific Relations, a scholarly research organization, which was charged with harboring Communists and following a Communist line in such of its publications as the *Far Eastern Survey* and *Pacific Affairs*. Under the influence of McCarthyism the investigation became an intolerable witch-hunt. Rumor and hearsay were accepted as legal evidence of Communist affiliations, guilt by association was given the widest credence, and the committee appeared to be far more interested in newspaper headlines than in facts. It kept Owen Lattimore, on whose guilt McCarthy said he would "stand or fall," on the witness stand for twelve long days of minutely detailed questioning.

The institute was not wholly innocent of the charges brought against it; among its members and the contributors to its publications were a number of card-carrying Communists as well as Communist sympathizers. The McCarran committee, however, ignored the broad scope of the IPR's activities and the generally objective character of most of its reports. In the case of Owen Lattimore, a number of contradictions in his testimony led to an indictment for perjury (later dismissed in the courts), but no evidence was produced showing he was either a Soviet spy or the "chief architect" of Far Eastern policy. The committee nonetheless concluded he was "a conscious articulate instrument of the Communist conspiracy."

The full report reflected the prejudice and bias that had marked the hearings. It stated that under the influence of its Communist-oriented members, the Institute of Pacific Relations was disseminating propaganda favorable to the Soviet Union and attempting to exercise influence on the State Department that would promote Russian rather than American interests in eastern Asia. Granted some Communists were enrolled in its membership, nothing in the report satisfactorily demonstrated that the IPR was itself engaged in any activity other than seeking to provide, through the publication of all points of view, a comprehensive record of Far Eastern developments.

While this investigation was dragging on, a Senate hearing in September 1951 provided Senator McCarthy with still a further opportunity to press home his claims of Communist penetration of the State Department. It concerned the nomination of Ambassador Jessup as the United States delegate to the annual meeting of the United Nations Assembly. McCarthy was a principal witness and he was out to prove his accusation that the State Department's chief troubleshooter in the Far East had an affinity for Communist causes. He cited little more as evidence of guilt than Jessup's membership in the Institute of Pacific Relations and the Russian-American Institute. Jessup denied any Communist sympathies whatsoever and heatedly characterized the charges as "barefaced falsehoods, distortions, and misrepresentations."

His accuser could not be stopped. Browbeating anyone who tried to contradict him, refusing himself to answer questions put to him by his Senate colleagues, conducting himself so outrageously that an irate Senator William Fulbright, Democrat from Arkansas, declared he had never seen a more arrogant or rude witness, McCarthy gave a first exhibit of that brutal behavior which the public was soon to witness at the famous televised army hearings. Flailing about at one point against his suspects in the State Department, he angrily answered the request of one of the committee members that he be more explicit about names and dates by blurting out, "I am dealing with too many of these slimy creatures to keep all the details in mind."

The extent to which McCarthy succeeded in making trouble was demonstrated when the Senate subcommittee, while far from convinced of the truth of the charges against Jessup, nonetheless refused by a vote of three to two to confirm his nomination as a UN delegate. The majority felt that the controversy had raised such clouds of doubt over Jessup's suitability that, although he had on three earlier occasions gone to the United Nations, he might not under these new circumstances be an effective spokesman for his country. President Truman, however, refused to accede to such pressure. He gave his special ambassador a recess appointment, and Jessup duly went to the UN.

The disruptive effects of McCarthyism were everywhere apparent in the spring of 1950, but its greatest impact continued to be on the conduct of Far Eastern policy. If it significantly served to paralyze any further moves toward disengagement from the Chinese civil war, it also led to the dispersal of many veteran China experts in the State Department at a time when their first-hand experience could hardly have been more needed. The investigations and loyalty reviews that the department felt constrained to make in the face of McCarthy's attacks did not turn up a single Communist. Nevertheless McCarthyism was greatly responsible for the transfer to less sensitive posts of the men most knowledgeable about China and in a number of cases to their dismissal or forced retirement as security risks. The effect upon morale throughout the foreign service was shattering.

These moves to cleanse the Far Eastern Division were initiated before Senator McCarthy himself came on the scene, as a result of the earlier right-wing pressure on the State Department growing out of General Hurley's charges that Communist sympathizers influenced our policy during China's civil war. Among the more important men transferred in this first period were John Paton Davies, the outspoken adviser to Stilwell at Kunming; John Carter Vincent, counselor at the embassy at Chungking and later head of the Division of Far Eastern Affairs; and John S. Service, third secretary at Chungking. In each case their flagrant error was realistically and honestly reporting the weakness of the Nationalists and the mounting strength of the Communists. Somewhat ironically, Davies was transferred to Moscow (where his knowledge of China, George Kennan was later to write, made him "a rock of strength to us"); Vincent was first moved to Switzerland and then made minister to Morocco and diplomatic agent at Tangiers; and Service was appointed consul general in Calcutta.

When McCarthy launched his attacks on the State Department, he made no direct charges against Davies but specifically singled out Service and Vincent as being pro-Communist. Summoned home to answer these allegations, both men were completely cleared after a series of investigations and loyalty reviews. However, the pressure was too great to allow them to remain in the department. Service found himself ousted in 1951 on grounds of "reasonable doubt" of his loyalty (to be reinstated six years later as a senior departmental officer after further court proceedings), and Vincent, whom Acheson tried to protect, was forced to resign two years later because of failure "to meet the standard which is demanded of a Foreign Service officer." Finally catching up with John Paton Davies, the legions of McCarthyism secured his dismissal on the vague score of "lack of judgment, discretion and reliability," though like Service and Vincent he had been fully cleared in all loyalty reviews.

No better example could be found of the heavy hand of McCarthyism on the operations of the State Department than the loss of such men, among others, against whom no valid evidence whatsoever was produced of Communist sympathies. The resort to such patent subterfuges as doubts of their loyalty could hardly have illustrated more clearly the timidity in official circles. Commenting on this situation in his *Memoirs*, George Kennan was to single out the case of Davies as demonstrating the humiliation and harassment to which foreign service officers were subjected at the hands of congressional and other investigating committees. "That this could happen to a man without an ounce of Communist sympathies," Kennan wrote, bespeaks "the nightmarish quality of the world of fancy into which official Washington, and much of public opinion, can be carried in those times when fear, anger and emotionalism take over from reason in the conduct of our public life."

The wide publicity given to McCarthy's accusations of disloyalty, whether or not they had any basis in fact, and the ever-present danger that such charges might lead to dismissal or the wrecking of a diplomatic career continued to have devastating consequences for the staffing of the Far Eastern Division. Even before McCarthy came on the scene the Washington *Post* wryly commented that "sooner or later the country will find that no man with any regard for his reputation let alone his career will touch a job having to do with China with a 10-foot pole." This happened sooner rather than later. By 1953 only two of the prewar foreign service officers concerned with China policy were still in the State Department. The next year Edgar Snow wrote that the department was left without a single experienced China expert on the policy-making level. In his recent book *To Move a Nation*, former Assistant Secretary for Far Eastern Affairs Roger Hilsman has said that "before the McCarthy business had run its course, the twenty-some China Specialists in the Foreign Service had either resigned, retired, or run to cover in jobs dealing with other parts of the world."

Dean Acheson could not have been more unhappy over this situation, and realizing the imperative need to establish public confidence in the State Department, he moved in September 1950 to place at the head of the Division of Far Eastern Affairs a man whom even Senator McCarthy could not suspect of having Communist sympathies. This was Dean Rusk. He had but recently been appointed Deputy Undersecretary of State and when he volunteered for what was in effect a demotion, Acheson happily accepted his offer. On record for his outspoken anti-Communist views, and having had no part in the previous formulation of China policy, Rusk was free of any taint of mistrust or suspicion. Promptly hailed as "a new stalwart" in the State Department, he was expected to command—and indeed did—far more confidence among members of the congressional China bloc than any of his predecessors in the Far Eastern Division.

Senator McCarthy's assaults were of course first directed against the Truman Administration, concentrating on the President, his Secretary of State, and Ambassador Jessup, but the momentum of his hysterical anti-Communist crusade carried over to the new Republican Administration after the election of General Eisenhower in 1952. The Wisconsin senator soon found its foreign policy no less "weak, immoral and cowardly" than that of the Truman Administration. With the transpiring of further events in eastern Asia, the Eisenhower program became in his fevered mind one of "appeasement, retreat, and surrender."

On first taking office as Secretary of State, John Foster Dulles, like Acheson, felt very much on the defensive in regard to possible security

Secretary of State Dean Acheson appearing before the Senate Investigation Committee, June 1951. Seated opposite him are Senators William Knowland (left) and Harry Cain. (United Press International)

Acting Secretary of State Walter Bedell Smith (right) with Senator Styles Bridges of the Senate Appropriations Committee, which investigated charges that Communist atrocities against American prisoners in Korea were suppressed by the Pentagon, April 1953. (United Press International)

Vice-President Richard Nixon with Generalissimo Chiang Kai-shek on Formosa, November 1953. (United Press International)

Foreign Minister George Yeh of Nationalist China and Secretary of State John Foster Dulles at the signing of the Mutual Security Treaty, December 1954. (Wide World)

Secretary of State John Foster Dulles (second from left) and Assistant Secretary of State Walter Robertson with Generalissimo and Mme. Chiang Kai-shek on Formosa, March 1958. (United Press International)

President John F. Kennedy with Assistant Secretary of State W. Averell Harriman prior to Harriman's departure for India in November 1962 to see whether military aid was needed to repel the Chinese invasion of that country. (United Press International)

Secretary of State Dean Rusk (left) and roving ambassador W. Averell Harriman upon their return from a tour of Southeast Asia, January 1966. (United Press International)

President Lyndon Johnson flanked by Secretary of State Dean Rusk and Defense Secretary Clark Clifford at a National Security Council meeting prior to the President's October 31, 1968, announcement of a halt to American bombing of North Vietnam. (United Press International)

Secretary of State George C. Marshall (center) confers with Senator Tom Connally (left) and Senator Arthur Vandenberg prior to Senate Foreign Relations Committee discussions of the world crisis, March 1948. (United Press International)

Secretary of State Dean Acheson with the State Department White Paper on China, August 1949. (Wide World)

Owen Lattimore (left) and Senator Joseph R. McCarthy during a recess of the Senate Foreign Relations Subcommittee hearings, April 1950. (United Press International)

Secretary of Defense George C. Marshall arrives at the White House for a conference with President Truman on the Korean situation, November 1950. (United Press International)

John S. Service (lower left) testifies before the Senate Foreign Relations Subcommittee, June 1950. Senator McCarthy is at upper right and other senators are Henry Cabot Lodge, Jr. (second from left), Bourke B. Hickenlooper, and Millard F. Tydings. (Wide World)

President Harry S. Truman and General Douglas MacArthur at Wake Island, October 1950. (United Press International)

Left to right, Wu Hsiu-chuan, head of Communist China's delegation to the United Nations, Kenneth Younger, of the United Kingdom, and John Foster Dulles, Republican adviser to the Secretary of State, at a General Assembly meeting, November 1950. (Wide World)

Senator Robert Taft in a speech in New York in April 1951 warned against appeasing the Communists. (United Press International)

Senator William Jenner, who in April 1951 said from the floor of the Senate, "The only choice is to impeach President Truman." (United Press International)

General Douglas MacArthur on the witness stand in May 1951, during the Senate Investigation Committee hearings. (United Press International)

Patrick J. Hurley, former ambassador to China, testifying in June 1951 before the Senate Investigation Committee hearing on General MacArthur's dismissal. (United Press International)

risks within the State Department. He insisted on "positive loyalty," and under the pressure of McCarthyism appointed as a special security officer Scott McLeod, a former FBI agent and administrative assistant of the reactionary Senator Bridges. McLeod brought to his assignment of assuring complete loyalty within the department a ruthless zeal that soon became a cause of considerable personal distress to the essentially fair-minded Secretary of State.

Protests against what was happening came from various sources. Former Secretary of State Henry L. Stimson had in March 1950 written in a letter to the *New York Times* that McCarthy's attacks on the State Department were a dangerous threat to our whole foreign policy, compounded by the fact that his real target was the Secretary of State. As the right-wing assault continued, five distinguished career diplomats, in another letter to the *Times* on January 17, 1954, deplored its crippling consequences for rational policy making. For fear of being accused of disloyalty, these diplomats said, foreign service officers were becoming increasingly reluctant to express any strong opinions that might differ from those of their superiors. George Kennan wrote that things were becoming so bad that he could not in good conscience advise any young man to enter the foreign service.

Not bothered by anything of this sort, Senator McCarthy knew where his duty—and political advantage—lay. He insolently followed his own course without the slightest regard for how his ill-conceived and unsupported charges might affect conscientious members of the foreign service. In his study of the Communist controversy in Washington during these years, Earl Latham has asserted that "with the acquiescence of the Secretary of State, he [McCarthy] wrought with brute brilliance, a catastrophe of sick apprehension in the Department of State and the destruction of its morale." In a later testament to the Wisconsin senator's influence, Louis Halle has written that "the whole apparatus through which the foreign relations of the United States had to be conducted was, in large measure, wrecked."

A further consequence of McCarthyism was the virtual suppression of objective reporting on China by the best-informed specialists in the journalistic and academic worlds. Their egregious mistake was that they agreed with the State Department experts on the bankruptcy of the Nationalist regime, the futility of extending further aid to Chiang Kai-shek, and the advisability of complete disengagement from the Chinese civil war. This automatically made them pro-Communist—Senator Brewster declared they were doing "as successful a selling job for Communism as has ever been done before"—and in the temper of the times, magazines and newspapers became very wary of publishing articles that might be attacked as disloyal.

The China experts were a small, tightly knit group closely associated through their common interest, and included such scholars and writers as Owen Lattimore, John Fairbank, Edgar Snow, Nathaniel Peffer, Joseph Barnes, Harold Isaacs, and T. A. Bisson. Their books; their articles in the publications of the Institute of Pacific Relations and in such magazines as *Harper's*, the *Atlantic Monthly*, the *Saturday Review of Literature*, the *Reporter*, and the *New Republic;* and their book reviews in the major newspapers provided the best available information on Far Eastern developments for the general public. But when timid editors felt unable to stand up against the charge that these writers were parroting Communist propaganda, the China experts often found their usual publication outlets closed to them. In a study of China policy published in 1961, Robert Newman reported that whereas between 1945 and 1950 the above group of writers reviewed in the *New York Times* twenty-two of thirty books dealing with China and in the *Herald Tribune* thirty out of thirty-five, between 1952 and 1956 not one of them appeared in the book-review pages of either newspaper.

The restraints imposed on these writers left the way open for a quite different set of publicists to inform the public on Asian affairs. Among them were John Flynn, a right-wing journalist and author of *While You Slept*, a fierce indictment of what he considered the Truman Administration's record of betrayal and treason; Felix Wittmer, who in his *Yalta Betrayal* attributed American policy making in the Far East to "the pinks and reds in Washington"; and Freda Utley, one-time British Communist, whose *The China Story* viciously attacked what she called "a powerful combine," including members of the Institute of Pacific Relations, which was spreading throughout the country "the gospel according to Mao Tse-tung."

"This was not history," Hanson Baldwin, the military correspondent of the *New York Times* and actually a severe critic of our China policy, wrote scathingly of these books. It was, he said, "a particularly reptilian form of politics which would have us believe that . . . our mistakes . . . were part of a Great Conspiracy to hand the country over to Communism on a silver platter." In this literature of suspicion, innuendo, and hate, McCarthyism was expressing itself in its most virulent and dangerous form.

If there had always been a wide gap between myth and reality in both official and popular understanding of China, the virtual suppression of factual reporting on the Far Eastern scene in the early 1950s greatly widened it. The public had little means for judging such critical issues as the underlying strength of nationalism in China, the goals and purposes of the Peking government, or the relationship between the Chinese People's Republic and Soviet Russia. In the circumstances it became highly suspect to hold any view other than that the international Communist conspiracy fully accounted for China's revolution and for the Chinese people's new hostility toward the United States.

"Not until the late 1950s," one of McCarthy's State Department's victims wrote somewhat ruefully a decade later, "could one suggest without loss of respectability that self-assertive nationalism might exist in, for example, Communist China." It was far safer to hew to the conventional line and accept the conspiratorial thesis which so easily explained everything that had gone wrong with our Far Eastern policy.

Another factor in the situation, a disturbing influence on policy and a source from which Senator McCarthy drew much of his material in developing his charges of Communist infiltration in the State Department, was that vague, mysterious, indefinable entity—that "mythical dragon," as a skeptical *Time* magazine called it—which became known as the China lobby. Not to be confused with the congressional China bloc, although often in close association with it, this lobby was composed of officials from the Nationalist embassy in Washington, their paid propaganda agents, and a number of rabid anti-Communists drawn from the ranks of American businessmen, retired army officers, and conservative "old China hands." Together they made up one of the most relentless pressure groups in the capital in their zealous promotion of Chiang Kai-shek and the Nationalist cause.

In August 1949, Senator Mike Mansfield, the Montana Democrat, first affirmed that money Congress had appropriated for military and economic aid to the Nationalists was being "siphoned off" by this China lobby to finance a propaganda campaign directed against the Secretary of State and the foreign service officers responsible for the conduct of our China policy. Soon afterward, a number of probing articles began to appear, including an editorial in the *New York Times*, which inquired into the lobby's undercover and possibly illegal activities. It was Senator Wayne Morse of Oregon, however, who was most instrumental in exposing the lobby to public scrutiny. Breaking into the questioning of Secretary Acheson at the hearings in 1951 on General MacArthur's recall from Korea, he declared that the China lobby, using funds provided by the Nationalist embassy, was responsible for an improper campaign to influence American foreign policy. He called for an immediate investigation.

Acheson, acknowledging that the public had a right to know what was going on, returned the next day to the Senate committee hearing to say that President Truman had agreed that an investigation should be made. The State Department soon afterward announced that it did not have the facilities to conduct such an inquiry. It turned the entire matter over to the Department of Justice, but the latter in turn found itself unable to carry out the assignment and let the whole thing drop.

Senator Morse stuck to his guns and about a year later, in April 1952, he renewed his demand for an investigation and introduced into the *Congressional Record* a number of messages that the counselor of the Chinese embassy, Chen Chih-mai, had allegedly sent to Chiang Kai-shek reporting on lobby activities. Their general purport was that in promoting its interests in the United States the Nationalist government should concentrate its energies on trying to influence Congress in view of the unfriendly attitude of both General Marshall and Secretary Acheson. One message, dated June 24, 1949, which was signed by Chen and addressed to the generalissimo, was very specific:

"As far as our activities in the United States are concerned, it seems that [while] we should cover the administration, as well as the legislative branch, we should especially strive for a closer relationship with the latter. There is no danger at all if our procedure follows the laws of the United States, but Dr. Hu Shih [former Chinese ambassador] is opposed to getting in touch with the legislative branch. His opinion is off the beam."

Other documents, showing that the embassy followed this proposed procedure in trying to influence Congress, revealed the rather questionable aspects, to put it mildly, of this willingness on the part of a foreign embassy to interfere in the domestic affairs of the host country. They referred to making contacts with Senator Taft, obtaining secret information from Representative Judd (which he indignantly denied), and hiring as a legal adviser an unnamed figure in Democratic circles "capable of reaching the highest levels of the proper authorities." They also referred vaguely to Nationalist air force officers in Washington seeking to spy out atomic secrets.

The documents disclosing these activities—some appeared to be of doubtful authenticity, but others were verified—still left open the question of who actually signed them. An air of mystery hung over what the China lobby was doing and especially over the source of its funds. When in 1960 Ross Y. Koen included in *The China Lobby in American Politics* the purported details of the lobby's financial transactions, his publishers felt compelled to withdraw the book when the Nationalist embassy threatened legal action.

Lacking an official investigation, the most responsible source for the origins and development of the China lobby, its association with many members of the congressional China bloc, and what became its close ties with Senator McCarthy is a series of articles in the *Reporter*. Published in April 1952, these articles cited chapter and verse in describing a propaganda campaign that in the view of the magazine's editors "managed to jam the rudder of our Far Eastern policy."

According to this account in the *Reporter*, the initial instigators of the China lobby were two prominent Chinese in this country, H. H. Kung and T. V. Soong, brothers-in-law of Chiang Kai-shek and important members of the four families that constituted the ruling group within the Kuomintang. They fled China in 1949 and were deeply involved in the transactions relating to the employment of funds transferred to this country from the Nationalist treasury. Whatever their role in these proceedings, both Kung and Soong, together with Dr. T. F. Tsiang, the Nationalist delegate to the United Nations, were agreed on the need for an intensive campaign to win American support for Chiang Kai-shek. They were ready to finance the program that the counselor of the Nationalist embassy envisaged for building up congressional opposition to the administration's policy of disengagement.

Following this line, the Chinese embassy hired in 1949 as a public relations expert William J. Goodwin, a former member of the Christian Front, a notorious anti-Communist, pro-Fascist organization. With a handsome salary and liberal expense account, Goodwin was soon "pushing ahead feverishly" in making available to members of the China bloc information to help them in undermining Secretary Acheson's position. Goodwin staged a series of dinners that were attended by such leaders in this congressional group as Senators Knowland, Bridges, Wherry, and McCarran, and he met also with numerous other members of both the Senate and House. He was later to boast that in making contacts with some one hundred Congressmen, he converted fifty of them to the Nationalist cause. He also said with equal satisfaction that he had "helped materially" in paving the way for McCarthy's charges against the State Department.

The China lobby further embraced two pro-Nationalist organizations, the one headed by Alfred Kohlberg, a New York importer of Chinese embroidery, and the other by Frederick C. McKee, a casket manufacturer from Pittsburgh. Both men were in effect professional anti-Communists and devoted themselves to support of Chiang Kai-shek with zeal and passion. Kohlberg's organization was called the American China Policy Association and included on its board of directors Representative Judd and Clare Boothe Luce; William Loeb, the reactionary editor of the Manchester (New Hampshire) *Union Leader;* and such former Communists as Max Eastman and Freda Utley. McKee's group was the Committee to Defend America by Aiding Anti-Communist China and had on its board several of the directors of the China Policy Association and also such disparate figures as David Dubinsky, of the International Garment Workers; Jay Lovestone, one-time secretary general of the American Communist Party; and former Postmaster General James A. Farley.

Working in close cooperation with officials in the Nationalist embassy and with William Goodwin, these groups played a significant role in widely distributing pro-Nationalist literature—news releases, newspaper advertisements, and pamphlets. But while this effort was all part of the China lobby's general campaign, neither the organizations nor the individuals concerned were very closely coordinated. In a postscript to the articles in the *Reporter,* Max Ascoli, the magazine's editor, commented that one of the most astonishing things about the China lobby was that as far as could be discovered, "it has no leaders, only mouth-pieces." Yet he still felt that somehow it was strong enough "to cramp our national leadership."

Kohlberg was probably the lobby's most direct link with McCarthy. The two men met for the first time in February 1950, and a little later, by his own testimony, Kohlberg was happily doing everything he could to forward McCarthy's attacks on the State Department. "I am proud," he once testified, "to have given Senator McCarthy a small part of the information he needed for his fight." In his turn the senator acknowledged this debt, and in Owen Lattimore's phrase became "the China lobby's 'willing tool.'"

After the advent of a new administration in 1953 and the conclusion of the Korean war, the Nationalist government's embassy continued its propaganda, hiring a new public relations firm, the Hamilton Wright Organization, to which it allegedly paid $300,000 a year. The China lobby as it was originally constituted, however, faded away; the organizations founded by Kohlberg and McKee became inactive. Their place was taken by a group initially called the Committee for One Million Against the Admission of Communist China into the United Nations. It sprang from

a movement on the part of a number of pro-Nationalists, headed by former President Hoover, to block what for a time appeared to be a possibility that the United States would reverse its position on the China representation issue. With such familiar figures as Senator Knowland and Representative Judd playing a major role, and with the powerful backing of
the American Legion, the American Federation of Labor, and the General
Federation of Women's Clubs, the committee succeeded within nine
months in collecting one million anti-Communist signatures.

Having played its part in preventing any change in American policy
in 1953, the original committee disbanded, but its members then reorganized as the Committee *of* One Million to throw its weight behind a
broader campaign to ensure the complete political isolation of the People's Republic of China. Its tactics whenever danger threatened were to
launch a nationwide postcard campaign, supplemented by full-page newspaper advertisements throughout the country, to rally popular opinion
against any concessions to the Communists.

In an article in January 1960 the *Nation* described this pressure group
as "the lobby of a million ghosts," but it could not be so easily dismissed.
The committee enrolled on its lists a wide spectrum of important political figures, including in 1966 no less than 334 members of Congress. Its
secretary, Marvin Liebman, stated that its purpose was to arouse congressional and public opinion—"If there is a China Lobby, we are it"—
not only against the admission of Communist China to the United Nations but against diplomatic recognition or trade relations.

The Committee of One Million, in its own words, represented "the
responsible voice of the American people united in opposing any steps
which would strengthen the political, economic or aggressive power of
the Peking regime."

It is impossible to unravel the tangled threads that bound together the
congressional China bloc, Senator McCarthy, the mouthpieces of the
China lobby, and such anti-Communist pressure groups as the American
China Policy Association and the later Committee of One Million. They
worked together and separately. Yet always in the background was the
same hard core of anti-Communists who remained convinced that American policy should fully support Chiang Kai-shek and make no concessions whatever to Mao Tse-tung.

McCarthyism above all else provided the emotional cement that solidified the widely accepted view that any accommodation with the Chinese
Communists was appeasement in the most pejorative sense of that much

misused term. It embodied and magnified all the exaggerated and irrational fears of the Cold War. Its impact on other phases of our national life—its stifling of free speech and civil liberties—was notorious, but it may be repeated that one of its most unhappy consequences was the caution it forced upon the State Department in dealing with the new issues of eastern Asia.

Dean Acheson in *Present at the Creation* stoutly denied this so far as his own term of office was concerned. "A good deal of nonsense," he stated, "has been written about the attack of the primitives [his word for his detractors], before and during McCarthy's reign, on the China policy of the Truman Administration. Whatever effect it had on our successors, it had little on us." He maintained that "between the bungling incompetence of Chiang Kai-shek's Kuomintang and the intransigence of Mao Tse-tung's Communists, our choices for policy decisions were small indeed."

Yet the gestures to conciliate the China bloc by approving continued economic aid to the Nationalists, the hesitations in carrying through President Truman's affirmed policy of complete disengagement from China's civil strife, and some few later concessions surely demonstrate that the Truman Administration was not as free from McCarthyist influence as its Secretary of State would maintain.

On the eve of the President's statement in January 1950 declaring that the United States would not pursue a policy leading to involvement in China's civil conflict, Acheson wrote his daughter a most interesting letter with reference to what Truman was going to say. "So much that is foolish, disloyal, and generally contemptible has been going on," he told her, "that it is good that we are—I hope—free to go ahead on a clear and sensible course."

But Senator McCarthy gave renewed life to the China bloc's vehement attacks on this clear and sensible course. In playing so outrageously on the public's fears and prejudice in his charges of Communist influence in the State Department, he greatly limited the administration's options. Whether under any circumstances a policy could have been implemented leading to complete disengagement from China's civil war and final dissociation from Chiang Kai-shek may be doubted. As things stood, the opportunity to carry through any such policy in the spring of 1950 was lost.

And then came Korea.

7

The Impact of Korea

WHEN THE NORTH KOREANS attacked across the Thirty-eighth Parallel on June 25, 1950, the whole situation in eastern Asia changed dramatically overnight. For this was not just a case of Communist subversion or a threat of possible aggression. It was the challenge of war, and a war universally accepted in the United States as precipitated and directed by Moscow in support of the world strategy of international Communism.

The likelihood of an attack by Communist forces in some part of the world in the spring of 1950 was anticipated by the National Security Council. In a highly secret document (NSC-68) initialed by President Truman in April—a document Dean Acheson has characterized as "one of the great documents in our history"—the council stated that the Soviet Union was poised to extend its power in either Europe, the Middle East, or Asia and that the United States should be fully prepared to resist the thrust of any such attack, in cooperation with its allies if possible, but if necessary by its own force of arms. Although little thought was given to the chance that the selected target might be Korea, the Truman Administration was ready for prompt reaction to any Communist threat.

The United States was not at this time greatly concerned over the status of Korea in the alignment of power in the Far East. That unhappy country was in early 1950 still divided as a result of the agreement reached five years earlier for its military occupation. In the south was the

Republic of Korea, recognized by the United Nations, and in the north the Communist-controlled People's Democratic Republic. However, both the Russian and American occupation forces had been withdrawn and the demarcation line along the Thirty-eighth Parallel seemed to be a relatively stable one. What might happen in Korea certainly had little interest for the American people, if they thought about it at all.

The Joint Chiefs of Staff, reporting on Korea prior to the withdrawal of our forces in the south, stated that "the United States has little strategic interest in maintaining the present troops and bases in Korea . . . and in the event of hostilities in the Far East they would be a liability." It was in adopting this stand that Secretary of State Acheson excluded Korea from the American defensive perimeter in the western Pacific. Even the Asia Firsters, so deeply convinced of the strategic importance of Formosa, bothered little about Korea. In one congressional debate involving an appropriation for economic aid to Korea, Representative Vorys stated that in comparison with helping Chiang Kai-shek, giving assistance to Korea's Syngman Rhee was pouring money down "a rat hole." "What kind of policy for the Far East would put economic aid into Korea, which bears no relationship to our national defense, and at the same time refuse a request to put aid into Formosa?" asked Representative Donald L. Jackson, another member of the China bloc, in this same debate.

Nevertheless, the Truman Administration took the view that the North Korean attack endangered the fundamental principles of our global policy and potentially threatened our national security. Recalling Japan's attack on Manchuria in 1931 and the fateful consequences flowing from inaction in that crisis, the policy makers in Washington were convinced that the North Korean assault was a challenge to the free world and to the whole postwar system of collective security that had to be met by all possible means.

In his bold and decisive measures to do so, President Truman was thus acting in support of the preservation of international peace as well as in what he believed to be vital American interests in the Far East. The State Department and the military establishment, regardless of their previous concepts in regard to Korea's strategic importance, were united in recommending and then fully supporting Truman's decision in this grave emergency. The entire country (public opinion polls showed favorable majorities of 73 percent) rallied behind him; even the most severe Republican critics of Far Eastern policy were ready to back up his stand.

"When the time came for you to act in behalf of free men and a free world," Senator Vandenburg wrote the President, "you did so with a spectacular courage which has revived the relentless purpose of all peaceful nations to deny aggression."

Truman was away from Washington when news was received of the North Korean attack. His advisers hastily got in touch with him by telephone, and he approved their recommendation to call a special meeting of the United Nations Security Council to submit a resolution terming the action of the North Koreans a breach of peace and calling for their immediate withdrawal behind the Thirty-eighth Parallel. The Soviet Union was still boycotting the UN, and in its absence the Security Council approved this resolution by a vote of 9 to 0, with Yugoslavia abstaining.

Returning to Washington, the President then met with his advisers at Blair House on the evening of this same day—Sunday, June 25—and a number of further steps were agreed upon to meet the emergency. They included authorization to General MacArthur, as Commander in Chief of the United States Forces in the Far East, to provide arms and ammunition to the South Koreans and protect the evacuation of all Americans. Then as the situation worsened the next day, without waiting for another meeting of the Security Council the President ordered MacArthur to dispatch air and naval forces directly to South Korea's aid.

Certain that the North Korean attack was instigated, mounted, and supplied by Soviet Russia, the President and his advisers had no hesitation in taking these unilateral moves, but they were anxious to secure a broader sanction for them from the United Nations and also establish an unassailable foundation for extending still further aid to South Korea. The American representative on the Security Council, Warren Austin, was consequently instructed to introduce a second resolution, recommending that all members of the UN furnish such assistance to South Korea as might prove necessary in repelling the aggression and restoring peace. The council adopted this resolution on June 27 by a vote of 7 to 1, Yugoslavia now in opposition and India and Egypt abstaining. The way was clear for more direct intervention, and three days later, in response to the recommendation of General MacArthur, President Truman authorized the employment of United States ground forces to reenforce the badly battered South Korean army.

So it was that under the aegis of the United Nations but itself taking the initiative at every turn and in some measure anticipating the approval of the Security Council, the United States became involved in the Korean war, with all its subsequent heartbreak, successive retreats and advances, immense cost in war material, and tragic loss of lives.

Quite as important from the long-range point of view as our intervention in Korea was the impact of this crisis on our policy toward China. In making his decision that the United States should do whatever was necessary to combat Communist aggression in Korea, President Truman took a parallel step in relation to Formosa. Wholly independent of the United Nations, acting on his own responsibility, he ordered the Seventh Fleet into the Formosan Straits to prevent the Chinese Communists from seizing the opportunity to attack the Nationalists.

Secretary Acheson, with the full support of the Joint Chiefs of Staff, proposed this move at that first memorable conference at Blair House on Sunday night. President Truman did not immediately agree—he said he wanted "to sleep on it"—but the next day he accepted the recommendation as a matter of elemental security. In announcing on June 27 his instructions to General MacArthur to employ United States air and naval forces to support the South Koreans, he also made public his orders in respect to Formosa.

Since Communism had resorted to armed invasion in Korea, the President said, occupation of Formosa by Communist forces would be a direct threat to the security of the Pacific and the United States forces there. Accordingly he had instructed the Seventh Fleet to prevent any attack on the island, and, as a corollary to this step, he was also calling on the Nationalist government on Formosa to cease all air and sea operations against the mainland. "The Seventh Fleet," Truman stated, "will see this is done." He then added that determination of the future status of Formosa would have to await "the restoration of security in the Pacific, a peace settlement with Japan, or consideration by the United Nations."

Although it may not have been what the Truman Administration had in mind during the immediate emergency, this vital decision led to the complete reversal of American policy toward Formosa as enunciated by Truman only six months earlier. As future developments progressively demonstrated, it undermined his stated position that we did not intend to interfere in China's civil strife through the interposition of our armed forces: while the United States was ostensibly seeking no more than Formosa's neutralization to avert the further spread of Far Eastern hostilities, it was in effect throwing military support to the Nationalist regime against the Chinese Communists. The ban on possible operations against the mainland by Chiang Kai-shek was virtually meaningless—he was in no position to mount such an assault—but the interdiction of any move against Formosa by the forces of Mao Tse-tung was all important because Peking was prepared, with troops assembled on the adjacent mainland, to attempt a final liquidation of the Nationalist regime.

Whereas in January 1950 official American policy was based on the postulate that Formosa lay beyond our strategic line of defense in the western Pacific, the Korean war brought it within the area whose military defense the United States was henceforth to consider vital to its national interests. The Truman Administration undoubtedly hoped that the immediate necessity of safeguarding Formosa might in time give way to some international guarantee of the island's status that would enable the United States to follow through with its original program of complete disengagement from China's civil war. The President had spoken of possible action by the United Nations. However, we were assuming a responsibility in June 1950 to which the later course of events gave ever greater weight. The Joint Chiefs of Staff were soon recommending renewed military assistance to the Nationalists, such aid was progressively increased, and ultimately the United States formally aligned itself with the Nationalist government on Formosa through conclusion of a mutual security treaty. A critical turning point in our whole policy toward China occurred almost fortuitously when the Seventh Fleet took up its battle station in the Formosan Straits.

These developments represented acceptance of the thesis so long maintained by the congressional China bloc that support for Chiang Kai-shek as the representative of free China was essential in barring the further expansion of Communist power. "It was not long after this," Roger Hilsman has written, "that the State Department became the captive of its critics and swung over to the position that the Nationalist regime on Taiwan was still the government of all China." No longer were we prepared to write off Formosa's possible subjection to the Chinese Communists as not seriously damaging to the interests of either the United States or the free world. It had become a vital outpost; it was to be defended at all costs.

Urgent military considerations relating to the Korean war were primarily responsible in persuading both the State Department and the Joint Chiefs of Staff to adopt this new policy, but domestic politics also had their influence. The need to neutralize Formosa to avert the spread of hostilities was reenforced by the need to neutralize the administration's foes. To assure Republican support, and especially that of the China bloc, for intervention in Korea, something had to be done to meet the continuing demand for active support of the Nationalists. President Truman's orders to the Seventh Fleet, which the Republicans lauded as finally drawing that defensive line in the western Pacific they had so long urged as vital to American security, were a key factor in winning the bipartisan support necessary for our action on the Korean front.

Acheson's change of heart in accepting a policy toward Formosa that he had formerly rejected did not end his difficulties with Congress. Senator Taft declared that a Secretary of State so significantly reversed by his superiors, as the Ohio senator interpreted events, "had better resign and let someone else administer the program to which he was, and perhaps still is, so violently opposed." And in spite of the Truman Administration's defiant anti-Communist stand in Korea, unreconciled members of the China bloc could not rid themselves of the illusion that sinister influences were still operating within the State Department. Senator Wherry once again insisted the President should fire his Secretary of State and "get rid of the alien-minded radicals and moral perverts in his Administration." Indiana's equally reactionary Senator Jenner turned his guns against General Marshall, who was now Secretary of Defense. Singling him out as a front man for the administration's Communist appeasers, Jenner incredibly charged that Marshall's appointment was to give respectability to a new sell-out of Chiang Kai-shek.

The Chinese Nationalists naturally enough welcomed the shift in American policy, which gave them a new lease on life at a time when the United States had appeared about to abandon them to the tender mercies of a Communist invasion. Chiang saw in this new situation a fresh opportunity to weld closer bonds between his government and the United States, and also a magically revived possibility of his ultimate return to the mainland. To win additional American sympathy and support, he promptly offered to provide up to 33,000 troops for military operations in Korea. Although President Truman was at first inclined to accept this offer, he was persuaded to reject it from wholly practical considerations—the difficulties involved in training, transporting, and providing logistical support for the Nationalist forces.

Where the Chinese Nationalists rejoiced when the Seventh Fleet moved into the Formosan Straits, the Chinese Communists angrily condemned the intervention. Premier Chou En-lai immediately declared that this move "constituted armed aggression against the territory of China and total violation of the United Nations charter." He demanded the fleet's withdrawal and stated his country's firm determination to free Formosa from the "tentacles" of American occupation. In his biography of Mao Tse-tung, Stuart Schram has written that this was the real turning point in the Communist leader's attitude toward America. The United States "openly exposed its imperial face," he reported Mao as saying, "and China had no alternative to resisting this policy and aiding North Korea."

In spite of repeated statements by both Truman and Acheson that the

United States did not have any territorial ambitions and that Formosa's neutralization was without prejudice to the island's future status, the Chinese Communists remained convinced we had no purpose other than to thwart their rightful goal of liberating the one part of Chinese territory still remaining in Nationalist hands. The lines were thus drawn for a confrontation between the United States and Communist China, the one committed to Formosa's defense and the other to its conquest, which time has done nothing to ameliorate.

The policy decisions reached in June 1950 thus marked a new phase in the over-all containment policy in eastern Asia. Our action in Korea was both to halt armed aggression and to block the spread of Communism, while in respect to Formosa we had undertaken to prevent loss to the Communists of the one remaining area of free China. At the same time, to round out this picture, President Truman took a further step, on the advice of Secretary Acheson, with momentous consequences for the future: he directed "an acceleration in the furnishing of military assistance to the forces of France and the Associated States in Indo-China."

The war in Korea led to near disaster before the United Nations troops, under the unified command of General MacArthur, succeeded in halting the North Korean onslaught, launched their own counteroffensive, and after a sensationally successful amphibious landing behind the enemy lines at Inchon, drove northward to recapture Seoul on September 26, 1950. The question then arose whether they should advance beyond the Thirty-eighth Parallel. Whereas the original intention of intervention was no more than to repel aggression, restore the Republic of Korea to its status prior to the invasion, and reestablish peace, the idea was now broached that forceful means might be employed to achieve the ultimate United Nations objective of uniting all Korea under an independent and democratic government. The military were confident that the North Koreans could be soundly defeated and their territory successfully occupied by the UN forces.

The one possible check on any such program was intervention by the Chinese Communists. However, the likelihood of any such move was generally discounted. President Truman confidently stated his belief that the Chinese would not be misled into fighting Americans, who were still their friends, when the only ones to gain from their entry into the war would be the Soviet imperialists whose goal was China's dismemberment. Still, there were divisions of opinion on the advisability of crossing the parallel. The Joint Chiefs of Staff definitely favored it; somewhat more cautious, the State Department's Far Eastern Division thought it should not be precluded; and some among the policy advisers in Washington, including George Kennan, strongly opposed it.

After much discussion the National Security Council agreed that an advance might be made beyond the parallel provided there were no indications of intervention by either Communist China or Soviet Russia. President Truman approved this recommendation, and on September 27, with the stipulation that non-Korean troops should not approach the Manchurian border, he authorized General MacArthur to carry the war into North Korea.

Official support for this decision still had to be obtained from the United Nations. With the confidence born of Inchon, our allies were generally approving. Great Britain's foreign minister, Ernest Bevin, hopefully predicted that soon there would be "no South Koreans, no North Koreans: just Koreans." UN Secretary General Lie agreed that it was not enough to force the enemy beyond the Thirty-eighth Parallel; the UN's aim remained a united Korea, and the opportunity to achieve it was at hand. India and others among the unaligned nations had serious misgivings, but the general mood within the United Nations was for going ahead. In accordance with the provisions of the "Uniting for Peace" resolution, which Secretary Acheson had introduced to allow the UN to circumvent a veto in the Security Council, the Assembly took up the issue and vigorously debated it for a week. Then on October 7, by an overwhelming majority of 47 to 5, with seven abstentions, it adopted an eight-power resolution recommending that "all appropriate steps be taken to ensure conditions of stability throughout Korea."

The passage of this resolution, providing through such ambiguous phraseology for the extension of the war into North Korea, was of course to have unforeseen and ultimately disastrous consequences. Its implications were never given the consideration they should have received. Candidly admitting that "I must bear a measure of responsibility," Dean Acheson has retrospectively written in *Present at the Creation* that the resolution increased the hazards of our intervention in Korea and encouraged General MacArthur's adventurism.

Both the United Nations and the United States were acting in this extension of the war beyond the Thirty-eighth Parallel in the face of repeated and emphatic warnings from Communist China. Premier Chou En-lai had earlier declared that "the Chinese people absolutely will not tolerate foreign aggression, nor will they supinely tolerate seeing their neighbors savagely invaded." On the eve of the Assembly's passage of the fateful resolution, he summoned the Indian ambassador in Peking to an urgent conference and told him that should the UN forces actually cross the Thirty-eighth Parallel, Communist China would be compelled to intervene. Following the resolution's passage he publicly warned that while "the American war of invasion has been a serious move from its very start," in the face of these new developments the Chinese "cannot stand idly by."

The diplomatic and military authorities in Washington, the UN command in Korea, all ignored these warnings. Their view was expressed by Secretary Acheson when he stated that Chinese intervention would be "sheer madness." Wholly miscalculating the risks involved in pushing into North Korea and grossly underestimating both Communist China's resolve and its potential military strength, the United Nations forces advanced northward in complete confidence. Dispatches from the front soon reported they were racing "unopposed toward the Manchurian border," and on October 23 an editorial in the *New York Times* was complacently headed, "Mopping Up."

Yet about this same time other newspaper dispatches began to appear stating that the Chinese Communists were massing troops, many of them transferred from the coastal area opposite Formosa or from the Manchurian border, and that some of them were believed to be infiltrating into North Korea. Spokesmen of the American forces ridiculed these reports. When the Joint Chiefs of Staff expressed their concern that should the allied forces approach too close to the Yalu River, the Chinese might in fact intervene, General MacArthur played down any such risk. Committed to a quick military victory that he felt securely within his grasp, he resented any restraining influence on his operations—which, he apparently felt, could only stem from Communist sympathizers in the State Department. Even should the Chinese intervene, MacArthur insisted, the danger was minimal, as they would at best be able to put no more than 60,000 troops in the field. Everything was under control.

The Truman Administration was having trouble with its flamboyant field commander. It had started in late July, when MacArthur first showed that independence of his superiors in Washington in regard to Far Eastern policy that was to become more and more embarrassing. At a time when Acheson was doing everything he could to assure both the Communists and our allies that the United States had no ulterior designs in neutralizing Formosa, the general paid a visit to Chiang Kai-shek that gave rise to grave doubts over American policy both abroad and at home. In their statements at the conclusion of their talks in Taipei, MacArthur stressed the importance of defending Formosa and praised Chiang for his "indomitable determination" to resist Communist aggression, and the generalissimo even more significantly declared that "the foundation for Sino-American military cooperation has been laid."

Deeply disturbed over the implications of these statements as they might be interpreted by our allies, Truman decided to send Averell Harriman, now serving as a special assistant to the President, to Tokyo to brief General MacArthur more fully on American policy. The general was told, Harriman later reported, that since it was well known that Chiang's burning ambition was to return to the mainland, the greatest care should be taken against giving him any encouragement in initiating hostilities that might drag the United States into a world war. Our allies already had misgivings over the thrust of American policy, and no public statements should be made that might serve to increase them. MacArthur remained very skeptical of the validity of our official policy ("We have not improved our position by kicking Chiang around"), Harriman further reported, but he definitely promised that he would obey all orders from the President.

Nevertheless, a month later, in a message to the Veterans of Foreign Wars at the close of August, which the President too late tried to have withdrawn, MacArthur again emphasized the great importance of Formosa—"an unsinkable aircraft carrier"—in American strategy. Playing into the hands of Communist propagandists who were affirming that the United States intended to retain control over the island, he stated that in unfriendly hands it would become "an enemy salient" in the center of our defensive perimeter with possibly catastrophic consequences. "If we hold this line," MacArthur said in outlining a strategy that included the defense of Formosa, "we may have peace—lose it and war is inevitable."

Against the background of these difficulties, the general's reckless attitude toward carrying the Korean war to the Chinese border finally convinced President Truman that he should himself talk with MacArthur in an effort to bring him into line with the more cautious policy the administration was following in order to maintain allied unity. The two men met on Wake Island on October 11. MacArthur denied any intent to deviate from policies laid down in Washington and promised the President his fullest cooperation. He again gave his assurance that there was no real danger of Chinese intervention in Korea and stated his firm belief, as Truman later wrote in his own *Memoirs*, that all resistance in both North and South Korea would be over by Thanksgiving.

This, it is hardly necessary to say, proved to be an illusory hope. The Chinese Communists were in fact prepared to make good their explicit warning that they would not stand idly by if the United Nations forces approached their border along the Yalu. The so-called People's Volunteers were already infiltrating, and by the end of October official dispatches from the front told of Chinese units fighting alongside the North Korean troops.

The situation now became greatly confused, with reports from General MacArthur alternating between complete confidence and almost frantic alarm over the strength of enemy reenforcements. The Joint Chiefs of Staff were baffled, and grew increasingly worried over the danger of a spreading war. They called upon MacArthur to observe the utmost caution in order to prevent outright intervention by either Communist China or Soviet Russia, and they refused his request for authority to fly American planes over Manchuria or to bomb the Chinese electric installations on the Yalu River. Bitterly protesting against restrictions on his freedom of action, which, he said, provided the Chinese with "a complete sanctuary for hostile air power," MacArthur nonetheless remained determined to carry the war to the enemy as best he could. In mid-November he informed the Chiefs of Staff that on the twenty-fourth he planned to launch a general offensive aimed at "a massive and comprehensive envelopment of the new Red forces." Once again in a euphoric mood, he did not doubt the success of this maneuver and instructed his field commanders to tell their troops "they will eat Christmas dinner at home."

As the offensive commenced in these sanguine circumstances, with the *New York Times* reporting "Allies Sweep Ahead," disaster struck with sudden and crushing force. The Chinese People's Volunteers, which had for a time pulled back but whose strength was now augmented to some 200,000 troops, counterattacked in overwhelming strength. They split the allied front and sent both the South Koreans and Americans reeling back in a defeat that fell narrowly short of a complete and irremediable rout. In a communiqué issued on November 28 General MacArthur dramatically announced, "We face an entirely new war . . . [which] poses issues beyond the authority of the United Nations military command." Instead of victory, the year's end would find the United States Eighth Army engaged in what has been called the longest retreat in American history.

It may be interpolated that the reasons for the intervention of the Chinese Communists remain a matter of dispute. However, the weight of the evidence, particularly as brought out in Allen S. Whiting's careful study, *China Crosses the Yalu*, would clearly appear to indicate that it was a defensive move rather than an act of imperialist aggression dictated by Moscow or another gambit of the international Communist conspiracy against the free world. The repeated warnings of the Peking government, its efforts to make indubitably plain that it could not stand aside if China were threatened by enemy troops poised on the Yalu, and the deliberation with which it finally intervened were not the tactics of an aggressor.

The Chinese, it would seem, were convinced that by occupying Formosa and invading North Korea, as they interpreted American actions, the United States was threatening China with war. Their leadership rallied support by calling on the Chinese people to protect their homes and defend their country. Moreover, in the further fear that current negotiations over a Japanese peace treaty would lead to a Japanese-American military alliance directed against China, a friendly Korea undoubtedly became in Peking's mind a vital strategic consideration. Over and beyond any possible pressure exerted by Soviet Russia, the People's Republic thus felt driven to accept a challenge that from its point of view directly endangered China's national security.

While these developments were taking place in Korea, a political battle over Far Eastern policy was being waged in the United Nations. Our allies answered our appeal to resist aggression by cooperating with the UN command in the field, but they remained deeply concerned over the possible escalation of military operations. Together with the neutralist nations they desperately sought some solution of the basic conflict in eastern Asia—involving Formosa as well as Korea—that would end the fighting and bring Communist China into a more reasonable relationship with the international community before the momentum of events precipitated a broader war.

The only practical approach appeared to be general negotiations, and to this end India in July 1950 revived the question of the admission of the People's Republic of China to the United Nations. It did so on the grounds that the UN was responsible for reestablishing peace and that in seeking any over-all settlement of Asian problems the direct participation of the Peking government was indispensable. Soviet Russia, which in this same month finally ended its boycott of the United Nations, supported the Indian proposal, and then took the matter a step further, preparing a resolution of its own that would not only have accepted the People's Republic but expelled the Nationalist government.

The Chinese Communists had not yet intervened in Korea, but the United States actively opposed both the Indian and Russian proposals.

Even though they might be linked with a possible pacification program, the Truman Administration well knew that acceptance of any such approach to a Far Eastern settlement, implying the abandonment of Chiang Kai-shek, was politically impossible. Acheson also felt as he had previously that the UN representation issue should not in any event be settled under forceful pressure. "We do not believe," he wrote Prime Minister Jawaharlal Nehru of India, "that termination of aggression from northern Korea can be contingent upon the termination of other questions which are currently before the United Nations. . . . I know you will agree that the decision [on Communist China's admission] should not be dictated by an unlawful aggression . . . which would subject the United Nations to coercion and duress."

At the opening of the Assembly session in September, India and the Soviet Union officially submitted their respective resolutions. With the United States leading the opposition, both of them went down to defeat. The vote on the Indian proposal was 32 to 16, with ten abstentions; that on the Soviet's was 38 to 10, with eight abstentions. Yet the Assembly felt that the matter should not be dropped: the important role of the Chinese People's Republic in Far Eastern affairs could not be ignored. By a vote of 42 to 8 it accepted another resolution, submitted by the Canadian delegate, for appointment of a special committee to consider the issue further.

In the meantime political maneuvering continued within the Security Council and the Assembly over other means to bring hostilities to a close. Amid heightening tension as the threat of Chinese intervention materialized with the first reports of the infiltration of the People's Volunteers, the Truman Administration found itself caught in a heavy crossfire. Our allies, more than ever alarmed over what they felt was the aggressive militancy of General MacArthur, constantly urged greater caution in the conduct of the war and the exploration of every possible avenue to peace. At the same time the administration's domestic political foes, incensed by any suggestion of what they considered appeasement, insisted on an uncompromising stand by the United States whether or not it commanded support from our allies.

Two proposals now came before the United Nations, leading to acrimonious debate, deepening controversy, and new difficulties for the administration.

Taking up the Chinese Communists' earlier charge that in sending the Seventh Fleet into the Formosan Straits the United States had "committed direct armed aggression in the territory of China," the Soviet Union had in late August introduced a resolution in the Security Council calling for the immediate withdrawal of all United States forces from Formosa. It also proposed inviting a representative of the Chinese People's Republic to attend discussion of the resolution. Ambassador Austin promptly stated that the United States, having no territorial ambitions in Formosa, would welcome a full investigation of the Chinese charges but was opposed to Peking's participation in the Security Council debates. A first vote on the Russian proposal failed to obtain the necessary majority. The United States subsequently modified its position, and the council thereupon agreed to invite the Chinese Communists by a vote of 8 to 2, with Nationalist China and Cuba casting the negative ballots.

Before final action was taken on the Formosan resolution, the council received from General MacArthur, on November 6, his official report on the intervention of the Chinese People's Volunteers in Korea. The issue arose of inviting a representative from Peking for its discussion. Again the United States demurred—its delegate stated that rather than "invite" the Chinese, the UN should "summon" them to account for their action—but it reluctantly agreed to go along with this invitation as it had that for Peking's participation in the projected debate on Formosa. The Security Council thereupon adopted the appropriate measure by another 8 to 2 vote. Immediately thereafter Great Britain, with American concurrence, submitted a further six-power resolution to the Security Council. While pledging the inviolability of the Sino-Korean border, it called for the immediate withdrawal of the Chinese Communists and cessation of their aid to the North Koreans.

The American concessions in accepting these proposals to allow Chinese Communists to take part in United Nations debates awoke the greatest resentment among members of the congressional China bloc. "In the name of the Almighty, what is Acheson trying to do!" expostulated Senator Bridges. The Secretary of State—to answer this rhetorical question—apparently believed that while standing firmly against the Peking government's admission to the UN, the United States had to demonstrate at least this much flexibility in its policies in order to maintain allied unity.

The Peking government had accepted the invitation for the debate on the Russian resolution condemning American aggression in Formosa, but it now flatly rejected any idea of discussing its own intervention in Korea. Having set forth this position, it sent General Wu Hsiu-chuan as a special envoy to the UN—the first and only time a representative of the People's Republic of China participated in a session of the United Nations.

The Security Council was still wrangling over the proper procedure in dealing with what were officially designated as "complaints" over American actions in Formosa and Chinese actions in Korea, and the Assembly was excitedly debating other aspects of the involved Far Eastern situation when on November 24, 1950, General Wu arrived in New York. The Security Council decided to consider both complaints simultaneously as a two-part item on its agenda. General Wu would take part in the debate and was also invited to speak in the Assembly.

His appearance could not have been more dramatically timed. General MacArthur had announced his offensive against the new Red forces in Korea, and the allied advance appeared to be getting successfully under way. But on the very day that Wu Hsiu-chuan made his appearance in the Security Council, November 27, everything changed. The following morning a startling headline dominated the front page of the *New York Times:*

ALLIES ARE DRIVEN BACK IN KOREA
FOE HURLS SIXTEEN DIVISIONS INTO PUSH
CHINA REDS MAKE DEBUT IN UN

The Communists had launched their sweepingly successful offensive; the retreating United Nations forces had their new war.

As the Security Council proceeded with its planned debate, General Wu took the floor. Totally ignoring the new developments in Korea, he assailed the United States for its Formosan policy and demanded that the UN immediately impose sanctions for these "criminal acts of aggression against the territory of China." Rising in his turn, Ambassador Austin hardly deigned to answer these charges, and turning instead to current events in Korea, declared they fully demonstrated "aggression, open and notorious" on the part of the Chinese Communists.

Both in his appearance at the Security Council meeting and also on the floor of the Assembly, General Wu played out his anti-American role with little consideration of the underlying issues that the United Nations was seeking to resolve. His obvious assignment, which the *Times* reported him as carrying out with a ferocity hardly concealed by the mildness of his manner, was to attack the United States all along the line. "American imperialism," Wu declared at one point, "is hostile to all liberation struggles of Asian peoples, and is particularly hostile to the great victory of the Chinese people. It has therefore resorted to armed aggression to realize the fanatic desire of attacking the new China and dominating the whole of Asia."

This was the voice of Communist propaganda; it was also the voice of a newly aroused Chinese nationalism.

In this tense atmosphere the action of the Security Council was both predictable and anticlimactic. It rejected the Soviet resolution incorporating the Chinese Communist accusation of American aggression by a vote of 9 to 1. It then in a comparable vote endorsed the six-power resolution calling for the withdrawal of the Chinese Communists from Korea, but this action was nullified by a Russian veto. Completely stymied, the Security Council left any further consideration of what might be done to promote Far Eastern peace to the veto-free Assembly.

During this hectic week at the close of November, the press played up every angle of the military confrontation between the United States and Communist China in Korea and their political confrontation in the United Nations. There could be no denying the grave nature of the crisis or the danger that threatened the entire free world. News stories reported that the United Nations lines were shattered and that the American forces, trapped in a great enveloping movement of enemy troops, were desperately fighting their way to the sea. *Newsweek* characterized what was happening as "America's worst licking since Pearl Harbor," and *Time* declared it "the worst defeat the United States ever suffered." Reports from Washington said that the administration was planning air strikes against the home bases of the engulfing "Chinese hordes" and that the use of tactical atomic weapons was under "active consideration."

"The United States faces today the greatest danger in our history," the not usually alarmist Hanson Baldwin wrote in the *New York Times* on December 1. "Military, economic or political destruction of western civilization are definite possibilities if the danger from the East is not met boldly, imaginatively and with united effort."

These views were shared in official circles. Declaring that in view of the historic friendship between the peoples of the two countries it was particularly shocking to find the Chinese being forced into battle against Americans, President Truman flatly stated that "we are fighting. . . . for our national security and survival." Secretary of State Acheson said that the aggression on the part of the Chinese Communists "created a new crisis, a situation of unparalleled danger . . . no one can guarantee that war will not come."

The underlying fear in this country was that the United States might not only find itself at war with Communist China, but that the Soviet Union would take advantage of our deepening involvement in Asia to strike out against the West in some other part of the world. Washington still took it for granted that the Chinese were playing Russia's game and taking their orders from Moscow. Again ignoring any possibility that the Chinese might have been acting in self-defense when the UN forces advanced to the Yalu, Truman declared in a further statement on December 2 that the new assault was to further the designs of the Soviet Union as "part of a world-wide pattern of danger to all the free nations of the world."

With these ominous perils in mind, the President declared a state of emergency and announced a mobilization of the country's military resources. He asked Congress for vast new appropriations, which were to total $18 billion, to provide for national defense and for military aid to our Western allies. "If those who are challenging the United Nations believe that we will give up our principles because they threaten us with mighty force," Ambassador Austin told the Security Council, "let them know they are tragically mistaken."

Our allies nevertheless believed that the United States was overreacting to Communist China's intervention in Korea; they were convinced that Soviet Russia wanted nothing more than to see a broadening of hostilities that would bog down the United States in an impossible Asian war. They were more than ever concerned over the belligerency of General MacArthur, who was seeking authority to carry the war to China. They were deeply worried over an announcement by Truman that in taking whatever steps were necessary to repel aggression, the United States would be prepared to employ "every weapon that we have." This was of course interpreted to include the atomic bomb, and in spite of every effort to minimize the idea of an implied threat in the presidential statement, it had a frightening impact, especially in England. With Churchill declaring on the floor of the House of Commons that "the United Nations should avoid by every means in their power becoming entangled inextricably in a war with China," Prime Minister Clement Attlee hurried to Washington for talks with President Truman.

Arriving on December 3, Attlee promptly let it be known that in his opinion the position of the United Nations forces in Korea was extremely precarious and that withdrawal from Formosa and Korea, together with the admission of Communist China to the United Nations, would not be too high a price for a cease-fire. The United States could not accept this defeatist policy. "Its adoption would cause terrible divisions among our people at home," Truman told Attlee. In these circumstances the two leaders could neither reconcile nor conceal their divergent views. However, they sought as best they could to preserve a united Anglo-American front. In a joint statement on the conclusion of their talks they declared that there could be no appeasement of Communist China and that their two governments would back up any action on which the United Nations might decide.

The UN Assembly, taking over the Korean problem from the Security Council, was meanwhile desperately seeking a formula that might somehow encourage peace. Once again neutralist India (it had abstained on the votes in the Security Council relating both to Formosa and Korea) took the lead in this effort. Its delegate on December 6 introduced a resolution calling for a cease-fire in Korea and the appointment of a three-man committee to take up with the Chinese Communist envoy, who was still in New York, the idea of a general conference among the nations concerned that would discuss all the interrelated problems of eastern Asia. The Assembly adopted this proposal on December 14 by an overwhelming majority of 52 to 5, with only the Soviet bloc in opposition.

The special three-man committee duly presented this plan to General Wu. He categorically rejected it. The proposed cease-fire, he said, was nothing more than a "trap" unless his government received assurances that its political aims would be accepted. A week later the Peking government officially confirmed his position. Premier Chou cabled the United Nations that the only possible basis for peace in the Far East was the unqualified acceptance of China's demands for an immediate withdrawal of United States forces from both Formosa and Korea and the admission of the People's Republic of China to the United Nations.

The impasse was complete.

The United States responded to this rejection of peace overtures by freezing Communist China's financial assets in this country, establishing a complete embargo on all trade, forbidding United States ships to call at Communist ports, and refusing visas for any American travel in China. It then moved to introduce in the UN Assembly a resolution calling upon the United Nations to declare the People's Republic of China an aggressor for its intervention in North Korea.

Peking made no further political moves. Calmly stating that he was sure the United States would not want "to start a world war by aggression against Taiwan and intervention in Korea," General Wu made ready to leave New York. On December 19, sardonically wishing the American people a Merry Christmas and Happy New Year, he started on the long journey home.

8

The Lines Are Drawn

WITH THE COLLAPSE of the always very slim hope that any accommodation could be reached with the Chinese Communists in resolving the Korean conflict, the United States became all the more determined to resist not only Peking's aggressive course in that country but to combat any other possible effort on its part to extend its political control in other parts of Asia. With the *New York Times* reporting 400,000 troops of the People's Liberation Army massed opposite Formosa, 300,000 poised to invade Tibet, and another 450,000 on the borders of Indochina, the forces of Communism appeared ready to march. American policy was to be directed toward doing what it could to block their further advance on the Far Eastern front.

Secretary of State Acheson declared that the United States continued to oppose recognition of the Chinese People's Republic and its admission to the United Nations, that it would not allow Formosa to fall under Communist control, and that it would step up the military assistance it was giving to the French authorities in Southeast Asia. However, a more immediate political objective was to persuade our allies to take a comparably strong stand against any further extension of Chinese power. To this end the Truman Administration bent all its energy and exerted all possible pressure to have the United Nations declare Communist China an aggressor nation and thus subject to stern political and economic sanctions.

With this turn of events, whatever flexibility marked our attitude toward the Chinese People's Republic prior to its intervention in Korea gave way completely to the rigid and unyielding position that was the continuing hallmark of the 1950s. Containment was reenforced by a policy of political isolation.

In the immediate aftermath of the departure of Peking's delegate, our allies were in spite of this country's insistence still very reluctant to declare the Chinese People's Republic an aggressor and favored additional efforts to obtain a peaceful settlement in Korea. Britain, Canada, and India were the leaders in presenting a new set of peace proposals somewhat more specific than those the Chinese Communists earlier rejected. These proposals embraced a cease-fire, a phased withdrawal of all foreign troops from Korea, and a four-power conference. The latter would be composed of the United States, Great Britain, Soviet Russia, and the People's Republic of China, and would meet to consider not only a permanent settlement in Korea but also the status of Formosa and the possible admission of Communist China to the United Nations.

The decision whether the United States should support or oppose this plan, Acheson has written, was "a murderous one." The proposal immediately aroused vehement opposition within Congress and generally throughout the country as constituting a complete surrender to Chinese demands. While the Communists were still fighting the allied forces, even to discuss such issues as Formosa and UN membership was widely castigated as an irreversible step toward abject appeasement. On the other hand, the administration had to consider the broader aspects of American policy, the whole situation in Europe, and the free world's tense relations with Russia. From this point of view it was of utmost importance to preserve allied unity and to demonstrate America's sincere desire for peace.

The Secretary of State consequently decided to brave his domestic foes and announced that the United States would vote in favor of an Assembly resolution approving this new approach to Peking. Even though the China bloc was newly outraged, with Senator Taft declaring that this shocking move was "the most complete surrender in the history of the United States," Acheson held firm. He was actually playing his diplomatic cards very skillfully. He was certain, he later testified in defending his position before a congressional committee, that the Peking government would again reject a cease-fire. Having made a conciliatory move, which in reality cost nothing, the United States would then be in a much stronger position in demanding that the United Nations outlaw Communist China and take further sanctions against it as an aggressor.

The Assembly approved the cease-fire resolution on January 13, by a vote of 50 to 7, with the opposition oddly enough limited to Nationalist China, the Soviet bloc, and El Salvador. Acheson's evaluation of the situation then proved to be correct. The Peking government was no more willing than it had been in December to accept a cease-fire without a prior commitment on the UN's acceptance of its political claims. The Chinese were still on the offensive—"Red Troops Pour South of Seoul" the dispatches from the front reported—and they remained confident they could drive the United Nations forces out of Korea. Believing that a cease-fire would break the momentum of the advance and provide the allies a breathing spell, the Communist leaders had no idea of weakening their bargaining position for future negotiations. On the day after the United Nations appeal for peace, they flatly rejected it and again said they would not enter upon any talks until the allied troops were withdrawn from Korea and the United States gave up the protection of Formosa.

Acheson promptly labeled this refusal to consider negotiations "a contemptuous disregard of a worldwide demand for peace," and Ambassador Austin took the same line in the United Nations. The goal of the United States, Austin declared, was an end to the fighting but in the face of Communist China's intransigency "the time to draw the line is now." There could be no submission to political blackmail by allowing any country to shoot its way into the United Nations. What might be expected, Austin asked, if a peace conference were held and refused to accede to the demands of the Chinese? "Would they then break into the United Nations with mortars and grenades? . . . Really, this response is not Chinese; it is their master's response, that of the Soviet ruling circles."

Even though Peking's recalcitrance strengthened the case for stigmatizing Communist China as an aggressor, the United States could still find no co-sponsors for its proposed resolution. Our allies remained hesitant over taking such a drastic step, and a twelve-nation neutralist bloc headed by India vigorously opposed it. Sir Benegal Rau, the Indian delegate, advanced the view, so contrary to American opinion, that the Peking government's intervention in Korea might well reflect "suspicious Chinese nationalism and not aggressive communism" and that to brand Peking as an aggressor would isolate it more than ever at a time when its cooperation was vital to any peace settlement. Prime Minister Nehru issued a statement in New Delhi expressing his conviction that in spite of the Chinese Communists' obdurate stand, they wanted negotiations and that the American program would once and for all end any chance of a peace conference.

The United States refused to back down, and on January 20 Austin formally introduced the controversial American resolution. It nominally kept the door open to negotiations by recommending the appointment of still another good offices committee, but the substance of the resolution was in a clause stating that the People's Republic of China, by giving aid and assistance to those who were already committing aggression in Korea and by engaging in hostilities against the United Nations forces, "has itself engaged in aggression in Korea." The resolution then called upon Peking to withdraw its forces, and should it fail to do so, the members of the United Nations were requested to consider additional measures to repel its aggression.

With Austin pressing home the refusal of the Communists to negotiate on any terms, the opposition to the American resolution gradually eroded. The Assembly adopted it on February 1 by a vote of 44 to 7, with eight abstentions. The Peking government lost no time in condemning the United Nations action. This move, it acidly announced, was an insult to the Chinese people and blocked all prospects of peace. In the circumstances, it concluded, the appointment of a new good offices committee was "a naked deceit."

The United States had won out. Yet many of the governments that had felt obliged to accept the resolution under American pressure remained convinced that the way should have been kept open to negotiations. They believed that in spite of their tough attitude, the Chinese Communists might have been induced to make concessions in a general peace settlement and that a formula could have been discovered for bringing a more cooperative Peking into the United Nations. In their view Washington had allowed the pressure of American public opinion to slam the door shut to any such possibility.

While the United Nations was still debating the aggressor resolution, events in Korea took a new and more encouraging turn. The allied forces brought the Communist offensive to a halt, and the very real danger of their being driven off the peninsula came to an end. By the close of February, reversing the field in a replay of the counterattack made in the equally perilous days of September 1950, they were once more advancing northward. Changing hands for the fourth time, Seoul was recaptured on March 15.

Should the United Nations forces again carry the offensive beyond the Thirty-eighth Parallel? General MacArthur, warning of the dangers of a stalemate, argued vigorously in favor of a further advance. He was not only ready to take all necessary measures within Korea to defeat the Communists, but favored direct action against China. He proposed a naval blockade of its coast, bombardment of its air fields and bases in Manchuria, and the use of Nationalist troops in "diversionary action possibly leading to a counter-invasion."

The Joint Chiefs of Staff were now, however, wholly opposed to crossing the Thirty-eighth Parallel, and they also flatly disapproved MacArthur's other proposals. In their analysis, he was ignoring the risk of a more direct confrontation with Communist China and, even more important, that of possible intervention by Soviet Russia. President Truman consequently decided against carrying the war to North Korea and expressly vetoed any idea of either a blockade of the China coast or air strikes in Manchuria. Reversing the earlier decision in 1950 to attempt to bring about Korea's unification by force of arms, the United States, with the emphatic support of its allies, returned to the original UN objective of seeking no more than to repel aggression and reestablish the status quo.

The Truman Administration, that is, accepted the concept of a limited war. Through a holding action rather than military victory it sought to contain Communist expansion without inviting any broader Asiatic conflict. The United Nations forces would secure and hold an unassailable position, approximately along the Thirty-eighth Parallel, and this, it was hoped, would ultimately persuade the Communists of the futility of further fighting and make possible a political settlement.

In abandoning the idea of a military victory in favor of a negotiated political settlement, the Truman Administration was following a course that in certain ways foreshadowed that which the Johnson Administration was forced to accept seventeen years later in Vietnam. But the popular attitude in 1951 differed very much from that in 1968. The Korean war had become very unpopular; the American people desperately wanted an end to it. But they accepted it as being fought under the authority of the United Nations to repel aggression, and they believed it to be both strategically and morally justified. The idea of restricting our objectives and fighting under self-imposed limitations was hard to encompass. The greater part of the public, shocked by the reverses suffered on the battlefield and determined to redeem them, could only think in terms of unreservedly carrying the war to the enemy. They were baffled by any other strategy.

Republicans generally were a good deal more than baffled. They were persuaded that in rejecting General MacArthur's proposals for mounting an offensive against Communist China itself, the administration was reverting to a defeatist policy which again revealed an inexplicable softness toward Communism. The Secretary of State's success in forcing through the United Nations the resolution condemning Communist China as an aggressor did nothing to reconcile his critics; their resentment against the concept of a limited war grew ever more vehement. The members of the China bloc insisted that no matter what the attitude of our allies, the United States should not accept any restrictions on military operations whether in North Korea or against China. Senator Knowland was ready for all-out war even if it risked the intervention of Soviet Russia; Senator Bridges demanded American support for a Nationalist invasion of the mainland whatever the danger of broadening hostilities.

President Truman and his advisers were quite as convinced as these Republicans of the reality of the Communist menace in Asia. They still believed, however, that the attack on Korea was only one manifestation of the aggressive designs of the international Communist conspiracy. In combating the lesser danger of Communism in Asia as compared to the Soviet threat in Europe, the United States in their view could not afford any action that would undermine allied unity. Nor could it allocate to the Far East resources that would weaken its more vital defenses in other parts of the world.

Acting on the premise that the European theater was much more important than Asia, President Truman consequently called upon the country to give primary support to building up and strengthening the North Atlantic Treaty Organization. He appointed General Dwight D. Eisenhower as Commander in Chief of NATO's military forces, ordered the transfer of additional United States divisions overseas, and sought new congressional appropriations to increase the flow of military supplies abroad. The subordination of Asia to Europe was inescapable as the administration adopted this approach in safeguarding the nation's peace and security.

General Omar Bradley, chairman of the Joint Chiefs of Staff, expressed this concept of global strategy in an often-quoted statement he made in May 1951. He declared that Red China was not *the* powerful nation seeking to dominate the world, and that to become engaged in a major conflict with it would probably delight the Kremlin. "It would involve us," Bradley categorically stated, "in the wrong war at the wrong place and with the wrong enemy."

Every official announcement stressing the importance of developments in Europe, every statement insisting on the necessity of allied unity even at the expense of a more vigorous policy in the Far East, rubbed salt on the raw wounds of the Asia Firsters. To concentrate on building up NATO and fight a limited war in Korea was from their point of view an inexplicable betrayal of the national interest. They were even more convinced in 1951 than they had previously been that neither the caution of our allies nor any other consideration should be allowed to stand in the way of crushing once and for all the immediate Communist threat in Asia.

They again found their champion in General MacArthur. He had no hesitation in letting it be known that in his view the primary American task was to compel Communist China, which he described as "a new and dominant power in Asia . . . aggressively imperialistic," to forgo its expansionist ambitions. Here was the real danger. He was convinced that the United States should bring all the force it could muster to defeat Communism in Asia, and the concept of more limited aims was completely abhorrent to him.

In spite of his earlier promises to conform to the views of the administration in conducting operations in Korea, MacArthur bluntly spoke out along these lines in a letter to Representative Joseph Martin, the Republican leader of the House, which was released on April 5. "It seems strangely difficult for some to realize," he wrote, "that here in Asia is . . . where the Communist conspirators have elected to make their play for global conquest . . . that here we fight Europe's wars while the diplomats there still fight it with words." It was imperative to use maximum counterforce in the present conflict in Korea, he said, for should we lose the war in Asia, the fall of Europe was inevitable. Then, referring to the handicaps under which he labored in conducting the UN operations, the irrepressible general concluded with the pregnant phrase that in war "there is no substitute for victory."

This open challenge to administration policy brought to a final startling climax the long feud between the President and the Commander in Chief of the United States Forces in the Far East. Whatever the merits of their differing views on global strategy, MacArthur's public criticism could not be brooked. The President, fully supported by both his civilian and military advisers, was convinced he had no alternative to dismissing an officer in the field who defied his Commander in Chief. Any other course would have thrown away the principle of civilian control—in the person of the President—over the nation's military forces. On April 11, 1951, Truman took the decisive and politically courageous step of relieving General MacArthur of his command because of his inability, as the President phrased it, to give his wholehearted support to the policies of the United States and the United Nations.

The announcement created a furor. On his return to this country, playing to the galleries as he landed with the simple statement "God bless America," MacArthur became for his Republican supporters, and for a time a great majority of the American people, a hero sacrificed on the altar of politics. The Gallup polls showed some 69 percent of the public upholding him and only 29 percent backing the President. Frustrated by the agonizing experience of being unable to bring the Korean war to an end, swept by those passions that affected every aspect of the underlying China problem, the public eagerly accepted his simplified thesis that a war is fought only to be won. The enthusiastic reception given the returning soldier served as an emotional outlet for pent-up feelings long suppressed.

In a sensational appearance before Congress on April 19, MacArthur eloquently reviewed the past history of Sino-American relations and his own attitude toward American policy in the Pacific. In Communist China, he declared, the United States faced a nation with an insatiable lust for power. We should not permit a stalemate in Korea; we should not allow Formosa to be brought under enemy control. He repeated his demands for the removal of all obstacles to the winning of the Korean war. While no man in his right mind would advocate sending our ground forces into China, he told Congress, the military needs of the moment demanded a naval blockade of the coast, removal of restrictions on air reconnaissance of Manchuria, and logistical support for effective Nationalist operations against the mainland.

Having reiterated that in war there can be no substitute for victory, General MacArthur—his voice dropping, his eyes becoming misty—recalled the lines of an old ballad, "Old soldiers never die; they just fade away," and concluded his address: "And like the old soldier of that ballad, I now close my military career and just fade away—an old soldier who tried to do his duty as God gave him the light to see that duty. Good-by." The members of Congress and the spectators in the crowded galleries rose in rapturous applause.

Reactionary Republicans and members of the China bloc wholeheartedly took up MacArthur's cause. In the prevailing spirit of the times, they found in his recall certain proof of the Communist influences at work in Washington that they had been inveighing against for the past year and more. "This country today," Senator Jenner exploded on the day after MacArthur's congressional address, "is in the hands of a secret inner coterie which is directed by agents of the Soviet Union." Senator McCarthy, who termed the general's removal "perhaps the greatest victory the Communists have ever won," went even further in describing subversion in Washington. "How can we account for the present situation," the Chicago *Tribune* reported him as saying on June 15, "unless we believe that men high in this government are concerting to deliver us to disaster? This must be the product of a great conspiracy on a scale so immense as to dwarf any previous venture in the history of man."

In the meantime the Senate Armed Services and Foreign Relations Committees instituted official hearings on MacArthur's recall and on the whole military situation in the Far East. These hearings (from which so many quotations have been taken for this narrative) ran through most of May and June 1951. The lines were drawn between General MacArthur on the one hand, and on the other, such administration spokesmen as Secretary of Defense Marshall, Secretary of State Acheson, and General Bradley. The testimony was not limited to the more recent developments in Korea. The Republican senators supporting an Asia First policy grilled the witnesses so minutely that they turned the hearings into an inquest on our entire China policy since the beginning of the civil war between the Nationalists and the Communists.

General MacArthur in his testimony refurbished all the arguments for giving priority to the Communist menace in Asia and for taking direct action against Communist China. Again stressing the importance of defending Formosa, he flatly stated that should the United States lose or give up this strategic outpost, "we practically lose the Pacific Ocean."

The administration spokesmen naturally enough defended the current policy of fighting a limited war, and their arguments were equally familiar. In their view MacArthur gravely underestimated the potential strength of the Chinese Communists, and adoption of the hazardous measures he proposed would not ensure an American victory. More important, they reiterated that his program would have disastrous consequences for the global campaign against Communism. The extension of hostilities in eastern Asia, General Marshall declared, would risk war with the Soviet Union "at the expense of losing our allies and wrecking the coalition of free peoples throughout the world." But at the same time the Secretary of Defense emphatically denied that American policy contemplated any idea of surrender or appeasement in waging a limited war. The United States would continue to oppose a settlement of the Korean conflict that would in any way award the aggressor or allow it to shoot its way into the United Nations.

Nothing brought out during the long hearings, which received wide publicity, altered the views of either party in the controversy over China policy. From the start it was very clear that the Republicans were set on undermining the administration. Their obvious design in questioning its spokesmen was to demonstrate that the Truman-Acheson policies had paved the way for the Chinese Communist victory in China by deserting Chiang Kai-shek and also served to invite further Communist aggression.

While the investigating committees made no official report on the hearings, eight of the twelve Republican members issued a final vitriolic statement. Reverting to the China bloc's ancient theme, they declared that nothing in the testimony changed their view that "Chiang lost China for any reason other than that he did not receive sufficient support, both moral and material, from the United States." As to the current situation in Korea, Dean Acheson's policy was designed "to conciliate certain of our associates in the United Nations rather than to advance the security of the United States." On the ground that General MacArthur's proposals constituted the only positive plan for victory in Korea, these Republicans warned against negotiations with the Chinese Communists. Any peace short of the liberation and unification of all Korea would be a delusion, they asserted; a settlement along the Thirty-eighth Parallel would be a Chinese Communist victory.

Neither the stirring popular welcome given to General MacArthur on his return to this country nor the Republican attacks on current policy during the subsequent Senate hearings lessened the administration's determination to follow a world-oriented policy in seeking to contain Communism. In its view the importance of maintaining allied unity remained paramount. The United States could not risk alienating those nations that were the backbone of the defense of Western Europe by irresponsibly taking the offensive against China. "We cannot go it alone in Asia," President Truman summarized this view, "and go it in company in Europe."

After the first flurry of excitement making MacArthur a martyr to the cause of military victory, public opinion began to swing over toward support of the administration's more cautious policy in Korea. Just as when the Republicans overreached themselves in their willingness to risk hostilities with Communist China over the Formosan issue in early 1950, so did they now a year later champion action whose dangers the American people did not care to run. A military victory had a pleasing ring to it, but an extension of hostilities that might involve Communist China, and possibly invite intervention by the Soviet Union as a result of the Sino-Russian alliance, called up the terrifying prospect of a third world war. Unhappy as they were over the course of events in Korea, most Americans were prepared to accept present ills rather than fly to unimaginable others.

Also, by late spring the situation in Korea was gradually improving. General MacArthur had grimly predicted another Communist offensive that might again drive back the United Nations forces, and for a time the allies were hard put to hold their ground against the engulfing waves of the enemy's "human sea." But they successfully did so. Under the over-all command of General Matthew Ridgway, who had replaced MacArthur, they first traded ground for terrific enemy losses, finally regained the initiative, and by June had driven the enemy back once again beyond the Thirty-eighth Parallel. There—or more accurately, slightly to the north—they halted and consolidated their position.

The opposing lines were now virtually stalemated; a relative calm also descended on the diplomatic front. The United Nations instituted on May 18 the embargo on shipments of strategic goods to China that this country had long been urging. Nevertheless, our allies were still restless in their search for an end to the hostilities, and Washington's policy makers, as Acheson has recorded, "cast about like a pack of hounds searching for a scent." They were finally rewarded when on June 23 Yakov Malik, the Soviet delegate in the United Nations Security Council, suggested a possible cease-fire.

The United States eagerly seized on this suggestion, and a week later, in the name of the UN command, General Ridgway specifically asked for a meeting of the two sides in Korea to discuss possible armistice terms. The Communists accepted the offer, and talks began on July 10 at Kaesong, later transferred to Panmunjom. They were to continue for two interminable years during which active hostilities broke out repeatedly, with a heavy toll of lives on both sides. But although an end to the war was still so long in coming, the cease-fire in July 1951 was immensely important. It averted what was at that time the very real danger of a more direct clash between the United States and the Chinese People's Republic, which might have engulfed even more than all Asia.

During this period in which the major attention of both the American people and their government was focused on Korea and the commencement of negotiations for an armistice, our general China policy step by step took on its more rigid form and shape. The United States progressively hardened its attitude toward the Chinese People's Republic and strengthened its ties with the Nationalist government. This was a natural consequence of the direct clash between American and Chinese Communist troops on the Korean battlefield; it also reflected the impact of domestic politics. In waging a limited war the Truman Administration was under the heaviest possible pressure to demonstrate that this policy did not mean, as its critics so vociferously charged, any intent to appease but that on the contrary the United States was more than ever committed to Communism's containment along the entire Asiatic front.

Administration spokesmen emphatically reaffirmed time and again, as had both General Marshall and Secretary Acheson at the MacArthur hearings, that no concessions whatsoever would be made to the Peking government whether in respect to recognition, admission to the United Nations, or trade or cultural relations. Acknowledging that the original idea of simply seeking Formosa's neutralization during the Korean hostilities was no longer valid, they declared the United States would never permit that island to fall under Communist control. Prepared now to uphold Chiang Kai-shek rather than seek disengagement from the Chinese civil war, the administration also moved from words to deeds. In March 1951 it sent a 100-man Military Assistance Advisory Group to Taipei, and on this mission's recommendation resumed direct military aid, with a first allocation of $300 million. The aid agreement stipulated that such funds should be used only for internal security and legitimate self-defense. Chiang was nevertheless encouraged to believe that one day he would be able to return to the mainland with United States support.

The degree to which our policy was solidified in unrelenting antagonism toward the Chinese Communists and revived friendship for the Chinese Nationalists was revealingly illustrated in important speeches made before the China Institute in New York on May 18, 1951, by two prominent State Department officials who were also future Secretaries of State. One speaker was John Foster Dulles, at this time negotiating a peace treaty with Japan, and the other was Dean Rusk, the Assistant Secretary of State for Far Eastern Affairs. The two men could not have been more emphatic in their broad assertions that the United States should do nothing that might in any way strengthen Mao Tse-tung's regime in Peking but in every possible way support that of Chiang Kai-shek in Taipei.

What was even more significant about these two speeches in the light of the positions Dulles and Rusk would later attain was their fervid insistence that in dealing with Communist China the United States faced a hapless satellite of Soviet Russia. Neither man admitted any possibility that the Chinese Communists might reflect the indigenous forces of nationalism or could possibly be acting independently, whether in Korea or elsewhere.

"By the test of conception, birth, nurture and obedience," Dulles said, "the Mao Tse-tung regime is a creature of the Moscow Politburo, and it is on behalf of Moscow, not of China, that it is betraying the friendship of the Chinese people toward the United States." Foreshadowing his own later policy, he then declared that "we should treat the Mao Tse-tung regime for what it is—a puppet regime"; no act of ours should be allowed to contribute to its success in fastening "the yoke of Moscow on the Chinese people."

Rusk was even more outspoken in stressing the degree to which the Peking government was sacrificing the interests of the Chinese people to the ambitions of a Soviet conspiracy. "We can tell our friends in China," he stated, "that the United States will not acquiesce in the degradation which is being forced on them. We do not recognize the authorities in Peiping for what they pretend to be. The Peiping regime may be a colonial Russian Government—a Slavic Manchukuo on a larger scale. It is not the Government of China. It does not pass the first test. It is not Chinese."

That Dulles and Rusk held such views was immensely significant at that time; it was of far greater import for the future, for they were expressing intense personal convictions that they were later to carry over to their conduct of Far Eastern policy as Secretaries of State under Presidents Eisenhower, Kennedy, and Johnson. Their attitude toward Communist China, formed in the days when McCarthyism was building upon the fears and suspicions aroused by the Cold War, had an inflexibility that subsequent changes in the world picture hardly affected.

In the spring of 1951 the American public so generally agreed that Mao Tse-tung was taking his orders from the Kremlin that these views of Dulles and Rusk awoke little comment. What the newspapers seized upon was the emphasis upon the need to increase military assistance for the Chinese Nationalists. The *New York Times* went so far as to introduce its account of the meeting at the China Institute with the startling headline, "Rusk Hints U.S. Aid to Revolt in China." In this same vein an article in the *U.S. News and World Report* declared that "Mr. Rusk . . . has brought a new philosophy, a new approach, a positive course of action" to American policy. This article's author was thoroughly approving of more positive action, but accepting the same interpretation of Rusk's speech, other commentators were deeply concerned over any closer links with Chiang Kai-shek.

An editorial in the *New Republic* caustically asked, "Has Acheson surrendered?" Writing in the same journal, Harold Ickes said that on the assumption that Rusk spoke for his chief, no successor to the incumbent Secretary of State could "go as far as Acheson has gone to appease the clamant and unreasonable Republicans by yielding to their suicidal demands on foreign policy."

Acheson promptly denied any change in existing policy. "To build these statements into far-reaching conclusions of involvement in the Chinese civil war is not justified," a State Department spokesman asserted in his behalf. Yet in approving the substance of Rusk's speech, although he said he did not necessarily endorse all its language, the Secretary of State in effect confirmed what could hardly be interpreted as other than a further commitment to the Nationalists in their continuing conflict with the Communists.

The Truman Administration most certainly wanted no part in any mad adventure of invading the mainland. However, its new determination, as the President phrased it six days after Rusk's speech, to support "the Chinese armies on Formosa to help keep that island out of Communist hands," could hardly have contrasted more sharply with earlier statements promising the Seventh Fleet's withdrawal. On this count, if not on all other matters, the administration appeared to have fully accepted the views of General MacArthur. A spokesman was quoted in the *New York Times* as expressing the general's gratification with the "apparent orientation of Administration policy toward his basic views on the Far East."

During this same troubled spring, other developments in the Far East heightened American mistrust of Communist China. Although the Korean truce negotiations somewhat reduced existing tensions and moderated fears of a direct Sino-American conflict, Peking was providing fresh evidence of what appeared to be aggressively imperialistic policies.

In late May the anticipated attack on Tibet took place. Chinese troops, in what was described as a movement of "peaceful liberation," invaded this one-time Chinese dependency and quickly brought it under Communist control. Whatever justification might be found in past history for this extension of the boundaries of the new China, the United States vigorously condemned the use of military force. The invasion of Tibet was seen as a further demonstration of the Peking regime's mounting power, and raised the question of how much further it might be prepared to go.

The most likely direction appeared to be Indochina. There the insurgent forces of the Vietminh were pressing ever harder upon the French colonial authorities, and Peking was giving the Communist regime in Hanoi increasing military aid and assistance in its struggle to free all Vietnam from alien control. With new concentrations of troops of the People's Liberation Army along the Indochinese frontier, the possibility that Communist China might intervene directly in this war as it had in Korea appeared very likely.

Dean Acheson, it will be remembered, had given high priority to Indochina in extending the containment policy to Asia. In May 1950 he had taken the first step in implementing this program through economic and military assistance to the French colonial authorities, and on the outbreak of the Korean war President Truman ordered an acceleration of this aid. He was acting on the basic assumption, as he asserted, that subversive activities in Indochina as in Korea were "part of a pattern" in a general Communist conspiracy against the free world. Soon afterward the United States sent a military mission to Saigon and further increased the flow of American arms and ammunition.

Even in this early stage our involvement in Vietnam was proving to be a frustrating experience. The French were calling for American assistance on the ground that they were resisting a Communist advance, which if it were not halted would bring all Southeast Asia under Communist control. Suggesting the later "falling domino" theory, General de Tassigny, commander of the French forces, stated that "once Tonking [now North Vietnam] is lost, there is really no barrier before Suez." But the French were primarily interested in maintaining their own political influence in Indochina; they were unwilling to recognize or make any concessions to the nationalistic forces underlying the Vietminh revolt. They made no real effort to satisfy the aspirations of the Vietnamese people (nor those of Cambodia and Laos) for freedom and economic progress. In assisting the French, the United States declared that it wanted to contribute not only to the security of Vietnam but to "genuine nationalism," but it increasingly ignored this latter objective.

In allowing itself to become so closely associated with French colonialism, the United States was reacting to pressure arising from the situation in Europe. Ever since the end of World War II our policy had been greatly influenced by the importance of maintaining the full cooperation of France in the allied program for resisting possible Soviet aggression in Europe. We were particularly interested at this time in trying to induce the somewhat reluctant French government to join the proposed European

Defense Community. In these circumstances it seemed impolitic to try to force France to make any concessions to the Indochinese nationalists as a price for our continued military assistance in Vietnam.

In writing about all this in *Present at the Creation,* Acheson implied that the decision to increase our aid to the French in 1951 (it amounted to over $500 million) was not in approval of what they were doing in Indochina but because of this paramount need to maintain their cooperation in Europe. Asked in the already noted interview reported in the *New York Times Book Review* whether this was a justifiable interpretation of what he had written, Acheson answered, "Entirely fair. The French blackmailed us."

Within the State Department there had been for some time grave doubts about the wisdom of our involvement in Vietnam and some apprehension over where our program of military assistance might eventually carry us. But the momentum of events was already forcing the pace. "I decided," Acheson has written in a rather startling admission, "that having put our hand to the plow, we would not look back."

The American public had little realization of what was taking place; it had hardly heard of Vietnam. The alert members of the China bloc nevertheless characteristically believed that the United States should forge ahead in this new campaign against Asian Communism. True to form, Senator Taft had his own proposal. "Now that a Communist assault in Southeast Asia is on the horizon," he advised, "it should be clear to our government that the only chance to stop it is by a Chinese Nationalist invasion of the Communist-held territory. An invasion, well organized, might snowball rapidly." Never making clear how far he felt the United States should go in supporting Chiang Kai-shek on such a formidable venture, Taft soon dropped the whole idea in a further manifestation of his amazingly consistent inconsistency in matters of Far Eastern policy.

With American officials, in the words of the Council on Foreign Relations' annual survey, tending "to class Southeast Asia as the most seriously endangered spot on the entire Soviet-Communist periphery," the United States early in 1952 proposed international action should Communist China move to intervene. Our delegate to the United Nations, John Sherman Cooper, told the Assembly that in the view of his government any such aggression would be a matter of "direct and grave concern which would require the most urgent and earnest consideration by the United Nations." At the same time, proposals were advanced, anticipating the Southeast Asia Collective Defense Treaty, for a military agreement among the United States, Great Britain, France, Australia, and New Zealand for concerted action in the event of any overt Chinese moves.

Nothing came of these proposals for international action. However, the escalation of our military aid to the French, if not yet the escalation of a war we still had no idea of entering directly, gathered increasing headway. In response to repeated requests for more help and to constant warnings of the danger of Chinese intervention, our material contribution to saving Vietnam from Communism rose each year until by the end of the Truman Administration the United States was paying somewhere between one-third and one-half the total cost of the war. At the same time, our dissatisfaction over the inability of France to deal with the steadily deteriorating military situation was keeping pace with our expanded assistance. Vietnam was already casting a long and ominous shadow over the Far Eastern scene.

A further development, though in this instance not a threatening one, which had far-reaching implications for our policy in Asia was the conclusion on September 8, 1951, of a Japanese peace treaty. The principal American negotiator and chief architect of the treaty was John Foster Dulles. He originally thought that both Nationalist China and Communist China might be invited to send delegates to the final peace conference but abandoned this idea with the outbreak of the Korean war. Neither government had any part in the negotiations. It need hardly be said that the treaty was remarkably fair-minded and generous. Far more controversial—particularly in later years—was the concurrent mutual security treaty that the United States and Japan signed at the same time.

Since the peace treaty deprived Japan of the right to have its own military forces (other than those necessary to maintain internal order), the purpose of this second pact was to provide for the security of Japan against armed attack by allowing the United States, in effect, to take over responsibility for its protection. The mutual security treaty gave this country the right to dispose its land, air, and sea forces in and about Japan and Okinawa in order to maintain a defensive shield which was obviously directed against possible Communist aggression.

A further factor in this treaty making was that Japan agree to accept the general tenets of our Far Eastern policy. In mid-September a letter signed by fifty-six senators warned the President that prior to submission of the Japanese treaties for Senate approval, "we desire to make clear that we would consider the recognition of Communist China by Japan . . . to be adverse to the best interests of the people of both Japan and the United States." As a consequence of such pressure Prime Minister Shigeru Yoshida, on December 24, 1951, sent an explanatory letter to John Foster Dulles. He stated that Japan hoped to establish normal relations with the Nationalist government of China but had no intention of concluding any treaty with the Communist regime.

The United States and Japan were thus aligned in a common front against the People's Republic of China as well as against Soviet Russia. Peking interpreted this development as forging another link in an American policy aimed at China's military encirclement.

The Japanese peace treaty also had its bearing—although negatively—on the status of Formosa. When Roosevelt, Churchill, and Chiang Kai-shek discussed their war aims at the Cairo Conference in November 1943, they had agreed that after the defeat of Japan the island would be restored to the "Republic of China" ("Thoughtlessly tossed to China," George Kennan has written, ". . . before we had any idea of what the future China was going to be like, and without any consultation of the inhabitants of the island"). But what was the Republic of China in 1951? The ambiguities over the conflicting claims of the rival governments in Taipei and Peking led the peace negotiators to take a noncommittal position. The treaty went no further than to state that "Japan renounces all right, title and claim to Formosa and the Pescadores."

This failure to settle the issue of Formosa's status theoretically left the way open to a United Nations mandate, as President Truman had tentatively suggested in 1950, or to establishment of an independent state. Yet neither the Nationalist government nor Communist China could be expected to entertain either of these possibilities or any other idea that might suggest two Chinas. On one thing, and one thing only, Peking and Taipei were agreed: by history, geography, and the Cairo agreement, Formosa was an integral part of the state known as China. They differed only as to which regime represented this China and therefore had legal title to the disputed island.

While the Japanese peace treaty was a tremendous achievement in resolving the issues that a decade earlier had led to the Pacific war, it obviously did nothing to settle the new conflict in Sino-American relations. Renewed fighting in Korea, where General Matthew B. Ridgway reported that the armistice negotiations were in "a complete state of paralysis," the threatening situation in Indochina, and the latent controversy over the status of Formosa did not augur well for peace and stability in eastern Asia.

Whatever feelings of friendship between the American and Chinese people that might have survived the Communist revolution had disappeared with the fighting in Korea. The Chinese saw the Americans as barbarian invaders threatening their hearths and homes; Americans viewed the Chinese as ruthless aggressors creating a new yellow peril. Power politics had effected a strange transformation, as one historian has noted, in making over the one-time "darlings of missionaries, philanthropists, and capitalists from friendly smiling protégés into Oriental monsters of unspeakable brutality and cruelty."

In this emotionally charged atmosphere, the United States still refused to consider any official relations with the Peking government. Its representatives had to deal with those of Communist China at Panmunjom, and they agreed that once an armistice was concluded a general peace conference should be held for "the peaceful settlement of the Korean question, et cetera." But the State Department was determined that such negotiations would not lead to official recognition of the People's Republic. The use of the phrase "et cetera" in the communiqué relating to a possible peace conference reflected a stubborn refusal to make any commitment to discuss such key issues as Formosa or China's representation in the United Nations.

On the latter question, the United States was wholly unyielding and in 1951 adopted a special technique to block the Peking government's admission. When the Soviet Union introduced what was to become its annual resolution to expel the Nationalists and seat the Communists, the American delegate simply proposed that consideration of the issue be postponed until the next year. The Assembly accepted this moratorium by a vote of 37 to 11, with four abstentions, and it would continue to adopt a similar American resolution for the next decade.

Far Eastern policy inevitably entered into the presidential campaign of 1952. Neither the politicians nor the public faced up to the fact that behind everything else that was happening in eastern Asia was a confrontation between an America prepared to defend its historic interests there and a resurgent China determined to establish its own dominating influence. Republicans and Democrats alike talked in terms of Communism versus the free world rather than the strategic stakes of political power. The Cold War as an ideological struggle still obsessed the American mind.

The Republicans made all possible political capital out of the vulnerable Democratic record, which they held responsible for the loss of China, the aggression in Korea, and a general betrayal of our Far Eastern interests. Their platform declared that by denying more effective American aid to the Nationalists, the Truman-Acheson policies substituted "on our Pacific flank a murderous enemy for an ally and friend." They promised to end the neglect of the Far East, whose conquest Stalin had long since identified as the road to victory over the West. "We shall make it clear," the Republican platform stated in reaffirming the Asia First thesis, "that we have no intention to sacrifice the East to gain time for the West."

The Democrats were very much on the defensive in attempting to defend their record. Their candidate, Adlai Stevenson, tried to absolve the Truman Administration of responsibility for everything that had gone wrong in eastern Asia, but he could hardly claim its policy had been successful. Stevenson found in fact little to say about the past other than that he did not think "tearful and interminable post-mortems about China will save any souls for democracy." What was most significant in the Democrats' attitude was the extent to which they had swung over to their political rivals' position on the issue of support for Chiang Kai-shek. "Our military and economic assistance to the Nationalist Government on Formosa," their platform declared, "has strengthened that vital outpost of the free world and will be continued."

While General Eisenhower was to accept the views of the China bloc in affirming that the United States was involved in the Korean war because the Truman Administration "abandoned China to the Communists," he generally left to the vice-presidential candidate, Richard Nixon, the hatchet job of blaming the alleged pro-Communist clique in the State Department for this betrayal of the national interest. Nixon also attacked Stevenson for having previously expressed the unorthodox view that nationalism rather than Communism might be the dominant force in Asia. The Democratic candidate would forfeit all right to be even considered for the presidency, Nixon said, unless he explicitly renounced all such ideas and unequivocally expressed his opposition to recognition of Communist China and to giving away Formosa.

Nothing in the presidential campaign had an influence on Far Eastern policy except for General Eisenhower's statement "I shall go to Korea" as a pledge of his determination to end the war there. Neither party suggested any move to break through the wholly negative approach, commanding such popular support, that was implicit in a continued emphasis on the military containment and political isolation of the Chinese People's Republic.

The State Department, accepting all the assumptions of those who still saw Peking acting as an instrument of Communist imperialism directed by Moscow, saw no alternative to this policy. Its sense of frustration nevertheless was admitted on one occasion by the new Assistant Secretary for Far Eastern Affairs, John M. Allison, who succeeded Dean Rusk when the latter left the State Department in 1952 to become head of the Rockefeller Foundation. "Communist China," Allison said, "poses the most difficult question of all for American foreign policy. . . . Today the Chinese people are the pawns of a small group of ruthless Soviet-led Chinese. . . . Frankly we do not know what we can accomplish at this time."

Whether a more effective China policy could be developed, whether anything could be done to moderate the existing Sino-American conflict, was one of the many problems to which the incoming Eisenhower Administration fell heir.

9

The Eisenhower Administration Takes Over

SOME TWO WEEKS after coming into office, President Eisenhower made a first move on China policy. While more urgently concerned with other aspects of foreign affairs, particularly with getting the stalled negotiations in Korea once again under way, he nevertheless incorporated in his first State of the Union message, on February 2, 1953, the announcement of new orders he had given to the Seventh Fleet, still maintaining its station in the Formosan Straits.

Explaining that the fleet originally took up this position in June 1950 both to prevent a possible Chinese Communist attack on Formosa and ensure against any attempt by Chiang Kai-shek to invade the mainland, Eisenhower declared that circumstances were now greatly changed. Since the Peking government's intervention in the Korean war, there was no longer any sense or logic in requiring the United States Navy to assume defensive responsibilities in respect to mainland China. He had consequently given instructions, the President said, that the Seventh Fleet would "no longer be employed to shield Communist China."

Although he gave assurance that this order implied "no aggressive intent against Red China on the part of the United States," the press promptly labeled the action "unleashing Chiang Kai-shek" and it was widely interpreted as freeing the Nationalists for their projected return to the mainland.

Both congressional and popular opinion were sharply divided over the significance of the President's action. Democrats were fearful over its possible consequences in involving the United States in new hostilities; Republicans rejoiced in this evidence that the administration was implementing campaign promises to end neglect of our Far Eastern interests. General MacArthur extolled the new orders to the Seventh Fleet as finally correcting "one of the strangest anomalies known to our military history."

However varied the popular reaction at home, the President's statement awoke universal concern in other parts of the world. The *New York Times* reported that Tokyo was greatly worried, India dismayed, and England and France very uneasy. Our allies, always fearful of what they felt were the militant tendencies of the United States in pursuing its Asian policies, became freshly alarmed over the danger that the new administration might encourage an extension of the still unresolved Korean conflict.

The orders to the Seventh Fleet did not actually represent any basic change in policy or have any practical impact. The Truman Administration, as we have seen, had already shifted from a policy of seeking merely to neutralize Formosa to one of providing direct military support to the Nationalists. Chiang Kai-shek's forces were engaged in hit-and-run raids on the mainland, which had led to the temporary occupation of twenty-one cities; instructing the Seventh Fleet not to shield Communist China was no more than *de facto* acceptance of this new state of affairs. Moreover, it did not in any way increase the Nationalists' capability to conduct offensive operations or imply direct support for them. What President Eisenhower had in mind, he later wrote in his memoir, *Mandate for Change*, was simply to warn Communist China that unless it was prepared to negotiate seriously in Korea, the days of stalemate were numbered, "that the Korean war would either end or be extended beyond Korea."

Nonetheless, freeing the Nationalists for a possible mainland invasion had psychological consequences of far-reaching and lasting importance. It strengthened Chiang Kai-shek's determination to prepare for such an attack and again encouraged him to believe that he might count on American backing whenever he felt strong enough to undertake it. It further convinced Mao Tse-tung that in supporting the Nationalists the United States was the implacable enemy of the new China's aspirations for the fulfillment of its national destiny in bringing all Chinese territory under the control of the Peking government.

In spite of every effort to reassure our allies, their underlying mistrust of American policy remained very lively. The new Secretary of State, John Foster Dulles, hurried to London to tell Foreign Secretary Anthony Eden that the United States had no aggressive designs whatsoever, but so far as the British were concerned, his explanation of the President's orders to the Seventh Fleet was not wholly convincing. Eden continued to believe, as he stated on the floor of the House of Commons, that these orders could have "unfortunate political repercussions without any compensating military advantages."

The assumption of closer links between the United States and the Nationalist government demonstrated by the so-called unleashing of Chiang Kai-shek disregarded conditions within Formosa: Chiang's island domain was hardly a free and democratic country that could be ideologically considered a fit partner in the alliance against Communism. The generalissimo was maintaining what was in effect a dictatorship and largely ignored the interests of the Formosan people themselves. He governed as arbitrarily as he once had on the mainland. Internal reforms, as President Truman himself had once said, were subordinated to Chiang's own political ambitions and his undying dream of a return to the mainland. The one criterion that enabled him to command American support, as in the case of so many national leaders during the years of the Cold War, was an unwavering and resolute anti-Communism.

"Formosa was one of those countries," a contemporary writer stated with oblique reference to earlier controversy over China itself, "whose strategic importance was considered too important to the United States and the free world to indulge in rigid insistence on democratic purity."

Equally or even more significant than these indications of the new administration's approach to China policy were the nature and character of the policy makers taking over control in Washington. While President Eisenhower, with a deep devotion to peace, retained ultimate authority and was on occasion to exercise it decisively, Secretary of State Dulles was always the "prime mover." A conservative New York lawyer with extensive diplomatic experience, most recently in negotiating the Japanese peace treaty, he had his own very definite ideas. He commanded Eisenhower's full confidence—though the President sometimes overruled him—and went his own way with complete certainty of the rightness of his views.

Dulles was a controversial and in some ways paradoxical figure, but his attitude toward Communism could not have been less ambiguous. His religious and philosophic background convinced him that here was an evil—"atheistic Communism"—with which no compromise or accommodation was possible. Even neutralism, he repeatedly affirmed, was immoral. Anthony Eden once described Dulles as "a preacher in the world of politics." Undoubtedly the Secretary of State felt that he was acting as the conscience of the Western world in his unwavering stand for freedom against all the forces of Communist imperialism.

Tough-minded and determined, Dulles was at times quite ready to override his advisers within the State Department, but in his dealings with Congress he was far more skillful and diplomatic than Acheson had ever been. It has sometimes been said that in matters concerning the Far East he allowed the State Department to become the captive of its earlier critics. But in no area did the new Secretary of State more clearly follow his own convictions. He was not surrendering to the China bloc, for he basically shared its views.

In the contest between the free world and the enslaved world, the Far East had in his mind a very special importance. Dulles was not an Asia Firster in the tradition represented by General MacArthur and Senator Taft. He had a far broader global outlook and fully accepted the necessity of strengthening our defenses against the Soviet Union in Europe. Nevertheless, he stated his belief, in an article in *Foreign Affairs* before becoming Secretary of State, that "it is in Asia that Russian imperialism finds its most powerful expression." Soon after taking office he repeated this view, and emphatically said that in developing his foreign policy he intended to give "a new order of priority and urgency . . . to the Far East."

His acceptance of the political importance of Asia was reenforced by a deep sentimental attachment to the old China, which he strongly believed had been bound to the United States by the closest ties of enduring friendship. His grandfather, John W. Foster, after serving as Secretary of State under President William H. Harrison, became an official adviser to the Chinese government, and both this political heritage and his many missionary associations helped to account for this attachment. Dulles one time recounted his childhood thrill on meeting the great Chinese statesman Li Hung-chang, and this fleeting contact would appear to have had its part in awakening his life-long sympathy for China and its people. No one could have felt more keenly that sense of shock so many Americans experienced when the Chinese came under Communist control and, under the influence of Mao Tse-tung, turned so violently anti-American. Everything conspired to deepen in John Foster Dulles a sense of almost personal resentment against the Chinese Communists and to heighten a sincere sympathy for Chiang Kai-shek as a Christian, a symbol of the old order in China, and a dedicated anti-Communist.

Dulles could not accept the outcome of the civil war. In commenting on a proposed speech by the President in March 1953 that stressed the importance of Far Eastern peace, he wrote a memorandum to Eisenhower questioning a reference to halting hostilities in Asia. It gave him a little concern, he said, "lest it commit us to end the Chinese civil war and again 'neutralize' Formosa." Dulles would continue to believe that somehow, sometime, China would be restored to the rightful control of the Nationalists, and he stubbornly refused to acknowledge the Communist triumph as definitive. While he never actually encouraged a mainland invasion, Undersecretary of State Bedell Smith is quoted in Emmet John Hughes's *Ordeal of Power* as saying somewhat plaintively on one occasion, Dulles was "still dreaming his fancy about reactivating the civil war in China."

The Assistant Secretary of State for Far Eastern Affairs during the greater part of the Eisenhower Administration was cast in the same mold as his chief. Dulles brought to this post Walter S. Robertson, who had served in China at the close of the war as minister-counselor at the United States embassy in Chungking. Throughout his service with the State Department, Robertson remained an unfailing proponent of greater assistance to Chiang Kai-shek and an outspoken foe of any move toward recognition of the Peking government. His speeches as Assistant Secretary were an unceasing diatribe against the puppets in Peking, those "zealous consecrated Marxists in their loyalty to Moscow and haters of everything we are and stand for. . . . What do the Communists want?" he once asked. "The answer is 'the world'—their world, our world, everything."

Robertson was questioned at a congressional hearing in January 1954 as to the basic implications of his attitude. Had he been correctly understood, one committee member asked, as saying that the heart of our China policy was "to keep alive a constant threat of military action vis-à-vis Red China in the hope that at some point there will be an internal breakdown?" He unhesitatingly answered, "Yes, sir, that is my conception." Queried further as to whether this did not fundamentally mean that "the United States is undertaking to maintain for an indefinite period of years American dominance in the Far East?" Robertson again gave an unequivocal reply: "Yes. Exactly."

This was strong medicine. It may not have reflected accurately the views of Robertson's superiors, but it remains striking evidence of the thinking in the State Department as to how the United States should meet the challenge of Communist China.

Assistant Secretary Robertson had even less doubt than Secretary Dulles over the eventual victory of the Nationalists in restoring their rule on the mainland. He was certain how the Chinese people would react if ever given a choice "between a government rooted in Chinese tradition and one that has made China a handmaiden of an alien imperialism." When the United States transferred two American destroyers to the Nationalist navy, he officially expressed the hope that "these ships will contribute to bringing nearer the day when China will again belong unreservedly to the Chinese."

In his public statements and in his diplomatic contacts Robertson clung uncompromisingly to his fixed ideas; there was no room in his mind for any review or reconsideration of changing circumstances on the Far Eastern stage. He was present at the Geneva Conference dealing with Korea and Vietnam in 1954, and there came into direct contact with Britain's Foreign Secretary. Reporting on a meeting between the two men, Anthony Eden later wrote that Robertson's attitude was "so emotional as to be impervious to argument or indeed to facts." How influential were the views of this official who on his retirement from the State Department in 1959 could still say of the Communist regime in China, "It just cannot possibly endure," is impossible to document. However, President Eisenhower has said in *Waging Peace* that Robertson was "a tower of strength to Foster Dulles in the forming of policy."

During these same years our ambassador in Taipei was Karl L. H. Rankin, the former chargé d'affaires. Quite as much a zealot in the cause of Chiang Kai-shek as Robertson, he not only exercised all possible influence as a diplomat to strengthen our bonds with the Nationalists but cooperated closely with the China bloc in Washington in seeking to bring pressure to bear upon the State Department in support of this policy. He candidly related these activities in an account of his diplomatic career, *China Assignment*, published after his retirement.

Rankin's thesis was that peace was impossible in Asia until the "predatory regime" in Peking, which carried the "flag of Communist conspiracy," was replaced by a truly Chinese government. To this end the United States should in every way encourage Chiang's return to the mainland. Rankin apparently interpreted his responsibilities in his sensitive post at Taipei as the constant promotion of this objective rather than an objective evaluation of the situation in the Far East. "Some of these excerpts," he wrote, quoting in *China Assignment* from his official dispatches to Washington, "may sound unwarrantably alarming, or seem to support unduly the side of Nationalist China. This was done deliberately, for my pervasive policy was to assist those in Washington who shared my sense of urgency about China and the Far East in general and who believed that a positive and active policy was indispensable."

The attitude of these key figures, that is, Secretary Dulles, Assistant Secretary Robertson, and Ambassador Rankin, governed the Eisenhower Administration's China policy. Each of these men was so caught up in the fears and alarms of the Cold War, each was so fully convinced that a vital confrontation between international Communism and the free world was taking place in Asia, that they were incapable of an open-minded appraisal of the changing configuration of the power structure in the Far East. They could not appreciate that while the Chinese People's Republic was assuredly Communist, it also represented the new forces of Chinese nationalism. Certain that Mao Tse-tung was at the beck and call of the Kremlin, they were blinded to the shifting course of Sino-Russian relations.

The immediate unfinished business that the Eisenhower Administration faced in eastern Asia was settlement of the Korean war. Both the President and his Secretary of State accepted the basic conditions underlying the Truman-Acheson policy: no retreat or appeasement of Communist China but a willingness to accept a negotiated settlement even though it fell short of Korea's unification. At the same time, they were determined to exert maximum pressure upon the Peking government to resume the stalled truce talks, which appeared to be hopelessly bogged down over the involved issue of repatriation of war prisoners, and to bring an end to the continued fighting as a first step toward a political solution of the whole Korean problem.

A number of official statements from Washington clearly intimated that the United States would not countenance any further delaying tactics at Panmunjom and that if the Chinese Communists were not ready to negotiate in good faith, we would be compelled to adopt measures bringing the war directly to China. The Chinese Communists could expect a naval blockade of their coast and bombing of their industrial installations. Once again, as in January 1950, there were also hints of the possible use of atomic weapons. On a visit to New Delhi, Secretary Dulles undertook to see that, through the medium of Prime Minister Nehru, these warnings were directly conveyed to Peking.

Discussing these moves in a television interview sixteen years later, Eisenhower said: "I let it be known that if there were not going to be an armistice . . . I would no longer regard this war as being limited." He was ready to attack wherever the enemy challenged and would not feel bound by any choice of weapons. He never directly threatened the use of the atomic bomb, Eisenhower explained, but the Chinese Communists were informed that he would do whatever was necessary to bring them back to the negotiating table. "I don't mean to say that we'd have used those great big things and destroyed cities," the former President concluded, "but we would use them enough to win."

These warnings to the Chinese Communists may or may not have been decisive in persuading them to change their position. Dulles was convinced that they were, and subsequently said so. However, shortly before this, on March 5, 1953, Stalin died and with new leaders in power, Soviet Russia swung over to a more conciliatory policy toward the West, with an emphasis on peaceful coexistence. The Peking government may well have thought that in these circumstances, uncertain of continued Russian aid, it could no longer hope for a military victory over the United Nations forces in Korea, and was quite ready to accept a settlement along the Thirty-eighth Parallel. In any event, it now agreed to resume negotiations at Panmunjom, and on April 26 talks once again got under way.

The Korean story remains complicated. The vexed problem of the release of the war prisoners; the recalcitrance of Korea's president, Syngman Rhee, whose objective remained the military unification of all Korea; and the obstructive tactics of the Communists all hampered the negotiations. Fighting again broke out on a large scale, and the UN forces were hard-pressed to throw back the fierce Communist offensive. The United States renewed its warnings that it might feel compelled to broaden the war and employ whatever weapons it felt to be necessary in protecting its position. Then, at long last, on July 27, the two sides agreed on an armistice.

The armistice reestablished the old line of Korea's division approximately along the Thirty-eighth Parallel, set up a demilitarized zone from which all troops would be withdrawn, and provided for the release of prisoners without forcible repatriation. The agreement further stipulated that a political conference would be held within three months to conclude a more permanent settlement. Nothing about this was wholly satisfactory.

But the United States could assert that it had succeeded in repelling aggression, and Communist China could conclude that its security was reasonably safeguarded by having blocked allied control over North Korea.

The conclusion of the Korean armistice created the hope in some quarters that the Eisenhower Administration would feel that the time was at hand for a thorough review of our Far Eastern policy. The *New Republic* took the lead among liberal journals in raising the fundamental question whether it was really in the American interest to withhold recognition from the Peking government and commit ourselves so strongly to the Nationalists. "Are we planning to come to terms with the world's largest nation to determine its intentions, to influence its relations with Russia and promote its willingness to live in peace?" it asked. "Or do we prefer to harass the Chinese Government without really threatening it; feeding, clothing, equipping and training the Nationalist army, a dagger long enough to draw blood but too short to inflict serious wounds?"

The answer in official circles was clear and unequivocal. The new administration had no idea of curtailing assistance to the Nationalists. It was prepared to invigorate rather than ease the tough policy to which the Truman Administration had swung over during the Korean war. In seeking to assure the political isolation of the Chinese People's Republic and to build up the Nationalist regime on Formosa as the legitimate government of all China, the Eisenhower-Dulles policy would make no concessions.

With no lessening of the suspicion and hostility between Washington and Peking, the plans for a post-armistice conference over Korea collapsed. It proved impossible to agree even on what nations should attend the proposed meeting. Yet matters could not be left at this point; peace in Asia was too important. The risk that fighting might again break out in Korea was ever-present, and new dangers threatened in Indochina.

When the Big Four foreign ministers—those of the United States, Great Britain, France, and Soviet Russia—met in Berlin in January 1954, Far Eastern as well as European questions entered into their discussions. Soviet Foreign Minister V. M. Molotov consequently proposed a broader conference, to which the Chinese People's Republic would be invited, with the general purpose of trying to reduce tension in the entire field of international relations. Secretary Dulles unhesitatingly rejected the proposal, the obvious purpose of which was to bring Communist China to the council table as one of the great powers competent to deal with European as well as Asian problems. Nothing could have more offended his sense of the fitness of things than this patent Russian maneuver for Peking's official recognition.

"I would like to state here plainly and unequivocally," the Secretary of State said, ". . . the United States will not agree to a five-power conference with the Chinese aggressors to consider the peace of the world. . . . We do not refuse to deal with it [the Peking government] where occasion requires. . . . It is, however, one thing to recognize evil as a fact. It is another thing to take evil to one's breast and embrace it."

Still, the foreign ministers could not brush aside the Far East. On the initiative of Anthony Eden they finally agreed—and it was the only constructive development at this otherwise wholly inconclusive meeting of the Big Four—to a new approach. They called for a special conference among all the nations concerned, to be held in Geneva in late April, which would deal with both Korea and Indochina. The meeting would in the first instance be made up of representatives of those countries associated with the United Nations command in Korea on the one side, and on the other, delegates from Soviet Russia, Communist China, and North Korea.

Dulles gave his consent somewhat reluctantly. And once again he made it explicitly clear that in agreeing to sit at the conference table with the Chinese Communists, the United States had no intention of recognizing them diplomatically. They would be coming to Geneva, he said in somewhat the same phraseology Dean Acheson had earlier used in agreeing to the presence of a Chinese delegation at the United Nations, not "to be honored by us, but rather to account before the bar of public opinion." Dulles was under very strong domestic pressure to take this unaccommodating stand, but it reflected his own unalterable conviction that no move whatsoever should be made suggesting acceptance of the People's Republic of China in the world community.

In the months following the Korean armistice the United States found further cause for anxiety over what Peking might do next. The continuing war in Vietnam appeared to be approaching some sort of a climax, and reports that Chinese Communist troops were poised on the Indochina border, first current during the closing days of the Truman Administration, were again rife. Dulles took them no less seriously than had his predecessor. "A single Chinese Communist aggressive front extends from Korea in the north to Indochina in the south," he declared on September 4, 1953.

Acting on the premise underlying the Truman-Acheson policy that a Vietminh victory over the French might ultimately bring all Indochina under Communist control, the Eisenhower Administration did not hesitate to continue extending military aid to the colonial authorities. The Peking government was also expressly warned of "grave consequences" should it send its own army to the Vietminh's support. Taking a position comparable to that he held in respect to Korea, Dulles further elaborated on this warning by stating that in the event of overt Chinese intervention, hostilities might not be confined to Indochina.

In the fall of 1953 the so-called Navarre Plan, named after the new commander in chief in Indochina, revived hopes that the French might be able to get the situation in Vietnam under control. It provided for the additional training and use of native troops—something like a "Vietnamization" of the war—and, setting a precedent that would be followed with dismaying regularity down through the years, the local military authorities confidently promised that this new strategy would soon bring the war to an end—at least by 1955. But the promised victories did not materialize; the augmented Vietnamese forces remained incapable of halting the Vietminh. Then in early 1954 the on-driving insurgents began a massive assault on the French stronghold of Dienbienphu, and the whole military situation deteriorated disastrously.

Confronted with the likelihood that the French position in Indochina might collapse, the Eisenhower Administration became greatly alarmed. Contemplating the need for possible further action by the United States, both the President and the Secretary of State undertook to awaken the American people to what they declared to be the "transcendant importance" of Southeast Asia. They let out all the stops in describing the threat to the free world should Soviet Russia and Communist China succeed in imposing their political system on the Indochinese states. Eisenhower took up the falling domino theory: should Vietnam succumb to Communist control, he asserted, all the other countries of Southeast Asia were in danger of toppling over. The free world could not stand passively by while this happened but should adopt active measures to meet a common danger.

Yet Vietnam in the mid-1950s, as Acheson had discovered some years earlier, still presented many anomalies and contradictions. Was Southeast Asia actually of such "transcendant importance" to the free world that the United States should allow itself to become involved in underwriting French colonialism? The Vietminh forces, led by Ho Chi Minh, were admittedly receiving aid from both Communist China and Soviet Russia, but were they really prepared to promote these countries' interests rather than Vietnamese nationalism? Who was the real enemy? The Vietminh, who sought to establish an independent state? The Chinese Communists, supposedly bent on their own imperial aggrandizement? Or the international Communist conspiracy, trying to subvert another outpost of the free world?

The answers to such questions were no clearer in 1954 than in later years, and American policy consequently followed a highly ambiguous course. In an attempt to resolve the dilemma of how it could justify its stand in safeguarding Vietnamese freedom by giving its support to colonialism, the United States now tried to persuade France to "perfect" the independence of the Indochinese states. But Paris was still reluctant to move affirmatively in this direction, and the European situation again made it very difficult for Washington to exert the pressure necessary to force any action. Committed to our aid program, we consequently accepted the French view that the nationalistic elements within the Vietminh were being manipulated by the agents of international Communism.

Secretary Dulles took the lead in linking developments in Southeast Asia with the world Communist conspiracy. "In the present stage," he said on March 24, 1954, "the Communists in Indochina use national anti-French slogans to win legal support. But if they achieve military or political success, it is certain they would subject the people to a cruel Communist dictatorship taking its orders from Peiping and Moscow." A week later, commenting on new reports that Communist China's troops were actually fighting alongside the Vietminh, he told the House Foreign Relations Committee with equal assurance that the Chinese were utilizing Vietnamese aspirations for freedom as "a pretext for a major war of aggression."

The reports of Chinese troops in Vietnam were never confirmed; Ho Chi Minh repeatedly stated that he had no intention of using any foreign reinforcements. The difficulties in deciding American policy, as President Eisenhower was to admit in *Mandate for Change*, were compounded by this lack of evidence of any direct Chinese participation in the Indochinese conflict. Our approach to the situation nevertheless remained firmly based on the proposition that behind the Vietminh stood the aggressive power of Red China as the spearhead of international Communism.

In late March the French indicated that conditions at Dienbienphu had become desperate, foreshadowing the probable collapse of the whole war effort, and asked the United States to come to the defense of this key outpost with an air strike. Washington was faced with a vital decision, and opinion among President Eisenhower's advisers was divided. However, both Secretary of State Dulles and Admiral Arthur W. Radford, the new chairman of the Joint Chiefs of Staff, favored direct American intervention. On April 3 they held a secret meeting, approved by the President, with a group of congressional leaders to promote this program.

Dulles and Radford specifically proposed that Congress adopt a joint resolution authorizing the President to employ air and naval forces to support the French position. The Congressmen were startled and worried. As reported in a graphic account of this meeting, entitled "The Day We Didn't Go to War," which later appeared in the *Reporter*, they began to ask questions. Did our allies approve such a plan? Did the military fully support it? When they learned that Secretary Dulles had not even consulted with our allies about it and that only Admiral Radford among the Joint Chiefs of Staff endorsed it, their skepticism over running such risks hardened into certainty that the United States should not take unilateral action. They unanimously agreed that before anything was done, the Secretary of State should at least go "shopping for allies."

President Eisenhower accepted the Congressmen's position in recognizing that however serious the crisis in Vietnam, the United States should not act alone. He consequently sent his Secretary of State to sound out opinion in London and Paris, and he himself undertook to write a long letter to Prime Minister Churchill outlining his own views and urging a coalition among those powers that were most vitally concerned in checking Communist expansion in Southeast Asia. He had in mind, the President said, the United States, Great Britain, France, Australia, New Zealand, and the Associated States of Indochina (as first tentatively proposed in 1951), and he especially emphasized that "the coalition must be strong and it must be willing to join the fight if necessary."

While Secretary Dulles, who flew to London on April 10, was frantically trying to round up support for the anti-Communist coalition, Americans generally remained completely ignorant of what was going on. However, reports from Washington suggested that the United States might feel compelled on its own to intervene in Indochina and intimated that it was prepared if necessary to broaden the war by taking direct action against Communist China as the real force behind the Vietminh. A battle commenced this early between "hawks" and "doves" over our policy in Southeast Asia. Those who felt the United States had no business intervening in Vietnam were aligned against those who called for measures to repel further Communist aggression at whatever cost.

Among the hawks Vice-President Nixon was perhaps the most outspoken. In a dramatic speech on April 16 before the American Society of Newspaper Editors, he startled the entire country with his bellicose views. "If to avoid further Communist expansion in Asia and Indochina we must take the risk now of putting our boys in," Nixon stated in no uncertain terms, "I think the Executive has to take the unpopular decision and do it." Both Congress and the general public were so alarmed that Secretary Dulles felt compelled to calm popular fears of our being about to plunge into an Asian war. The Vice-President's statement was "hypothetical," he said, and the use of American troops in Indochina "unlikely."

President Eisenhower was certainly not prepared to take any such drastic step; he remained very much opposed to unilateral intervention. It was not that he did not feel much the same as Nixon about the Communist menace. He too saw looming behind the Vietminh the aggressive designs of the Chinese. As he recalled in *Mandate for Change*, he believed that if Peking actively came to the support of the Vietminh as they had to the support of the North Koreans, the United States, even without allies, could not avoid considering the necessity of "striking directly at the head instead of the tail of the snake, Red China itself." But he saw no need for such action under existing circumstances. Eisenhower felt that it would be a tragedy, as he later described his views, for the United States to become involved in another war in Asia and was determined to do everything possible to avoid it.

Secretary Dulles's mission to find backing for an anti-Communist coalition to safeguard Southeast Asia was making no progress. France now gave belated assurances that it would grant the Indochinese states full independence, but while favoring in principle an allied coalition, its attitude was skeptical and defeatist. More important, Great Britain had the gravest reservations. Foreign Secretary Eden felt that the idea should be examined very carefully. He believed the possible composition of such a coalition created many problems, and stated that in any event nothing should be done until the forthcoming Geneva Conference had the opportunity to study all phases of the Far Eastern situation. In urging immediate action Dulles sought to draw analogies between Communist China's designs in Indochina and Japan's invasion of Manchuria in 1931, and even with Hitler's occupation of the Rhineland in 1936. Eden was not overly impressed. He held to his position that the threat of retaliation implicit in the formation of an anti-Communist military coalition would be provocative and dangerous.

On his return to Washington the Secretary of State was nevertheless unwilling to abandon the coalition plan and called a meeting of the ambassadors of the countries involved to consider it further. Eden, who thought he had made his position clear, was incensed and immediately instructed the British ambassador not to attend the meeting. The whole business fell through. Dulles believed that Eden had surrendered to the pressure of neutralist India; Eden felt that Dulles was trying to force his hand. What Eisenhower tactfully described as a "misunderstanding" did nothing to smooth the way in maintaining Anglo-American accord.

In spite of this setback, the indefatigable Dulles would not give up. On the eve of the Geneva Conference he made another attempt to win over the British to some sort of joint action to restrain the Communists. Eden again refused to commit his government in any way. Great Britain remained opposed, he said decisively, to setting up any coalition or taking any joint military action until all the possibilities of attaining a peaceful settlement in Vietnam were completely exhausted.

Without allied support the administration finally gave up any idea of intervention. It did not send American planes to the defense of Dienbienphu or strike at the "head of the snake" in Communist China. With neither Congress nor the public ready to back proposals for "putting our boys in," President Eisenhower in effect overruled his Vice-President, his Secretary of State, and the chairman of the Joint Chiefs of Staff. The Vietminh in the meantime drove relentlessly ahead to the ultimate capture of Dienbienphu; France had to face the bitter reality of complete defeat of its military forces in Vietnam.

The Geneva Conference met under the darkening clouds of this crisis in Vietnam at the close of April. However, the initial item on its agenda, as originally decided by the Big Four ministers in Berlin, was a settlement in Korea, and it was to this the conferees first turned. With Chou En-lai heading the delegation from Communist China and John Foster Dulles that of the United States, the atmosphere was not very cordial. The two major protagonists did not engage in any diplomatic amenities. The correspondent of the *New York Times* reported that they neither looked at one another in the conference sessions, had any contact in the antechambers, nor made any effort "to disguise a deep-seated resentment." Eden was later to write that in a conversation with Molotov, the Russian delegate said "with a frosty smile that he had observed that Mr. Dulles had succeeded during his stay in Geneva in never once acknowledging Mr. Chou En-lai's existence." Another observer has written in discussing Dulles's attitude that "it was the most bizarre performance of his secretaryship."

There was little chance of the United States and the Chinese People's Republic breaking through such barriers to reach any general accord. Dulles took the position that what was at stake was the authority of the United Nations: Communist China should be compelled to accept the UN solution to the Korean problem. Chou En-lai insisted that Asian countries should settle the affairs of Asia and that American policy was one of unwarranted interference. The United States, he charged, was "dreaming to impose upon the Chinese people the power of the Kuomintang remnant clique" ruling on Formosa. No headway whatsoever was made in these circumstances, and the Korean negotiations collapsed. On May 5 Secretary Dulles glumly left Geneva saying that things were going "just as we expected."

The conference next turned to the problem of Indochina and invited to its further sessions representatives of the Associated States—Vietnam, Cambodia, and Laos—and also delegates from the Vietminh's Democratic Republic of North Vietnam. However, the United States delegation, with Undersecretary Bedell Smith taking the place of Secretary Dulles, withdrew from any further active part in the negotiations.

Dienbienphu had in the meantime, on May 7, fallen to the Vietminh, and a new ministry in Paris realistically accepted the inevitable. It agreed to the withdrawal of France from Indochina, with recognition of the full independence of the one-time French colonies. As for Vietnam, an armistice was projected temporarily dividing that country along the Seventeenth Parallel, between the Democratic Republic in the north and the State of Vietnam in the south.

The further negotiations at Geneva took time, only action by Communist China at one point breaking a complete impasse, but with the exception of the United States and South Vietnam, the participating nations finally reached a broad accord, which was embodied in an official declaration issued on July 21. They pledged themselves to respect the sovereignty and independence of Cambodia, Laos, and Vietnam, accepted the demarcation line dividing Vietnam along the Seventeenth Parallel, stipulated that elections would be held in 1956 for Vietnam's national unification, and acknowledged a prohibition on the introduction of foreign troops into Vietnam. To supervise the observance of these agreements the International Control Commission was established, consisting of representatives of India, Poland, and Canada.

In announcing that the United States was not prepared to join in this conference declaration, Undersecretary Bedell Smith nevertheless stated that his government would "refrain from any threat or the use of force" to disturb the agreements and would view any renewal of aggression in Indochina "with grave concern and as seriously threatening international peace and security."

The American public, with its attention at this time largely centered on the McCarthy army hearings, was not greatly concerned over the division of Vietnam or indeed any other aspects of the situation in Southeast Asia. But as always, the alert members of the China bloc were alarmed. Senator Knowland characterized the settlement at Geneva as "one of the greatest victories for communism in a decade." An editorial in the *Reporter* commented, "We stood aside, holding our noses, but the predestined truce was signed. The Communists have gained another smaller China."

The effect of the Geneva settlement on American policy was a prompt renewal of the drive for a collective defense treaty to prevent further direct or indirect Communist aggression in Southeast Asia. With North Vietnam lost to the other side, this appeared to the Eisenhower Administration as more necessary than ever. John Foster Dulles now felt assured of the British support that had not been forthcoming before the Geneva Conference, and he took up negotiations where he had left them off. His efforts were successful when some six weeks later, on September 8, 1954, eight nations meeting in Manila signed the Southeast Asia Collective Defense Treaty. The signatories were the United States, Great Britain, France, Australia, New Zealand, the Philippine Republic, Thailand, and Pakistan, and the treaty's stated purpose was to meet any threat of aggression by joint action in accordance with the individual members' constitutional practices. Through a special protocol the treaty's protective umbrella was extended to South Vietnam, Cambodia, and Laos should they request assistance.

What this treaty more clearly meant for the United States was underlined when in signing it an "understanding" was filed that the American commitment to act in meeting a common danger applied only to Communist aggression. Our target was then even more plainly designated in a further statement by Secretary Dulles. He declared that "open military aggression by the Chinese Communist regime" and "disturbances fomented from Communist China" were the twofold danger the United States faced in Southeast Asia.

The new pact, which led to the organization of the Southeast Asia Treaty Organization (SEATO), provided a very insubstantial basis for concerted allied action. It did not legally bind the signatories to anything more than consultation, and the refusal of such important Asian nations as Indonesia, Ceylon, Burma, and India to have anything to do with it further weakened its significance. With a confidence that the future hardly justified, President Eisenhower and Secretary Dulles were nevertheless highly satisfied. "The dilemma of finding a moral, legal and practical basis for helping our friends of the region need not face us again," Eisenhower wrote in *Mandate for Change* with somewhat dubious foresight.

The United States was not content with the establishment of SEATO in making good its resolve that "the time has come to end the retreat in Asia"; it was also prepared to extend military assistance to South Vietnam in holding the new line accepted at the Geneva Conference. After South Vietnam's first head of state, the former puppet emperor Bao Dai, abdicated in favor of Premier Ngo Dinh Diem, President Eisenhower made such a commitment to the new government in a letter of October 23, 1954. This was not unconditional. A cautious Eisenhower carefully informed President Diem that "the Government of the United States expects that this aid will be met by performance on the part of the Government of Vietnam in undertaking needed reforms."

Perhaps recalling the unfortunate consequences of providing unconditional aid to the French (and also to the Chinese Nationalists), the administration was trying to set up reasonable safeguards for the utilization of whatever funds it might provide the new Vietnam government. But these provisos were soon forgotten. In seeking to implement the doctrine of containment in Southeast Asia, the United States overlooked all the evidence of incompetence, dictatorial control, and corruption that increasingly characterized the Diem regime. That it was anti-Communist, as with the Chinese Nationalists, appeared to be quite enough.

In adopting the policy embodied in SEATO and a program of expanding military and economic aid to South Vietnam, the Eisenhower Administration was embarking on a course firmly believed to be in the interests of the entire free world as well as in the interests of the United States. But in so significantly extending our obligations in the Far East, it acted with little realization of what this might ultimately involve. "Europe offered a solid ground on which the United States could take a stand," Louis Halle has written in *The Cold War*. "By contrast Asia was a swamp."

Yet those responsible for this policy were hardly constrained by the possible limits of national power. The prevailing attitude at this time was illustrated in a speech President Eisenhower made in April 1954, when the Vietnam crisis was at its height. He said on this occasion: "We can stand up and hold up our heads and say, 'America is the greatest force that God has ever allowed to exist on his footstool.' As such it is up to us to lead this world to a peaceful and secure existence. And I assure you we can do it."

As these developments were taking place in Southeast Asia, the United States and the People's Republic of China found themselves involved in a direct and more threatening clash over Formosa. As during the Korean war each nation was convinced in this dispute that it was legitimately defending its national interests and accused the other of imperialist aggression. The Communists continued to consider Formosa a province of China temporarily in the hands of a rebel clique; the United States not only still recognized the Nationalist government as that of all China but now included Formosa within its defensive perimeter in the western Pacific. This issue would remain the all-important barrier—more than Korea, more than Indochina—to any moderation of the mutual mistrust and suspicion between the United States and China that had so completely replaced the old traditions of Sino-American friendship.

The first intimation of a dangerous confrontation in the Formosan Straits was a proclamation by Premier Chou En-lai on August 11, 1954. "The liberation of Taiwan," he declared, "is a glorious, historic mission of the Chinese people. Only by liberating Taiwan from the rule of the traitorous Chiang Kai-shek group . . . can we complete victory in the cause of liberating the Chinese people." He then added that "foreign aggressors" who might attempt to block the Peking government from fulfilling this mission would face "grave consequences."

Six days later President Eisenhower was asked at a press conference what would happen if the Chinese Communists actually launched their threatened assault on Formosa. The President answered very simply. The orders first issued to the Seventh Fleet in 1950 were still in force, he said, and therefore, "I should assume that what would happen is this: any invasion of Formosa would have to run over the Seventh Fleet."

A new crisis was in the making.

10

Crisis
in the Formosan Straits

IN A WIDELY PUBLICIZED ARTICLE in *Life* early in January 1956, which developed the thesis that John Foster Dulles had averted war in eastern Asia through the skillful practice of "brinkmanship," author James Shepley gave three examples of how this was done. The first was the threat of the possible use of atomic weapons should the Peking government refuse to conclude an armistice in Korea, the second was the warning that the United States would not stand aside if the Chinese Communists intervened in the war in Indochina, and the third was American policy in the Formosan Straits in 1954–55.

"The ability to get to the verge without getting into the war is the necessary art," Shepley quoted Dulles as saying. "If you try to run away from it, you are lost. . . . We walked to the brink and looked it in the face. We took strong action."

The validity of the Dulles thesis—both in its application in these three instances and in its consequent results—has often been disputed. The Secretary of State's critics have sometimes drawn a none too favorable comparison between his approach to foreign affairs and that of an earlier Republican policy maker who was also deeply concerned over the Far East: Theodore Roosevelt. Whereas, half a century earlier, Roosevelt believed in speaking softly and carrying a big stick, these critics pointed out, Dulles spoke out loudly (sometimes frightening our friends more than our foes) but, in terms of support either at home or abroad, his big stick was a very uncertain weapon should the enemy have ever called his hand.

Factors other than the exercise of brinkmanship most certainly contributed to the avoidance of war with Communist China during the critical period of the mid-1950s. The assumption that our warnings and threats prevented the miscalculations that might otherwise have led to war rests on a somewhat dubious foundation. Whatever else might be said of the Dulles policy, moreover, it contributed nothing to the settlement of the underlying causes of conflict in eastern Asia. On the contrary, it served to widen still further what was becoming the seemingly unbridgeable gulf in relations between the United States and the Chinese People's Republic.

This was well illustrated in the Formosan crisis in 1954–55. At no time since the triumph of the Chinese Communists—even including war in Korea—was there more controversy over what policy the United States should follow or more fear over where we were heading. For a time a distinct possibility of general war did exist. It was warded off because President Eisenhower stood firmly against any American move that might precipitate hostilities and because Chairman Mao Tse-tung was equally reluctant to present a direct challenge to the United States. These were the essential elements in averting war—not, as Dulles would have it, walking to the verge and taking strong action.

Shortly after the exchange between Premier Chou En-lai and President Eisenhower, in the last week of August 1954, words gave way to action in the Formosan Straits. The Communists raided the island of Quemoy; the Nationalists retaliated with sea and air attacks on the Chinese mainland; then from its coastal bases the People's Liberation Army commenced a heavy artillery bombardment of Quemoy.

This little island, or more accurately, group of islands, and also Matsu to the north—to become so well known as the "offshore islands"—lie just a few miles off the mainland coast. They were—and are—in Nationalist hands, determinedly held by Chiang Kai-shek as a possible springboard for an invasion of the mainland. Should they fall into Communist hands, they would conversely offer a stepping stone for an assault on Formosa. In 1954 their strategic value was not as important to either side as the psychological impact of any change in their status. Their loss would have seriously undermined Nationalist confidence in an eventual reconquest of the mainland; in winning control of them, the Communists would have felt they were that much further in liberating Formosa itself.

The bombardment of the islands appeared to be a probing operation to discover just how far the United States might be prepared to go in defending the Nationalist regime, and it posed what Secretary Dulles described as a "horrible dilemma." To rush to the islands' defense would involve this country even more directly in China's civil war, but to fail to do so might encourage the Communists to believe they could attack Formosa with impunity. As tension mounted in the straits, though there was no further immediate action, President Eisenhower met with his advisers on September 12. He found them, as usual, very much divided. The Joint Chiefs of Staff, with the single exception of General Matthew Ridgway, favored not only defending the offshore islands but also supporting the Nationalists in attacking the mainland; Dulles believed the United States should take a strong stand but proposed first taking the issue to the United Nations; and General Ridgway and Undersecretary Bedell Smith were reported to oppose any move that would involve military or naval operations unless Formosa itself were attacked.

The President threw his weight behind the counsels of restraint. He told the military, as he has written in *Mandate for Change*, that the discussion was not about a limited brush-fire war, for "we're talking about going to the threshold of World War III." He did not believe an attack on China could be limited or controlled as had been the case in the Korean war. In the existing circumstances he was unwilling to intervene to protect the offshore islands, let alone encourage the Nationalists to invade the mainland.

While the crisis simmered in the straits, the United States was adventitiously engaged in negotiations that were to put its basic commitment to defend Formosa squarely on the line. Returning from the Manila Conference, which had led to conclusion of the Southeast Asia Collective Defense Treaty, John Foster Dulles stopped off in Taipei in early September to discuss with Chiang Kai-shek a mutual security treaty. Further conversations over its terms were now proceeding in Washington against the background of this new threat to Far Eastern peace.

A major purpose of the proposed treaty was to supplement those that the United States had already signed with Japan, South Korea, the Philippine Republic, Australia, and New Zealand in securing its defensive line in the western Pacific. It envisaged joint action against either armed attack or subversive Communist activity. However, the ambition of Chiang Kai-shek to invade the China mainland involved a special problem.

If the United States allowed itself to become unreservedly committed to the Nationalist government, Chiang might well feel he could call on American aid in trying to reestablish his authority over all China. Little question existed of his desire to involve the United States. "Our plan for fighting Communism and regaining the mainland," he had said in February 1953, "will necessarily form . . . an important link in the general plan of the free world to combat world-wide Communist aggression." While in sympathy with Chiang's aims, Dulles was nevertheless as anxious as his predecessors had been to avoid a situation where Chiang could call the tune in making American policy.

The treaty between the United States and the Republic of China, as finally signed in Washington on December 2, 1954, provided for the mutual defense of the two parties' territories and gave the United States the right to dispose its forces about Formosa and the Pescadores as might be required for the defense of these islands. But to safeguard American interests against Chiang's impetuosity, there was a cautionary exchange of notes between Secretary Dulles and Foreign Minister Yeh. They stipulated that, other than in sustaining the legitimate rights of self-defense, the Nationalist government would not resort to force—clearly meaning force against Communist China—except in joint agreement with this country.

The new leash on Chiang incorporated in this exchange of notes was an elastic one, and there was little reason to believe that he took it very seriously. He had no idea of allowing his freedom of action to be restricted. He continued to talk belligerently not only of Formosa's importance to the free world, but also of his steadfast determination to carry the struggle for his country's future across the Formosan Straits. "The China mainland is an integral part of the Republic of China," he told the American correspondent Fulton Lewis, Jr., in an interview two months after signature of the defense treaty. "To recover the mainland is not only our supreme mission but our inherent right." In concluding this formal treaty with Nationalist China, the United States was to rediscover that it had an ally increasingly hard to keep under control.

The Chinese Communists, who had continued to concentrate their forces on the coastline opposite Formosa and were intermittently shelling Quemoy, promptly assailed this new treaty as "a grave warlike provocation." From their point of view it constituted intervention in China's internal affairs in that Chiang's regime on Formosa was in rebellion against the constituted authority of the Peking government. In supporting Nationalist China, they asserted, the United States was again demonstrating its imperialist ambitions in Asia.

While the Communists' anger was building up along these lines, American hostility toward Peking was exacerbated by another development, quite unrelated to events affecting Formosa. On November 22, 1954, a military tribunal in Peking imposed long prison terms on eleven United States airmen who had been shot down and captured during the Korean war, together with two civilian employees, on charges of espionage. The Chinese were holding a number of other Americans in prison, but this move against uniformed members of our armed forces aroused the American public even more than when Consul General Ward was arrested five years earlier.

Firebrands both within and without Congress demanded immediate action to secure the airmen's release at whatever cost, and Senator Knowland excitedly called for a blockade of the China coast. The Eisenhower Administration refused to be rushed off its feet by this clamor. The President declared that the United States would do everything it could peaceably in behalf of the prisoners but would not be driven to what would be an act of war; on the contrary, he was prepared to submit the issue to the United Nations. Recognizing the validity of American protests on the ground that Peking had violated the Korean armistice, the Assembly was ready to act. On December 10, by a vote of 47 to 5, it adopted a resolution instructing Secretary General Dag Hammarskjold to seek the prisoners' immediate release.

In the meantime, to pick up the thread of developments in the Formosan Straits, the bombing and raids on the offshore islands had continued without provoking more direct conflict. However, in early January 1955 the Chinese Communists launched their heaviest air attacks to date, not against Quemoy but against the Tachen Islands, lying some two hundred miles to the north, and their ground forces invaded still another little island, Yikiang, where they quickly overwhelmed a thousand Nationalist guerrillas.

Once again the Joint Chiefs of Staff called for immediate military action on the part of the United States, and once again President Eisenhower overruled his bellicose advisers. He did not believe that Yikiang or the Tachen Islands were of any strategic or political importance, whatever might be said of the other offshore islands, and decided that instead of trying to defend them the United States should assist in their evacuation. At the same time he was persuaded by Secretary Dulles that he should disabuse the Communists of any idea that this move marked a retreat and impress upon them that we were prepared to assist Chiang Kai-shek in holding Quemoy and Matsu should they invade these islands as a step toward the conquest of Formosa.

After instructing the naval command to aid the Nationalists in the evacuation of their 10,000 troops on the Tachen Islands, Eisenhower made ready to send a special message to Congress, drawn up by Dulles, relating directly to policy toward Formosa.

In this message, delivered on January 24, 1955, the President stated that the question of Formosa's status was one ultimately to be decided by the United Nations. Since the situation had become too critical to await such action, he was in the meantime asking Congress to grant him authority to employ the armed forces for the protection of Formosa and the Pescadores, together with other "closely related localities," when an attack on them was clearly recognizable as preliminary to an assault on Formosa itself. He did not need such a grant of authority on constitutional grounds, Eisenhower said; his purpose in coming to Congress was to make clear "the unified and serious intentions" of the government, the Congress, and the American people to fulfill their commitments and thereby prevent any miscalculation on the part of the Chinese Communists as to where the United States stood and its readiness to fight if necessary.

His proposals, as embodied in what became known as the Formosan Resolution, were only briefly debated in Congress. A number of senators questioned the necessity of a grant of authority which the President claimed he already had; others sought to exclude the offshore islands from the protective mantle thrown over Formosa. However, Senator Hubert Humphrey expressed the prevailing view, Democrat though he was, which assured the resolution's passage. Its rejection, he said emphatically, "would be to undermine the President's authority completely and totally."

So strong was this pressure (as on some later occasions) to uphold the President's hand and maintain national unity that skeptical Congressmen were persuaded it was politically useless even to question the proposed grant of authority. They fell in line and, as Senator Russell Long of Louisiana phrased it, were ready to back the President even if it meant war with Communist China. In these circumstances the House adopted the joint resolution by a vote of 410 to 3, and the Senate by 83 to 3. On January 29, 1955, stating that the country was at one in its determination "to defend an area vital to the security of the United States and the free world," the President signed the Formosan Resolution.

The significance of the Formosan Resolution, both in itself and in establishing a precedent for comparable open-end grants of authority in later years, was hardly appreciated at the time. But its adoption set a pattern that would be followed a decade later when President Johnson asked in the Tonkin Bay Resolution for comparable power to repel Communist aggression in Vietnam. Congress was in some measure abdicating its responsibility in the conduct of foreign affairs by giving the President a free hand that could lead to war. In the case of both the Formosan and Tonkin Bay resolutions, opposition was effectively silenced by appeals to patriotic unity. Nothing could have more graphically demonstrated the sway of emotion in dealing with these perilous issues.

The almost unquestioning bipartisan support Congress was now prepared to give the administration's Far Eastern policy was soon afterward even further revealed. Both the Southeast Asia Collective Defense Treaty and the Mutual Defense Treaty with Nationalist China were still waiting approval when Congress adopted the Formosan Resolution. The Senate now moved decisively. It accepted the first treaty on February 1 by a vote of 82 to 1, and the latter on February 9 by a majority of 75 to 6.

Although there was virtually no opposition to SEATO, the handful of senators opposed to the pact with Chiang Kai-shek assailed it as a fundamental shift in Far Eastern policy that in spite of all the arguments advanced for its immediate expediency was contrary to the national interest and increased the possibility of eventual war in the Pacific. Senator Estes Kefauver, Democrat from Tennessee, could see no reason at all for entering into treaty relations with Nationalist China. "I do not wish," he said, going directly to the heart of the matter, "to give the color of sovereignty and permanency to the government of Chiang Kai-shek on Formosa and the Pescadores." The mood not only of Congress but of the country as a whole gave no countenance to such a heretical view.

The rapidity and near unanimity with which Congress backed up these successive administration moves, whether affecting Formosa, Indochina, or other parts of Asia, appear in retrospect highly remarkable. It was a striking commentary on the times that the specter of Communist aggression could so easily lead the country to acquiesce in granting the President such wide latitude in enforcing the military containment of China. In the course of one fevered debate Senator Wiley of Wisconsin reflected this fearful spirit. "Either we can defend the United States in the Formosan Straits—now," he declared, "or we can defend it later in San Francisco Bay."

In one sense these commitments broke no new ground; they were fortifying the position represented by President Eisenhower's orders to the Seventh Fleet in January 1953. But in reaffirming the importance of defending Formosa as an outpost of the free world by accepting Nationalist China as a treaty-bound ally, they went a great deal further than earlier policy. In his correspondence with a somewhat skeptical Churchill in regard to these developments, Eisenhower very significantly gave a new weight to the idea that in maintaining its defensive position in the western Pacific, the United States was bound not only to defend Formosa but to support the Nationalists. "We must not lose Chiang's army," he wrote on February 19, 1955, "and we must maintain its strength, efficiency and morale . . . We cannot afford the loss of Chiang unless all of us are to get completely out of that corner of the globe. This is unthinkable to us—I feel it must be to you."

The Eisenhower Administration had taken its stand, and public opinion polls showed a large majority upholding its policy, even to the extent of approving use of the atomic bomb should the Communists attack in force. The American people could hardly be expected to look more deeply into the long-term implications of our commitment to the Chinese Nationalists than the policy makers in Washington. For the most part they went along with it on the easy assumption that in this aspect of his policy, as on so many other issues at home or abroad, Ike really knew best.

Our allies at the opening of 1955 became newly concerned as to where American policy as fashioned by these commitments might be leading. They were apprehensive over how Americans, in an angry mood induced by the Communists' imprisonment of the fliers, might react to any fresh incidents in the Formosan Straits. At the close of January the New Zealand delegate to the United Nations took the lead in trying to lessen tensions by introducing a resolution in the Security Council calling for a cease-fire in the straits and inviting a representative of the Peking government to take part in its discussion.

The United States had no objections to this proposal but first took occasion to clear itself of all charges of acting improperly. "It is not necessary for us to say," Henry Cabot Lodge, our UN delegate, stated with somewhat questionable accuracy, "that the United States has never interfered in the internal affairs of China." He then went on to rebuke Peking for having accused the United States of aggression and scored the presumption of Moscow in supporting such a charge. "The international Communist organization which his country controls . . . would certainly like to take over Formosa," Lodge said in reply to the Soviet delegate. He then announced that the United States was willing to discuss the whole issue and that it approved inviting a spokesman for the Chinese People's Republic to express his government's views.

The Security Council adopted the New Zealand resolution by a vote of 9 to 1 (the Soviet Union opposing, Nationalist China abstaining) and extended the appropriate invitation to the Peking government. Chou En-lai unhesitatingly rejected it. The status of Formosa, he stated in reaffirming his government's undeviating position, was an internal Chinese question that could not be submitted to review or discussion by the United Nations. The People's Republic of China would be more than willing to participate in any debate limited to the issue of American aggression, but it could take no part in any broader international consideration of what was a purely domestic matter. The Security Council did not see anything more that could be done and threw in its hand.

Great Britain continued to bring to bear such influence as it could in calling upon the United States to exercise restraint. Ready to support our policy so far as Formosa itself was concerned, the Foreign Office felt that extending American protection to the offshore islands might needlessly lead to war. It urged that their status, as well as the problem of the imprisonment of the American fliers, be kept open for negotiation. In his personal correspondence with Eisenhower, Churchill too was cautionary. He acknowledged that the United States could not permit its ally Chiang Kai-shek to be overrun and liquidated, as he phrased it, but he argued for our disengagement from the offshore islands. He did not believe them directly related to Formosa's defense and sought to reassure Eisenhower that with or without them, the United States could easily "drown any Chinese would-be invaders of Formosa."

Such foreign pressures upon the administration and the collapse of the UN's efforts to bring about a cease-fire led to a renewal of debate within official circles on American policy. In general the military maintained their tough stand. When Chiang took advantage of the situation to ask for promises of "material and logistic" support in invading the mainland, Admiral Radford was willing to give him a go-ahead signal and again advocated a blockade of the China coast. Even more bellicose was General James Van Fleet, the former commander of the Eighth Army in Korea. "We need a deed," he wrote in an article in *Life*. "And here in the offshore islands is the perfect opportunity to perform a deed." He proposed American occupation of Quemoy and Matsu, and then, if the Communists continued their shelling of the islands, the United States would be justified "to shoot back with atomic weapons and annihilate the Red effort."

General Ridgway continued to stand out against an interventionist policy. He held the view, which few Americans could ever accept, that in the light of Chiang's proclaimed desire to hold the offshore islands as a base for future invasion, the Chinese Communists might be influenced by defensive considerations. Recalling these days in his memoir *Soldier*, Ridgway wrote that the idea of an attack on the mainland was completely "repugnant" to him and that he felt a preventive war, as urged by other members of the Joint Chiefs of Staff, would "tragically demonstrate our complete and utter moral bankruptcy." He also pointed out what he believed would be the danger of creating a power vacuum in eastern Asia, which would bring the United States and Soviet Russia into direct confrontation. "I challenge any thesis," wrote the former commander of UN forces in Korea, "that destroying the military might of Red China would be in our long-range interests."

President Eisenhower held to his own middle-of-the-road course maintaining the thin line between provocation and retreat, but he was increasingly concerned over the gravity of the situation. Fresh reports of the imminence of a full-scale Communist assault were matched by disquieting news about the morale of the Nationalist troops. Returning from a trip to the western Pacific, John Foster Dulles warned that in his view Quemoy and Matsu could not be successfully defended without the use of atomic weapons.

With such rumors flying about, the President was asked at a news conference on March 16 whether the United States would employ atomic weapons in the event of general hostilities in Asia. He replied that against military targets, the answer was yes. This statement awoke a new uneasiness, and the State Department became greatly concerned over its effect on our anxious allies. Eisenhower's press secretary, James Hagerty, relayed to his chief a frantic plea from some of the department's members urging that because of the delicacy of the Formosan Straits situation, the President should not answer any more questions about it. Eisenhower's answer, as related in *Mandate for Change*, shows that he knew just what he was doing when he seemed to fumble at his press conferences—a failing his critics held up to scorn. "Don't worry, Jim," he reports telling his press secretary, "if that question comes up, I'll just confuse them."

Within Congress the old divisions that had bedeviled the formulation of Far Eastern policy ever since the revolution in China were again flaring up. In spite of the strong bipartisan support for both the Formosan Resolution and the Mutual Security Treaty with Chiang Kai-shek, opposition mounted to the apparent intent of the administration to defend the offshore islands. Everything appeared to suggest that without making a firm public commitment, Eisenhower had decided to take such action should the Chinese Communists launch any further attacks on Quemoy or Matsu.

A group of Democratic senators, including Wayne Morse, Hubert Humphrey, Herbert Lehman, and Russell Long, consequently introduced on April 1 a resolution specifically barring the President from employing American forces to defend these islands. The majority leader, Senator Lyndon Johnson, fully supported it. "It would be folly to jeopardize our future," he said, hardly foreseeing his own role in Vietnam a decade later, "through an irresponsible adventure for which we have not calculated the risks." The Republicans rallied to defeat successfully a move that would have tied the President's hands in a continuing emergency, but this did not silence the political criticism of his attitude.

Adlai Stevenson, who as its former presidential candidate was the titular head of his party, took up the offensive in a nationwide radio address on April 11. He did not consider the status of the offshore islands essential to the security of the United States or even to that of Formosa, he declared. "Should we be plunged into another great war," Stevenson said, "the maintenance of our alliances and the respect and good will of the uncommitted nations of Asia will be far more important to us than possession of these offshore islands by General Chiang Kai-shek ever could be."

The political disputes over policy, the reported divisions within the administration itself, and the President's own news conferences were bewildering a public largely ignorant of Far Eastern actualities. Yet the people still gave every indication of willingness to support the President. Writing in the *New Yorker*, Richard Rovere sought to analyze the conflict between what he called the "Dulles-Knowland-Radford" position on the necessity of protecting the offshore islands and the noninterventionist position, which favored abandoning them altogether. As between these two contesting policies, Rovere thought the American people were willing to let Eisenhower plot his own course in the conviction that his overwhelming desire was to maintain peace. "The whole trend of American policy, not as it has been discussed by Dulles but as in fact made by Eisenhower," he wrote, "has been toward disengagement."

In following his cautious policy, the President still did not say what he would do if the Chinese Communists actually invaded the offshore islands, but Rovere's theory that he would like to free the United States from any responsibility for their protection seemed to be substantiated in early April. He undertook to persuade Chiang Kai-shek to withdraw some of his troops from Quemoy and Matsu and evacuate the islands' civilian population.

Eisenhower explained his thinking on this move in a memorandum to Dulles, reprinted in *Mandate for Change*. He was not necessarily contemplating the surrender of the islands, he wrote, but of relieving both the United States and Nationalist China from any rigid commitment to their "full-out" defense. Consequently, whatever might happen, he added somewhat obscurely, "there would be no danger of a collapse of the free world position in the region."

The President soon discovered that persuading Chiang to reconsider his attitude was easier said than done. He chose Admiral Radford and Assistant Secretary of State Robertson, as two of the staunchest adherents of the generalissimo, to undertake this delicate mission. Leaving Washington on April 20, they found on their arrival in Taipei that Chiang was adamantly opposed to any shift in his policies. Completely impervious to both diplomatic and military arguments, he refused to consider the reduction of troops on Quemoy and Matsu because it would undermine morale by suggesting an abandonment of his goal to return to the mainland. The idea of drawing a new defensive line in the Formosan Straits excluding the offshore islands, Chiang told the American emissaries, would be tantamount to accepting the concept of "two Chinas" to which he remained unalterably opposed.

Eisenhower felt he had no alternative to accepting Chiang's decision— "The Americans knew they had a bear by the tail," Anthony Eden was later to write in his *Memoirs*—and he fell back on his program of maintaining a discreet silence on his future intentions. Reviewing these days and the conflicting advice he received as to what the United States should do, Eisenhower later wrote that "the hard way is to have the courage to be patient."

In spite of continuing tension in the Formosan Straits and the failure of the Radford-Robertson mission, the President's patience now unexpectedly appeared to be rewarded. Attending an Afro-Asian conference at Bandung, Indonesia, Chou En-lai dramatically announced on April 23, 1955, his government's willingness to enter into negotiations with the United States. "The Chinese people are friendly to the American people," he stated, sharply reversing Peking's usual anti-American propaganda line. "The Chinese people do not want to have war with the United States. The Chinese Government is willing to sit down and . . . to discuss the question of relaxing tension in the Far East and especially the question of relaxing tension in the Taiwan area."

The reasons for this shift in attitude were not entirely clear, but Communist China seemed to be adopting a more conciliatory foreign policy all along the line. At the Bandung conference, Chou En-lai was calling for a new Asian unity based upon the five principles: respect for territorial integrity and sovereignty, nonaggression, noninterference, equality and mutual benefit, and peaceful coexistence. If there was an anti-Western undertone to this program, the Chinese Communist leader eschewed the usual violent rhetoric of Communism and significantly moderated the hostile attitude Peking usually adopted. Soviet Russia was at the same time pursuing in Europe the more accommodating course adopted following Stalin's death. Within a few weeks it would sign the treaty restoring independence to a neutralized Austria and agree to a summit meeting of the Big Four in Geneva. Whether Communist China was following the example of its Communist ally or acting solely on its own initiative in seeking to change the political climate in Asia, Premier Chou made the first friendly gesture toward America since the Chinese Communists had set up their regime in Peking.

The United States nevertheless did not jump at this offer of negotiations. Secretary Dulles remained highly suspicious that the Chinese were "playing a propaganda game." A coldly correct State Department announced three preconditions for any possible talks. These were the participation of the Chinese Nationalists on terms of equality, the prior release of all American prisoners in China, and the Peking government's acceptance of the earlier UN invitation to take part in the Assembly's discussions over ending hostilities in the Formosan area.

Chou En-lai, not unnaturally in the face of such a highly qualified response, felt himself sharply rebuffed. He issued a further statement emphasizing that China's willingness to negotiate should not be construed as in any way affecting the right of the Chinese people to exercise their sovereign powers in liberating Formosa. Nevertheless, Pakistan's Foreign Minister, Mohammed Ali, reported from Bandung that while Chou thought that the State Department's reply to his offer had almost slammed the door shut and he himself had closed it a little more, it was still open at least a crack. "And I believe," Mohammed Ali added, "he wants to open it wider."

Dulles now modified his stand. At a press conference on April 26 he said that a cease-fire in the Formosan Straits must be a first step toward negotiations and that the United States would not talk about Nationalist China "behind its back." But he did not repeat the preconditions set forth in the original State Department reply. The next day President Eisenhower showed himself even more receptive to the proposed talks. Candidly admitting that the initial response "erred in not being as complete as it should have been," he expressed his hope that the talks would be held and would be productive in helping to strengthen the forces of peace throughout eastern Asia.

Although both sides remained mutually suspicious, they now gave further ground. Dulles agreed that a cease-fire would not be construed as prejudicing Communist China's legal claims to sovereignty over Formosa; Chou En-lai stated that the Chinese people were willing to pursue their goal of recovering Formosa through peaceful means so far as this was possible. As the hostilities in the straits now gave way to an informal truce, an agreement was reached to have the talks that had occasionally been held between the American and Communist Chinese consuls in Geneva raised to the ambassadorial level. A joint announcement on July 25 stated that they would be concerned with the release of American prisoners held in China and "other practical matters."

In this encouraging atmosphere negotiations commenced a week later between Wang Ping-nan, the Chinese ambassador to Poland, and U. Alexis Johnson, our ambassador to Czechoslovakia. A first hopeful development was an announcement from Peking that it was releasing the imprisoned airmen. Gratified by this move, the United States still remained concerned over the continued detention of some forty-one civilians. It insisted that freeing them was essential before the discussion of any other issues. "You do not negotiate—at least the United States does not negotiate," Secretary Dulles acidly declared, "with a pistol aimed at its head."

In spite of this setback, the talks continued and in September, Ambassadors Johnson and Wang were able to report further progress. A joint announcement stated that the Chinese People's Republic would "expeditiously" release all Americans who desired to return home, and in return the United States would facilitate the repatriation of all Chinese in its territories who wished to return to Communist China.

This highly promising development, which Dulles himself said found the Chinese going further than they ever had before, nevertheless did not prevent the negotiations from running into new snags. The United States was soon complaining that the Communists were still holding nineteen prisoners, and the Peking government rejoined that they had offended against Chinese law and "no time limit can be set for their release." Moreover, just at this juncture James Shepley's article praising Dulles's "brinkmanship" appeared in *Life*, and Chou En-lai angrily accused the Secretary of State of renewing "the clamor for an atomic war against China."

Underlying these difficulties was a complete deadlock over the basic issue of the status of Formosa, and on January 21, 1956, the State Department released a revealing account of the exchanges that had taken place between the two ambassadors during the previous three months. They were in accord on a general renunciation of the use of force in Sino-American relations but not on its specific application in the Formosan Straits. Ambassador Wang reiterated the Chinese contention that the status of Formosa (which he of course called Taiwan) was an "internal affair" and that consequently his government could not accept any limitation on its sovereign powers in handling a purely domestic question. Ambassador Johnson set forth the basic American position that the Republic of China was itself a sovereign nation and that through our treaty with its government the United States was legally justified in protecting Formosa from possible attack. The willingness of the Chinese Communists to renounce the use of force was meaningless, Johnson said, unless it applied to Formosa; they appeared ready to give up force "only if they are conceded the goals for which they would use force."

Wang spiritedly rebutted Johnson's thesis in again stating that Formosa was Chinese territory and that no question of its defense could arise so far as the United States was concerned. He accused this country of having itself resorted to force in the straits. For his government to acknowledge the American position, he said, would be to agree to Formosa's continued occupation. "The American side continues to demand that our side accept that the United States has 'the inherent right of self-defense' in China's Taiwan area. This," he added decisively, "is what our side absolutely cannot accept."

The talks were not broken off. Chou En-lai reaffirmed his hope that existing tensions might be relaxed, and Dulles, after commenting with admirable understatement that negotiations with the Communists were usually "slow and prolonged," indicated that the United States was still planning to go ahead. But with neither side willing to give way on its basic interpretation of the status of Formosa, the obstacles to any real agreement were insuperable.

The Chinese suggested that in the hope of making some real progress the ambassadorial talks might be replaced by direct negotiations on the foreign minister level. The United States promptly replied that this was impossible so long as the Peking government remained unwilling to accept "a meaningful renunciation of force" and continued to hold thirteen American citizens as prisoners. But behind these reasons for rejecting a meeting of foreign ministers was the objection that it could be construed as a move toward American recognition of the Chinese People's Republic. To this Secretary Dulles remained as implacably opposed as ever, regardless of what concessions the Communists might conceivably contemplate.

The critical situation in the Formosan Straits had by this time—the spring of 1956—subsided. The informal truce that accompanied the beginning of the ambassadorial talks continued in spite of the lack of progress in Geneva; the Chinese Communists did not renew their bombardment of the offshore islands. But in failing to respond more generously to the overtures of the Peking government for a further exploration of the Formosan problem on the foreign minister level, the United States blocked whatever chance there might have been of more productive negotiations. At the one time when the Peking government seemed to be in a conciliatory mood, the United States actually stiffened its own attitude. There was no surety that any solution could have come of a meeting of foreign ministers, but the opportunity to sound out Chinese intentions was lost.

Critics both at home and abroad were unhappy over this failure to pursue a course that might have led to some easing in Far Eastern tensions. They felt that in maintaining its uncompromising stand that the Chinese People's Republic must renounce all right and title not only to Formosa but even to the offshore islands, Washington was not contributing to the prospects of peace. On the contrary, they feared American policy was aggravating the perils of a conflict that could escalate into a third world war.

Anthony Eden has written in *Full Circle* that at the Geneva Conference of the Big Four in the summer of 1955, "our formal meetings were concerned with Europe, our private anxieties with the Far East." He felt strongly that the United States should have exerted sufficient pressure on Chiang Kai-shek to compel him to withdraw his troops from Quemoy and Matsu. So long as the offshore islands remained in Nationalist hands, he continued, the Communists were justified in maintaining that their occupation constituted a constant threat of Chiang Kai-shek invading the mainland with American support. Eden apparently thought that if the offshore islands had been given up, the Peking government might have been willing to renounce the use of force in seeking Formosa's liberation.

Critics in this country were of much the same mind. Adlai Stevenson, who had so vigorously attacked Far Eastern policy at the time of passage of the Formosan Resolution, again spoke out sharply. He assailed the concept of brinkmanship, declared he was "shocked that the Secretary of State is willing to play Russian roulette with the life of the nation," and deplored the rejection of Chou En-lai's proposal for raising the ambassadorial talks in Geneva to the foreign minister level.

Recalling these days in an interview quoted by Theodore White in *The Making of the President, 1960,* Stevenson reaffirmed his view that the surrender of the offshore islands might have not only persuaded the Communists to give up their idea of Formosa's subjection by military force but induced them to consider a plebiscite for the determination of the island's future status. Our policy, Stevenson told White, was predicated on the myth of Chiang Kai-shek's reconquest of China, and "so we have kept Quemoy and Matsu as landing stages back to the mainland." He was convinced that the President and the Secretary of State had played their cards very badly in dealing with the Chinese Communists. "The opportunity we missed in 1955," he said, "is the greatest political crime of our times, for in 1955 we had a chance to talk to them, to begin to resolve some of the problems there."

Contemporary criticism of the Eisenhower-Dulles policy was nevertheless very limited. Both Congress and the general public accepted it as effectively safeguarding American interests in eastern Asia. The overwhelming anti-Communist sentiment throughout the country, magnified and distorted under the continuing influence of McCarthyism, would not condone any retreat. The public was ready to support Dulles in his refusal to make any move that might allow the Chinese Communists to believe that their militant tactics were paying off.

By the same token, most Americans believed that the United States should expand its military and economic aid to the Nationalist government (between 1951 and 1956 it totaled no less than $500 million) as our most certain anti-Communist ally in Asia. They ignored the extent to which in committing itself to Chiang Kai-shek's cause, the United States might be allowing him to influence our policy. They accepted the thesis, as expressed in President Eisenhower's already quoted statement, that we could not afford the loss of Chiang's army unless we were to get completely out of that corner of the globe.

These popular sentiments were reflected in both the Republican and Democratic platforms in the presidential election of 1956. In spite of the inter-party feuding in the past the Far Eastern policy planks, which had drawn very close together four years earlier, were now virtually identical. They both stated unqualified opposition to either the recognition of the Chinese People's Republic or its admission to the United Nations, promised additional efforts to secure the freedom of all Americans imprisoned by the Chinese Communists, and called for continuing economic and military support for Nationalist China. American activities in eastern Asia consequently did not enter significantly into the presidential campaign; the reelection of President Eisenhower could be interpreted as a tacit endorsement of his policies.

As the year 1956 ended, the annual review of the Council on Foreign Relations reported something like a "breathing spell" in Asia, and a spokesman of the State Department was quoted as saying that he thought "we may fairly characterize our Far Eastern policy as a success to date." What were at best only uneasy truces existed in the major trouble spots of Korea, the Formosan Straits, and Indochina; such success as had been attained lay only in the fact that no actual fighting was in progress. In their persistent anti-Communist crusade, the American people were content that without active hostilities the United States appeared to be successfully holding China in check.

11

"*A State of Quasi War*"

THE RELATIVE CALM that prevailed in Asia as Eisenhower commenced his second term was largely owing to Communist China's continued restraint in its foreign policy and its apparent willingness to stand on the conciliatory program Chou En-lai had presented at the Bandung Conference. It was not threatening any of its Asian neighbors, and in spite of the impasse over Formosa, its muted propaganda still stressed the desire of the Chinese people for friendly relations with those of the United States. Nothing suggested that the Peking government had modified its goal of asserting its own political dominance in Asia, but the emphasis shifted from warlike moves or military intervention to more moderate political pressure.

Even in domestic affairs the Communist leaders seemed to be initiating programs that indicated a swing toward greater liberalization. Premier Chou, perhaps following the lead of the "de-Stalinization" movement in Soviet Russia, spoke of enlarging "the democratic base of our system of government." Widely noted throughout the Western world was Mao Tse-tung's famous declaration, "Let a hundred flowers blossom . . . let a hundred schools of thought contend." This was a fleeting moment. The Peking government soon discovered that in this permissive atmosphere what sprang up were "poisonous weeds," and the intellectual thaw quickly gave way to new restrictive measures. China was soon to be caught up in a host of internal problems, with a badly faltering economy; these domestic troubles were in turn to lead to a stiffened foreign policy and a new aggressiveness. Still, for a brief time, the Communist establishment seemed to be on a less dictatorial and more reasonable course.

In the United States the view was expressed in some quarters that in the light of this more favorable atmosphere, the Eisenhower Administration might reconsider those aspects of our China policy so harshly directed toward the Peking government's political isolation. A number of critics in Congress, as well as among editorial writers, again raised the question of the validity and practicality of our position in seeking to ostracize the Communist regime. Such influential senators as Hubert Humphrey and J. William Fulbright took the lead in saying it was high time for a fresh look at our policy. The venerable Senator Theodore F. Green, Democrat from Rhode Island and chairman of the Foreign Relations Committee, wrote President Eisenhower saying that he believed the United States should sooner or later recognize the Chinese People's Republic. Other spokesmen of liberal persuasion called for reconsideration of our attitude on its representation in the United Nations.

It soon appeared, however, that the changing conditions within China did not bear upon the policy makers to adopt a new approach to the problems of the Far East, nor were the critics at home of any more influence than they had been in 1953. They stood firmly by the established line that the United States could not afford to make any move that might lead the Chinese Communists to believe their policies were paying off or would serve to build up their position in the international community.

In his frequent public talks Assistant Secretary of State Robertson kept up a constant barrage against "the defiant Marxist imposters" who had made China "an outlaw nation." Far from seeking to create a more rational attitude toward the Chinese Communists, he played upon popular fears of their worldwide aggressive designs. "Red China . . . is the mighty instrument of Communist power in Asia," he said on one occasion. "With its dedicated international Marxist leaders it is like a giant octopus with tentacles of infiltration and subversion stretching into every corner of the area."

From Ambassador Rankin in Taipei came a flood of dispatches not so much stressing the iniquities of the Communists as glorifying the virtues of the Nationalists: Chiang Kai-shek was still the great hope of anti-Communist Asia; his ultimate triumph over the subversive forces in Peking was inevitable. "Free China today leads a crusade against the malignant influence of international Communism which far transcends the conception of a purely military counterattack against the mainland," Rankin said in one talk widely publicized in this country by the State Department.

Robertson and Rankin were subordinates, but Secretary Dulles was no less certain that the United States should follow a policy of exerting "inflexible" pressure against the Chinese Communists and do everything possible to strengthen Chiang Kai-shek's government on Formosa. In an important address on June 28, 1957, he emphatically reasserted the position he had taken on first coming into office four years earlier:

"We can confidently assume," the Secretary of State said, "that international Communism's rule of strict conformity is, in China as elsewhere, a passing and not a perpetual phase. We owe it to ourselves, our allies, and the Chinese people to do all that we can to contribute to that passing. . . . Under present conditions, neither recognition, nor trade, nor cultural relations, nor all three together would favorably influence the evolution of affairs in China."

Further elaborating on this fixed, unyielding, and completely negative approach, Dulles added that American recognition would make it probable that the Chinese People's Republic would obtain China's seat in the United Nations and thereby win additional prestige at home and abroad. "Under these circumstances," he reiterated, "it would be folly for us to establish relations with the Chinese Communists which would enhance their ability to hurt us."

The most striking example of the Secretary of State's stand was his attitude in respect to a possible exchange of American and Chinese newsmen, an issue that first came up in the summer of 1956 and dragged on under increasing controversy for over a year. At a time when the Chinese were in a seemingly amenable mood, Dulles maintained a stubborn opposition to what might otherwise have become a significant breakthrough in Sino-American relations.

In reply to their requests, Chou En-lai offered on August 6, 1956, to grant visas to fifteen accredited representatives of the American news media. They were not handpicked left-wing radicals but correspondents of such established agencies and papers as the Associated Press, the *New York Times*, the *Christian Science Monitor*, and *Newsweek*. Here was an unexpected chance to raise the bamboo curtain, which, except for what had now become the wholly inconclusive ambassadorial talks in Geneva, so completely cut off all direct contacts between the United States and Communist China. Yet the very next day after Chou En-lai's offer, the State Department replied that in accordance with the standing ban on travel in Communist China, adopted during the Korean war, it would not validate the passports of these American newsmen to visit the mainland.

In justification of this surprising action the Department stated that the Peking government was still holding ten Americans in prison and that so long as they remained "political hostages," the United States would not relax the existing travel regulations. Somewhat later in further explanation of this policy, Undersecretary of State Robert Murphy set forth a different thesis. He told the Senate Foreign Relations Committee that Chou En-lai's invitation appeared to be the start of a dangerous cultural offensive that sought to induce "our scholars, our musicians, our artists, and our writers" to go to Communist China solely to win greater respectability for the Peking regime. To obtain our acceptance for this program, the Communists were holding out the promise of releasing the remaining American prisoners, and it was because of this maneuvering that the United States could not consider any modification of the travel ban. "To do so," Murphy said, "would be yielding to extortion. There would be no end to it."

The American newspaper community, which believed that the opportunity to get direct, firsthand reports on China would be of great benefit to this country, forcefully challenged this obstructive policy which seemed irrelevantly to drag in the issue of the Chinese-held prisoners. Its spokesmen asserted that the State Department's refusal to permit correspondents to visit China represented an attempt to make news reporting an instrument of foreign policy in denial of the basic principles of free information and free speech. The chance to find out more about developments within Communist China, they said, should be welcomed, whatever policy the State Department might choose to follow on diplomatic recognition or any other issue.

Dulles refused to back down. In a press conference on February 6, 1957, six months after Chou's offer, he returned to the charge that Communist China was using the detention of American prisoners as a lever to try to force the State Department to allow reporters—"preferably those it picked"—to go to China for Peking's own propaganda purposes. The United States, he said, repeating Murphy's point, did not like the idea of having its citizens used as a means of extortion: "That kind of blackmail I don't propose to satisfy."

The news reporters, baffled by these ideas of extortion and blackmail and insisting that the presence of American correspondents in China would benefit the United States more than the Communists, continued to needle the Secretary of State. Shifting his ground, Dulles thereupon said that what he really feared was that through a "cultural exchange" the Peking government was hoping to create among other countries a more favorable attitude toward the Communist regime. "And one of our problems," he explained somewhat obscurely, "is not to set an example which would be bearable by us but if it was generally extended would have dangerous consequences in other areas." He made no concession to the importunities of his journalistic critics other than to say that the State Department would be willing to study any other means to satisfy the demand for better news coverage of China that would not involve dropping the official ban on American travel.

President Eisenhower backed up his Secretary of State. At his own news conference three days later, he said that he could not at the moment promise any change of policy. He added, however, in affirming the point Dulles had made, that the State Department was studying "very earnestly to see how we could secure from China more news without appearing to accept Red China on the same cultural basis as we do . . . other nations."

The newspapers and the press associations were far from persuaded that these bland assurances meant anything at all. They remained highly indignant. As they intensified their pressure on the State Department, Dulles finally intimated on April 23 that it might be possible to allow a special pool of correspondents to take advantage of Peking's offer, but he still insisted that this could be done only if a way were found to do so without relaxing the general travel ban. The issue presented very special difficulties, he said in frank revelation of his own attitude toward Communist China, because it involved relations with a country with which "we are in a sense in a state of war."

As he still made no move to resolve the problem, his critics returned to the attack, and at a press conference a month later they asked him point-blank whether he was still "unswerving" in his attitude. "Well," Dulles answered, "I continue to hold the position I have enunciated several times. Whether you call that unswerving I do not know." Then returning to the matter of the American prisoners, he bypassed the argument that the Chinese had invited the correspondents for propaganda purposes and in admitted contradiction of his earlier position said that if Peking released the prisoners, "we would certainly take a new look at the situation." The press remained baffled and angry.

In the meantime three correspondents, including William Worthy, a reporter for the Baltimore *Afro-American*, visited China in defiance of the State Department ban, and then in August some forty young Americans who had attended the World Festival of Youth and Students in Moscow journeyed on under Communist auspices to Peking. The State Department roundly condemned these unauthorized visits and declared its intention to invalidate the passports of anyone violating its proscription against travel in Communist China. Newspaper editorials almost universally protested this arbitrary action, and questioning of the existing travel regulations spread to the Senate. Fulbright introduced a resolution calling on the State Department to encourage and facilitate the entry of correspondents into China or failing this, to refrain from seeking reprisals against those who visited the mainland on their own responsibility.

The badgered Secretary of State was driven to concede some ground. The State Department now announced that it would agree to the authorization, on a seven-month trial basis, for representatives of twenty-four specified news media (including the radio-television networks) to visit Communist China. But Dulles simultaneously imposed a condition that he must very well have known would make it virtually certain that these correspondents would not receive the necessary travel permits from Peking. "It is understood," the State Department said, "that the United States will not accord reciprocal visas to Chinese bearing passports issued by the Chinese Communist regime."

Peking reacted as might have been expected. An editorial in the *People's Daily* spoke out in terms of outraged scorn, declaring the State Department's plan completely unacceptable and denouncing the "insufferable arrogance" of the United States in agreeing to send its correspondents into China but refusing reciprocal visas to Chinese newsmen who might wish to visit the United States. "The day has passed," the editorial concluded, "when the Chinese people can be treated like pawns."

The issue came up in Geneva, where Ambassador Wang proposed a mutual exchange of correspondents only to have Ambassador Johnson immediately reject it. Johnson stated that the question of reciprocity was not raised when Chou En-lai made his original offer to accept American newsmen and he was "astounded" that Peking now brought it up. To soften the impact of our stand Johnson said that although the State Department could not give blanket permission for Chinese correspondents to visit the country, it might be willing to consider individual applications. This hardly served to satisfy Ambassador Wang. His concern was the principle of reciprocity in defense of the dignity and honor of his own country.

The Secretary of State's critics resented a gesture toward letting down the travel bans when its practical effect remained meaningless. They pointed out that in meeting Peking's reasonable protests, the State Department could have secured waivers to admit Chinese correspondents under the existing law, as it had repeatedly done in the case of those from

Soviet Russia and the countries of eastern Europe. Even Senator Knowland, no advocate of propitiating Communist China, acknowledged that "temporary news certificates" could be granted without giving up the general ban on travel in China. Yet in spite of the rising clamor in the press—"Let's have no curtain here," said the New York Times—the Secretary of State was not moved. He stated emphatically on August 26 that reciprocity was denied because "we wanted to obviate any claim by the Chinese Communists that they would be entitled as a right to send a corresponding number of Chinese reporters to this country."

Immediately following the Secretary of State's authorization for a specially selected pool of correspondents to visit China, the appointed newsmen had hurried to Hong Kong. There they waited in the hope that in spite of the denial of reciprocity the Peking government might agree to grant them visas. It was a futile hope. On September 7 Premier Chou let it be known that the State Department had "put an end to the matter by refusing reciprocal rights of coverage to Chinese reporters."

One exception was Edgar Snow, who was admitted three years later. As a result of his being so well and favorably known to the Chinese leaders through his earlier association with them after the Long March in the mid-1930s, the Peking authorities in 1960 granted him a travel visa as a correspondent for Look. He was in China for five months, had a long interview with Mao Tse-tung, and recorded his experiences both in his articles for Look and in his book The Other Side of the River. On his return the State Department asked him to come to Washington for an interview. Its antagonistic attitude toward any exchanges with Communist China was reflected in Snow's report that this meeting lasted only ten minutes. "It shocked me," he wrote, "that the American instrument to whom Mao Tse-tung had bothered to talk for nine hours—obviously with the expectation that he might reach an ear in the White House—could be so completely wasted."

Throughout this controversy, standing virtually alone, John Foster Dulles adhered to his position that any benefit that might accrue to this country from an exchange of newspaper correspondents was completely overshadowed by the extent to which it would build up the prestige of the Chinese Communists. His belief that Peking was trying to use the possible release of the American prisoners as a form of blackmail to force American concessions affected his attitude emotionally, but it had other, still deeper roots. Acting on his assumption that Communism in China was only a passing phase, Dulles remained convinced that American policy should sternly refrain from any move, even an exchange of correspondents, that might seem officially to acknowledge that the Peking government actually existed.

As this business came to its unhappy conclusion, Communist China's general attitude was going through something of a transformation, and in a mood of revived belligerency Peking was soon to challenge once again the American position in the Formosan Straits. This new crisis, arising at the close of August 1958, followed much the same pattern as the hostilities three years earlier. The Chinese Communists renewed their shelling of Quemoy, the United States reacted sharply, our allies became alarmed, Peking apparently experienced a change of heart, and the crisis gradually subsided.

China's new militancy in foreign affairs developed obscurely out of both internal and external developments. At home the country embarked enthusiastically on the "Great Leap Forward." Through a massive socialistic program reorganizing both agriculture and industry, all economic problems were to be solved and China overnight to become a modern industrialized nation. The central government's plans envisaged the esta lishment of communes to mobilize the peasantry in boosting farm production and the creation of new small-scale industries in the villages—workshops and "backyard steel furnaces"—to increase the manufacturing output.

It was a sweeping, grandiose, utopian scheme. But the Chinese lacked adequate experience in economic planning, and the country was soon mired in insurmountable social and economic difficulties. To combat the consequent discontent, Peking adopted further repressive measures, which only fed the unrest they were supposed to alleviate. In their zealous fanaticism the Communists forced the pace far beyond the capacity of China's economic or human resources; they were soon compelled to acknowledge that the Great Leap Forward was a disastrous failure.

Partly to direct popular attention away from these domestic ills by the time-honored method of busying "giddy minds with foreign quarrels," and at the same time taking advantage of what seemed to be propitious circumstances on the world stage, the Peking government swung over to a more aggressive stance in foreign affairs both in relation to its Asian neighbors and toward the West. On his visit to Peking in 1960, Edgar Snow reported Chou En-lai as saying that Communist China's more militant policies had been adopted only after three fruitless years of maintaining a conciliatory attitude. But it would appear clear that the need to inspire national unity in a time of troubles and the impact of events abroad were the basic factors in launching China on its new course.

Europe was in disarray in 1958 as a consequence of the divisions among the allies following the Suez crisis and the new difficulties in the Middle East, which had led the United States to intervene in Lebanon. At the same time, the Soviet Union seemed to be gaining ascendancy; the whole cause of socialism received a tremendous impetus with the launching of Sputnik, which so spectacularly demonstrated Russia's scientific and technological skills. "The East Wind," Mao Tse-tung triumphantly proclaimed, "is prevailing over the West Wind." Communist China was encouraged to believe that it could further build up its influence and power not only in Asia but throughout the world.

Yet in spite of all this, China may well have been motivated in resuming the offensive in the Formosan Straits quite as much by a defense complex as by a revived aggressiveness. For once again the Chinese Nationalists, believing that the internal troubles the Communists were facing made them vulnerable to attack, were threatening invasion. In complete disregard of all American advice, Chiang Kai-shek had concentrated more and more of his troops on Quemoy and Matsu until they totaled some 100,000 men, and he was using the offshore islands as a base for commando raids against the Communists. Naturally, he said that his transfer of troops was necessary for the defense of Formosa, but he continued to preach his holy crusade of a return to the mainland.

With advices from Taipei reporting that the generalissimo was "restless and uneasy," Washington grew deeply concerned over what he might be plotting. As President Eisenhower phrased it mildly in discussing Formosa in *Waging Peace*, "Chiang Kai-shek had helped to complicate the problem." It was never certain at what point he might decide to precipitate the hostilities that the United States was so anxious to avoid.

Whatever the motive, self-defense or aggression, the Chinese Communists opened a new offensive, once again probing American intentions in the defense of the offshore islands. On August 23, 1958, four years to the day after their initial raid on Quemoy, they began shelling that island and set up a naval blockade to cut it off from all supplies or other assistance. With the Peking radio blaring forth warnings of their intent to "smash the American paper tiger and liberate Taiwan," the Communists called upon the Nationalists to surrender.

President Eisenhower promptly ordered the Seventh Fleet to take up a position where it could assist the Nationalists in trying to run the Communist blockade of Quemoy and declared that the United States would not "desert" its responsibilities. Secretary of State Dulles warned the Peking government, through the medium of an open letter to the chairman of the House Foreign Relations Committee, that a direct attack on the offshore islands could not be considered a "limited operation" but would be viewed as a threat to the peace of the entire area of Formosa.

Whether these statements meant that the United States was prepared to take forceful action to protect Quemoy was nevertheless left very much in the air, as it had been in 1955. The statements of both the President and the Secretary of State kept the Communists guessing, and they also confused the American public and our always nervous allies. Nor was the situation clarified by further pronouncements following a conference at Newport, Rhode Island, on September 3 and 4. Dulles stated then that the United States would not hesitate to employ armed force to protect Formosa, repeated that the offshore islands were more than ever related to its defense, and declared that "the naked use of force" by the Chinese Communists "would pose an issue far transcending the offshore islands and even the security of Formosa." He went on to say that the President had not as yet made a decision whether in existing circumstances the employment of United States forces was either required or appropriate, but should he find this necessary, our action would be both "timely and effective."

This was all rather ambiguous. However, at the same time a further statement emanating from Newport, attributed by the press to a "high administration official," declared specifically that the United States would forcefully repel any invasion of Quemoy or Matsu. This source was universally accepted as being the Secretary of State himself (Dulles, "flushed and ill at ease," as the press reported, later acknowledged this), and in its account of the Newport conference the *New York Times* felt justified in heading its story: "U.S. Decides to Use Force If Reds Invade Quemoy."

The prospect of possible war with Communist China over possession of the offshore islands created widespread consternation. This crisis suddenly appeared far more serious than that of 1954–55. Former Secretary of State Acheson, who had been greatly responsible for originally extending the containment policy to eastern Asia, was shocked by its possible application to Quemoy and Matsu. He believed that the United States had been maneuvered by Chiang Kai-shek into an impossible situation that it could no longer control. We appeared to be "drifting, either dazed or indifferent," Acheson protested, "toward war with China, a war without friends or allies, over issues which the Administration has not presented to the people, and which are not worth a single life."

Adlai Stevenson and Senator John Kennedy also attacked the policy, Stevenson calling it "clumsy, erratic and self-righteous," and Kennedy declaring it contrary to "the weight of military, diplomatic, political and historical judgment." Nor were Democrats alone in taking up the cudgels against the administration. Many Republican leaders were equally concerned. Their point of view was expressed by Senator John Sherman Cooper of Kentucky, who said that the United States should make it clear that "we will defend Formosa with everything we have but I do not believe it is in the national interest to go to war over Quemoy and Matsu."

Dulles made no immediate reply to this criticism, but Vice-President Nixon sprang to the administration's defense. Believing that under no circumstances should the United States be allowed to appear a "paper tiger," he saw far more at stake than just possession of the offshore islands or even Formosa. "What is under threat," he stated emphatically, "is the entire position of the United States and that of its free world allies, in the Western Pacific."

Amid this confusion and controversy, with no further official word from President Eisenhower as to whether the United States was indeed ready to employ its armed forces to defend Quemoy, Premier Chou En-lai moved, as he had in 1955, to bring the issues in dispute to the conference table. While reaffirming Peking's determination to use all its military resources to resist American imperialism, he suggested on September 6 that the ambassadorial talks (they had been recessed for some time) be reopened in Warsaw to consider "the Sino American dispute in the Taiwan area." Without the hesitations that had marked its response to the similar proposal in the earlier crisis, the State Department promptly replied that it welcomed this idea.

While a resumption of talks was still in the making and the shelling of Quemoy continued, Secretary Dulles was questioned at a long news conference on every aspect of the Far Eastern situation. Again the picture that emerged was far from clear. Dulles reiterated the undeviating intention of the United States to defend Formosa, but parrying the inevitable inquiries about the offshore islands, he said no more than that while they would not be protected "as such," should a Communist attack on them threaten Formosa the United States would "meet that attack at that point." Pressed on this issue in the light of the strong opposition, both at home and among our allies, to any step that might lead to war with Communist

China, he answered that he did not believe there would be war if the United States stood firm but that it was vitally important for the government to maintain a free hand.

Answering additional questions dealing with the criticism of current policy, Dulles stated that he saw no need "to require that all our allies should agree with everything we do," and then turning to his domestic critics, bitingly asserted that "there lies a responsibility upon the President and his principal advisers which cannot be shared with the general public."

The Secretary of State also expressed the hope that the proposed ambassadorial talks might lead to a cease-fire or a modus vivendi, declared that the key issue remained Communist renunciation of force in the Formosan Straits, and vaguely hinted that although the United States would do nothing behind Nationalist China's back, it might itself make some concessions should the situation in the straits really ease.

This press conference did not relieve popular anxieties (that same day James Reston wrote in the *New York Times* of a new "Dulles Doctrine" to resist aggression in Quemoy and Matsu as part of an expanded containment policy), and the President decided to take his turn in trying to clarify matters through a special television address to the nation on September 11. Realizing, as he later wrote in his memoirs, that the administration's method in dealing with the situation "was hardly blessed with unanimity of opinion," he tried to counter what in a later period would have been called a credibility gap by setting the whole record straight.

Three background developments appeared to make this all the more necessary: Premier Nikita Khrushchev, who had earlier gone no further than to assure the Chinese Communists of Russia's "moral and material aid," had written President Eisenhower on September 8 to state that his government would consider an American attack on the Chinese Communists as an attack on the Soviet Union; our allies again intimated that while they would support our defense of Formosa, they could not go along with protection of the offshore islands; and Ambassador Rankin in Taipei warned that Chiang Kai-shek was becoming very worried over American intentions.

The President was anxious to prevent any Communist miscalculation over our policy and at the same time calm popular anxieties. The bombardment of Quemoy, he said, appeared to be a part of "an ambitious plan of armed conquest" and the United States would not be either "lured or frightened into appeasement." Our policy was designed not only to save Formosa and the offshore islands from Communist control, he declared, but had the further objective, implying a parallel with Korea, of upholding the basic principle that "armed force shall not be used for aggressive purposes." He then shifted ground to express his full support for negotiations with the Chinese Communists; held out the hope that a way might be found to settle the status of Quemoy and Matsu so that they would not remain "a thorn in the side of peace"; and sought to reassure both the American public and our troubled allies by stating his own firm belief that "there is not going to be any war."

In these circumstances the talks in Warsaw between the two ambassadors to Poland—Wang Ping-nan and Jacob D. Beam—got under way on September 15. Yet no more than in 1955 was there any real basis for agreement. Beam insisted on Communist China's renunciation of force in the Formosan Straits; Wang refused a commitment that would sacrifice the principle that the status of Formosa was a wholly domestic question. Moreover, the Nationalists were letting it be known offstage that they would not accept any limitation on their sovereign rights in the offshore islands. "Talks with the Communists under any circumstances are futile," declared an unregenerate Chiang Kai-shek, "and the Warsaw talks are no exception."

Still, the parleys continued. Neither side was prepared to break them off. When the U.N. Assembly took up the dispute over Quemoy and Matsu at a meeting on September 18, Secretary Dulles successfully urged postponement of the discussion pending the final outcome of the negotiations.

Unlike the situation three years earlier, however, the Communists were still shelling Quemoy and tension in the Formosan Straits was unabated. The American public became restive. It was fearful that things might get out of control and that Chiang Kai-shek would make some move which could drag the United States into war by the back door. Although the administration continued to command popular support for its stand on Formosa, fewer and fewer people felt that the United States was in any way bound to rush to the protection of the offshore islands. At the close of September a leak from the State Department disclosed that 80 percent of the letters it was receiving were highly critical of current policy and fearful of the possible consequences.

Secretary Dulles, stung by this disclosure of the letters his department was receiving, retorted that "certainly you cannot allow your foreign policy to be dictated by public opinion." But as statesmen before and since have realized, it could not be ignored. Dulles knew this very well. Stoutly denying that he had any intention of changing or modifying policy, he began to back away from the unquestioning support he had previously given Chiang Kai-shek. At a news conference on September 30 he admitted that it had been "rather foolish" for the Nationalists to insist on maintaining so great a part of their military forces on the offshore islands. He even went so far as to suggest that if the Chinese Communists agreed to a cease-fire, the United States would favor a reduction in these occupation troops. In a further effort to allay the suspicion that Chiang could bend American policy to his own purposes, the Secretary of State pointedly stressed that the United States had no commitment whatsoever to support the Nationalists in the "hypothetical contingency" of their attempting an invasion of the mainland.

An irate Chiang Kai-shek rose in wrath. Saying that he was "incredulous" over this statement of the Secretary of State and that it was "incompatible with our stand," he categorically rejected any idea of redeploying his troops on the offshore islands. Quick to take advantage of this apparent rift in the relations between Washington and Taipei, the Chinese Communists stepped up their propaganda to convince their fellow countrymen on Formosa that the Americans would sooner or later abandon them altogether. They again stated that the status of Formosa was an internal question and proposed direct negotiations with the Nationalists for its settlement. To emphasize their desire for peace, they also announced a one-week cease-fire to enable the Nationalists, on condition American ships did not escort their convoys, to ship supplies to beleaguered Quemoy.

Chiang Kai-shek spurned this offer of negotiation because the Communists "never will keep their word." In an anniversary message to his armed forces on October 10 he declared that the Nationalists had in fact won the first round over Quemoy and would soon win the second. "And then," the generalissimo told his troops, "we can further launch our counterattack to deliver our compatriots on the mainland from Communist tyranny."

Finding Chiang's belligerency even more of an obstacle to reducing tension than during the earlier Formosan crisis, the Eisenhower Administration again felt the need to bring pressure on him to modify his policy. As in 1955 its approach, as Secretary Dulles had already hinted, was to provide a basis for a general cease-fire by persuading Chiang to withdraw his troops from Quemoy and Matsu and thereby obviate Communist fears that he intended to use the islands as a staging area for a mainland invasion. Dulles stated for the record that the Communists were attempting to drive a wedge between loyal allies; the United States had no idea of coercing

Chiang into any change of policy. Nevertheless, he now felt the situation sufficiently serious to undertake a special mission to Taipei himself in the hope of exercising a restraining influence on Nationalist ambitions.

After three days of talks Dulles and Chiang issued, on October 23, a joint communiqué. It made no mention of a reduction of troops on the offshore islands. The Secretary of State had been unable to sway the Nationalists from their "almost pathological devotion" to Quemoy and Matsu. The best he could obtain was a generalized promise from Chiang Kai-shek to follow a peaceful course in the Formosan Straits. The joint communiqué stated that while the Republic of China considered the restoration of freedom to its people on the mainland its sacred mission, it believed "that the principal means of successfully achieving its mission is the implementation of Dr. Sun Yat-sen's three principles [nationalism, democracy, social well-being] and not the use of force." In again seeking to leash Chiang Kai-shek—to use the old phrase—the United States found him, as always, a very tough customer. His obdurate insistence on maintaining his forces on Quemoy and Matsu spoke more eloquently of his own hopes for some day reconquering the mainland than this vague pledge not to resort to force.

Dulles had to be content. Returning to Washington, he spoke of the new understanding as "eminently satisfactory." He praised the Nationalist government as dedicated "to peaceful accomplishment of its high mission as spokesman for the aspirations and traditions of China." But he also emphasized that the United States would not support or tolerate an attack by the Nationalists against continental China.

While these somewhat contradictory moves were being made on the diplomatic front, the Chinese Communists were following an erratic course in respect to Quemoy. Having found the United States determined and Soviet Russia cautious about developments in the Formosan Straits, they gave over military means to achieve their objectives and returned to political methods to prevent any "two China" solution of the Formosan problem. However, to keep up the pressure they did not entirely halt their shelling of Quemoy. Having first extended the initial cease-fire, they resumed the bombardment during Dulles's visit to Taipei with greater intensity than ever before, and then on October 25 announced that for "humanitarian reasons" they would shell the island only on the even days of the month. "I wondered," Eisenhower recalled in *Waging Peace*, "if we were in a Gilbert and Sullivan war."

Nevertheless, the danger of any further escalation of hostilities seemed to have ended. The ambassadorial talks went on, however inconclusively, and this partial truce prevailed in the straits. But nothing was settled. Asked at a news conference what he thought were the Communists' intentions, Dulles frankly answered, "What they will do next, I don't know."

Here matters rested in the autumn of 1958. Neither the Nationalists nor the Communists abandoned their respective missions to liberate the other's territory. The former maintained their heavy troop concentrations on the offshore islands and gave only lip service to the concept of employing peaceful means to achieve their goal; the latter, accepting no limitation on their right to settle what they termed a domestic issue by whatever means they chose, continued intermittently to shell Quemoy. The potential powder keg of the Formosan Straits was not defused. The United States remained as deeply involved as ever. There was little doubt that should the Communist forces actually invade the offshore islands, American air and naval power would come directly to their defense.

In later unofficial comments both Secretary Dulles and Premier Chou En-lai underscored the sharp conflict in the American and Chinese positions. In a transcribed record of conversations with the Secretary of State, Andrew H. Berding quoted Dulles as saying that the United States could not surrender the offshore islands, let alone Formosa, without disaster, for this would mean that the Communists had attained their objective of driving the United States out of the western Pacific. Edgar Snow has recorded Chou En-lai as telling him in their 1960 conversations that unless the United States acknowledged that the status of Formosa was an internal Chinese affair and withdrew the Seventh Fleet, it was inconceivable that friendly relations could ever be established between the two countries.

Apart from its stand on the Formosan Straits, the United States was seeking in every other way during this period to implement its fundamental policy, as set forth by John Foster Dulles, to do nothing that could possibly contribute to acceptance of the Peking regime as China's legitimate government. We have seen that the Secretary of State refused to countenance even Sino-American cultural exchanges because they might be considered a step toward recognition. For the United States to move in that direction, he thought, would have an adverse effect on other governments in Asia and this "could be disastrous to the cause of the free world." Dulles also insisted on maintenance of the trade embargo adopted during the Korean war, and having long since abandoned his original position that the United Nations should operate on the principle of universalism, he conducted an unrelenting campaign to block the admission of the Chinese People's Republic.

On matters of trade with Communist China, the United States stood virtually alone. Our allies had accepted a ban on the shipment of all strategic goods during the Korean conflict, but on its conclusion they were anxious to relax these restrictions by narrowing the definition of what might be considered materials of war. They wanted to place trade with China on the same basis as that with the countries of eastern Europe. The United States did everything possible to resist this approach, employing the provisions of the Battle Act, which called for the termination of American aid to any country shipping strategic goods to a Communist-controlled state, but it was a losing cause. At the close of May 1957 the State Department felt compelled to accept so far as our allies were concerned a substantial modification of the original restrictions. At the same time, it announced that the United States would continue its unilateral embargo on all trade with Communist China whether or not it involved so-called strategic goods.

Some members of Congress, responding to the age-old dream of the immense potentialities of the China market and reluctant to see our commercial rivals develop a thriving trade from which Americans were barred, considered our embargo unrealistic. Senator Warren G. Magnuson of Washington, chairman of the Interstate and Foreign Commerce Committee, called for at least some modification of existing bans. "We can't keep 400 million people behind an economic bamboo curtain just because we don't like their government," he stated. But while he had some support, including that of Senator Lyndon Johnson, general sentiment in the Senate opposed any change in policy that might serve to strengthen Communist China's military or industrial potential. "The stakes are too high, the dangers too great," said Senator Charles Potter of Michigan, for the United States to assume "the calculated risk of trade with Red China."

The latter view was, of course, shared by Secretary Dulles. He was deeply disturbed over the expanding trade of other nations with Communist China and all the more determined that the United States should steadfastly maintain its embargo. In his opinion this was essential whatever other countries might do. For the United States to encourage any trade with the Communists that might strengthen China's industrial base would be "to gamble with our national security."

Whatever differences of opinion might exist on this issue, the administration, the Congress, and an overwhelming majority of the American people were united in their opposition to Communist China's representation in the United Nations. Every year when this question was about to come up in the UN Assembly, both the Senate and the House adopted resolutions expressing this view—and adopted them unanimously. Moreover, both William Knowland and Lyndon Johnson, as their respective party's Senate leaders, were on record as stating that if the United Nations accepted the Peking government the United States should withdraw its support from the world organization.

President Eisenhower, who believed that 95 percent of the American people shared his conviction that the Chinese Communists should not be admitted, maintained that the administration's stand was based not on a "strange emotionalism" but was "soberly rational." The continuing influence of McCarthyism, however, was to a great extent responsible for the failure of any Congressmen to take the political risk of challenging the majority view. No change was observable in what George Kennan once called "the savage enthusiasm many Americans have worked up over the cause of keeping the Chinese Communists out of the United Nations."

Secretary Dulles now held that since the UN had condemned Communist China as an aggressor during the Korean war, the People's Republic could not be even considered as a member until it had completely purged itself of such aggression. This it had failed to do, the Secretary of State repeatedly stressed; it was encouraging war in Indochina and maintained a threatening posture in the Formosan Straits. Moreover, he stated emphatically on one occasion, the United States could never approve of seating delegates from a government that was not only guilty of aggression but was "consistently and viciously hostile to the United States."

Throughout the Eisenhower Administration the American delegation to the UN consequently exercised all its influence in lining up opposition to the usual Soviet resolution for replacing the Nationalists with the Communists. Every year the Chinese People's Republic was assailed as an outlaw nation whose admission would vitiate if not destroy the United Nations as an instrument of international peace. "If some of us here think that this Assembly, this United Nations," said Henry Cabot Lodge, serving as a delegate in 1957, "should become a cockpit in which the criminal and the law-abiding nations are indiscriminately scrambled up, the thing for them to do is to go and get an amendment to the charter." On another occasion Walter Robertson, as the American spokesman, accused the Peking government of keeping itself in power only through a series of bloody purges. To admit such a state to the United Nations, he said, "would make a mockery of our charter and rob it of all moral authority."

The technique used to carry out our policy remained the annual submission of a resolution calling for postponement of any action to the next year. The Assembly adopted it with consistent regularity. However, the opposition was slowly gaining. The vote in favor of the moratorium in 1954 was 43 to 11, with six abstentions, and in 1960 it was 42 to 34, with twenty-two abstentions. Or to put it in a more revealing way, the votes cast against excluding the Chinese Communists, in spite of the fervid oratory of the United States delegate and more subtle political pressures, rose in this period from some 18 percent of the total to nearly 35 percent.

Our comparable stand in opposing any move to draw Communist China into negotiations on the limitation of arms was even more significant. The accelerating arms race, with the progressive development of bigger and better atomic bombs, had inspired the drive for a nuclear test ban treaty. The question posed was whether any international agreement to limit or control arms could be effective without the participation of the People's Republic of China. Both among our allies and in some quarters in this country, the view was held that Chinese delegates should be brought into the early stages of the talks. The Eisenhower Administration saw no need for this. It argued that an invitation to a world arms meeting would imply recognition of the Peking regime and only serve to enhance its international prestige.

Assistant Secretary of State Robertson acknowledged that if a system for controlling armaments or banning further nuclear tests could ever be set up, then Communist China might be included. But the idea that it should have any part in the negotiations for such a system was not seriously entertained, and the possibility that the Peking government might in the meantime itself develop nuclear weapons was casually ignored. As late as March 1960 President Eisenhower said that while Chinese armaments might eventually have to be taken into account, a great deal more progress would have to be made in general disarmament talks "before we are into the stage of worrying too much about Red China."

During the final years of the Eisenhower Administration, the course Communist China was following in foreign affairs served to stiffen rather than ameliorate the determination in Washington to seek its complete political isolation. Indications of a rift in Sino-Russian relations were already apparent. John Foster Dulles admitted that the Peking government could no longer be considered a satellite of Moscow; rather, both "the Soviet Union and Communist China are under the domination of what might be called international Communism." This frightening bogey was not defined in terms of the physical source of its power, but as one of its major instruments Communist China became in the eyes of the Secretary of State an ever more dangerous threat to the free world.

In spite of a realistic refusal to press matters too far in the Formosan Straits, Peking was indeed following a less restrained course around China's borders which belied the spirit of Bandung. The Chinese Communists strongly backed Ho Chi Minh and the Vietcong in a revived campaign to overthrow the Diem regime in South Vietnam, and they openly supported the Communist-controlled Pathet Lao in a complicated power struggle in Laos. Seizing upon the pretext of a revolt in Tibet, which they may well have instigated themselves, they charged the rebels with having "colluded with imperialism" and suppressed their uprising with cruel savagery. After driving the Dalai Lama into exile, they dissolved his government, set up their own rule under the puppet Panchen Lama, and brought to an end Tibet's supposed autonomy. And finally, Peking precipitated an acrimonious border dispute with India, marked by frequent military clashes along the frontier, which set the stage for the more direct attack on that country in the brief Sino-Indian war of 1962.

On a broader front the Chinese were also contriving to impress upon the Communist world that they were the true heirs of Marxism-Leninism. In opposition to the more conciliatory policies of Soviet Russia, they were prepared to take the unprecedented step, in the light of Chinese history, of reaching out overseas and proclaiming support for all revolutionary movements directed against the capitalistic West. Whereas the Russians maintained that socialism could triumph through peaceful competition and without war, the Chinese Communists now declared that only through militantly supporting the peoples of Asia, Africa, and Latin America in their wars of liberation could the forces of socialism overcome American imperialism, the arch enemy of peace.

In sharp reaction to Peking's newly aggressive policy, Washington renewed its own attacks on the Chinese Communists as threatening world peace. Assistant Secretary of State Robertson, to quote once again that rabid foe of the Chinese Communists, was more vehement than ever before. He let out all the stops in a speech in March 1959 as he assailed "the fanatical, aggressive, hostile, and threatening International Communist regime of Peiping, an implacable enemy dedicated to the destruction of all the foundations upon which a free society rests."

In this atmosphere—this "state of quasi war" in Undersecretary of State Christian Herter's phrase—the 1950s came to an end. President Eisenhower, visiting Formosa on a Far Eastern tour in June 1960, reaffirmed the policy, both in respect to the Chinese Communists and the Chinese Nationalists, that his administration had inherited on coming into office seven years earlier and had ever since maintained with such unrelenting firmness. He told a popular rally in Taipei that the United States did not accept "the claim of the warlike and tyrannical Communist regime in Peking to speak for the Chinese people." Nothing had lessened the American determination, he assured his Chinese Nationalist audience, "to stand with you, and with all our free neighbors of the Pacific, against any aggression."

On the basis of all contemporary evidence, the American people continued to uphold the Eisenhower Administration's position. They were not too interested in the Far East. Except during the Formosan crisis their attention was more generally directed to other parts of the world. When they did consider the affairs of Asia, they saw no alternative to a policy of containment and isolation to restrain the Chinese Communists. Not yet fully recovered from the traumatic shock of the loss of China, they were still fearful that any different approach would invite another Munich.

With the advent of a new administration under President John F. Kennedy in 1961, it remained to be seen whether the Democrats would continue along the same road or try to initiate a new approach.

12

The Kennedy Years

As EVENTS UNFOLDED in the early 1960s the new Kennedy Administration found itself involved in the field of foreign affairs with more immediately critical issues than its China policy. The renewed conflict with Soviet Russia over the status of Berlin, the dramatic Cuban missile crisis, and the negotiations for a nuclear test ban treaty greatly overshadowed developments in the Far East. But while they might be relegated to the background, Sino-American relations could never be ignored.

The United States saw the Peking government's aggressive stance during these years—in Korea, in the Formosan Straits, in Indochina—as a continuing threat to the peace of Asia. As Communist China further asserted its ambition to expand its sphere of influence and built up its own military power, President Kennedy was to state that such policies might lead "to a potentially more dangerous situation than any we have faced since the end of the second World War." For its part, the Chinese People's Republic again declared that American support for the anti-Communist nations on its borders, with the presence of United States forces in Korea, Formosa, and Indochina, seriously affected "the security of China and the peace of Asia." There were charges that through intrusions in Chinese territorial waters and air space, the Kennedy Administration was "more obsessed and malignant" than the Eisenhower Administration in "pursuing an aggressive policy which is stubbornly hostile to the Chinese people."

Some hope initially existed that the new policy makers taking office in 1961, with a fresh outlook and uninhibited by the repressive forces of McCarthyism, might find a way to ease Far Eastern tensions. But nothing of the sort happened. While American relations with Soviet Russia improved following the Cuban missile crisis, those with Communist China appeared to worsen.

Prior to his election the new President's views on Far Eastern affairs had been somewhat shifting and ambivalent. Although his immediate reaction to the victory of the Chinese Communists in 1949 reflected the popular sense of outrage over "the loss of China," he came to regret his charges that what "our young men had saved, our diplomats and President have frittered away." At a press conference in November 1961 he said that his current views were more in accordance with the facts than those he had held in 1949, and in respect to his early speeches he told Arthur M. Schlesinger, Jr., as the latter has recorded in *A Thousand Days*, that he was sorry he had ever made them. During the 1950s he repeatedly acknowledged that Communist China's policies posed a grave threat to American interests in eastern Asia, but he also expressed his misgivings over the inflexibility of our policy in meeting this challenge. At the time of both Formosan crises, he was ready to uphold our treaty commitment to defend Formosa against possible Communist attack but opposed extending protection to the offshore islands.

Kennedy elaborated on his position in an article in *Foreign Affairs* entitled "A Democrat Looks at Foreign Policy," which appeared in October 1957. He deplored what he considered the shift in our national attitude "from a hyperbolic image of a free China to the brittle conception of a shiftless, totalitarian China" and assailed the consequent policy toward the Peking government as "exaggeratedly military" and "probably too rigid." He obliquely attacked Secretary of State Dulles, who was at this time deeply involved in the controversy over the exchange of American and Chinese news correspondents. "There have been—and still are—compelling reasons for the nonrecognition of China," Kennedy wrote, "but we must be very careful not to straight-jacket our policy as a result of ignorance and fail to detect a change in the objective situation when it comes."

Asked in an interview two years later what he would himself do about China policy, he was more specific. In his opinion the defense of Quemoy and Matsu should be abandoned, both in the interests of allied unity and because allowing Chiang Kai-shek to garrison these islands provided a needless irritant in our relations with Peking. He believed the door should be always kept open for possible negotiations with the Chinese Communists. "We should indicate our willingness to talk with them when they desire to so do," Kennedy said, "and to set forth conditions of recognition which seem responsible to the watching world."

China policy entered at least briefly into the presidential campaign in 1960. Kennedy called for reassessment of a stand that "has failed dismally in its principal objective of weakening Communist rule on the mainland." His Republican opponent, Richard Nixon, naturally enough defended the record of the administration in which he served as Vice-President.

Somewhat by chance, the more immediate issue of Quemoy and Matsu was brought into the two candidates' famed television debates. Kennedy's position was that while the United States was most certainly not going to allow the Chinese Communists to dominate the Far East and would neither retreat nor appease under pressure, it should not ignore the provocation from the Chinese point of view of the presence of hostile troops so close to the mainland. For this country to commit itself to the defense of the offshore islands, he maintained, was dangerously to limit its options, play into the hands of the Communists, and bring the whole world closer to war. "I do not intend," he said forcefully, "to let Chiang Kai-shek and the Chinese Communists decide whether our troops shall fight on these islands." Moreover, he added, Quemoy and Matsu were neither strategically defensible nor essential to Formosa's security.

Nixon's emphatic rejoinder was that protection of the offshore islands was a matter of principle; the United States was not interested in them as real estate but somewhere a line must be held against further Communist expansion. He was against "handing over to the Communists an inch of free territory." To retreat from the stand the United States had taken in relation to Quemoy and Matsu would be appeasement and would be so interpreted by friends and foes alike. The Chinese Communists want not just these islands, not just Formosa, Nixon fervently declared, "they want the world."

Although these statements accented the conflicting views within this country over the offshore islands, further discussion in the television debates engendered a good deal more heat than light. Nixon attacked his opponent for "woolly thinking" and for following a "soft line" toward Communism; Kennedy countered that the Republican candidate was "foolhardy and reckless" in espousing a policy that might well lead to a wholly unnecessary war. However, the question was at once so controversial and so peripheral to the main issues of the campaign that as the debates proceeded, both men cautiously backed away from it and the original sharp differences in their views became blurred. Nixon retreated to a less aggressive stand over the importance of the offshore islands' defense, and Kennedy modified his originally explicit position in favor of their abandonment.

The public was not very much interested.

On assuming office after his narrow electoral victory, Kennedy gave some signs that he would like to take a new look at the whole situation in eastern Asia. Eschewing the emotional rhetoric of the Cold War and the moral condemnation of both Communism and neutralism so familiar during the Eisenhower Administration, he made plain that the basic interest of the United States in the Far East, as in Europe, was to prevent any alteration in the existing balance of power, which was serving to maintain, however precariously, general peace. Kennedy fully accepted the basic assumption governing our policy; that is, the necessity to contain Communist expansion, but everything suggests that he would have liked to break through the Sino-American deadlock. A number of his associates have recalled that he believed there was something "irrational" in the relations between the United States and the Chinese People's Republic and that something should be done about it.

However, the new President felt his hands were tied. Popular hostility toward the Chinese Communists had not really lessened. Any shift in our attitude toward them still threatened to raise the old charges of appeasement. With his political position so insecure, Kennedy persuaded himself he could not take the risks of any new approach on an issue still so emotionally explosive.

Whatever his private ideas, he hewed to the old line. In his first State of the Union message he declared in brief reference to Southeast Asia that "the relentless pressures of the Chinese Communists menace the security of the entire area—from the borders of India and South Vietnam to the jungles of Laos." In subsequent press conferences he pointed out that the Peking government was still refusing to admit American newspaper correspondents, held American citizens in jail, and was assailing the United States in attacks that were "constant, immediate, and in many cases malevolent." These were familiar pronouncements. Kennedy made no real effort either to modify existing policies or to prepare public opinion to accept a more realistic attitude toward Communist China.

His appointment of Dean Rusk as Secretary of State also strongly militated against any shift in our position in the Far East. Rusk's wartime and subsequent diplomatic experience had been largely in Asia, and he had amply demonstrated his hard-line approach in dealing with Communist China while serving as Assistant Secretary of State during the Truman Administration. Nothing in 1961 indicated that he had in any way modified his earlier views. Rusk was indeed very much of the same persuasion as John Foster Dulles in interpreting the conflict between Communism and the free world as one of fundamental moral principle: no compromise should be made with the forces of evil.

Rusk appeared unable to free himself from the bonds of his original conviction that the Chinese Communists were the willing instruments or, at least, the helpless puppets of the international Communist conspiracy directed from Moscow. This imposed a fixity on his outlook almost impervious to new developments. Largely ignoring the forces of Asia's revolutionary nationalism in his absorption with Communism, very certain of himself in his cool, composed attitude, the imperturbable Rusk allowed nothing to sway him from his determination to see that the United States refrained from any move that might augment Communist China's international status.

At the Senate hearings on his confirmation as Secretary of State, Rusk admitted with his genius for calm understatement that "the China question is a very complicated one at the present time," but his only answer as to how it might be handled was in a continuation of current policies. He saw no possibility of bringing about a normalization of Sino-American relations. Appearing a little later on the "Today" television show, he emphatically reaffirmed his opposition to either diplomatic recognition of the Chinese People's Republic or its admission to the United Nations.

He drew strength from the Far Eastern Division. James C. Thomson, Jr., at this time a special assistant in the Department of State, has written that it was the most rigid and doctrinaire of any regional division. Its members were generally committed to the one policy line: the close containment and political isolation of mainland China, enforced through American military power and a network of alliances with our anti-Communist client states on China's periphery.

Although the new President was to face more important Asian issues, one that significantly brought out both the differences of opinion within his administration and Kennedy's own conflict between his personal impulses and his political caution was the perennial question of Chinese representation in the United Nations. How touchy a subject it had become is suggested in an account by Arthur Schlesinger, Jr., of a meeting at the White House in the summer of 1961 dealing with general strategy for the forthcoming session of the UN Assembly. Various other matters were discussed and "next came the question of China—at which point," as Schlesinger tells the story, "the President, calling forward, said, 'Jackie, we need the Bloody Marys now.'"

In the background were some complicated considerations.

Adlai Stevenson, whom the President had appointed as ambassador to the United Nations, was highly critical of current China policy. He believed the United States should face up squarely to the Communists' complete control of the mainland. As a private citizen he had argued in favor of finding a solution to the representation issue which would provide for seating in the Assembly delegates from both the Peking government and the Nationalist government. The new Undersecretary of State, Chester Bowles, was also publicly on record in favor of such a solution. "Only when we move off dead center in East Asia, beginning with the creation and implementation of imaginative policies based on the reality of the two Chinas, will we start to exert a constructive influence on the shape of events to come," he wrote in an article in *Foreign Affairs* in April 1960. After the election of Kennedy, Bowles reaffirmed these views on a television program in England in which he again definitely advocated a broad policy based on acceptance of an independent mainland and an independent Formosa.

Even the suggestion that such ideas might get a hearing was enough to alarm Republican conservatives and the successors of the old China bloc. A revived Committee of One Million, disproving any idea that it was merely a lobby of a million ghosts, promptly launched a massive propaganda campaign condemning Communist China and all its ways in order to bring pressure to bear on Congress to resist any change in UN policy. With such familiar figures as former Senator H. Alexander Smith of New Jersey and former Representative Walter Judd of Minnesota in command, the committee placed advertisements in newspapers throughout the country opposing any move toward reconsideration of Communist China's recognition or its membership in the United Nations. Both the House and Senate responded as they had in past years with the unanimous passage of concurrent resolutions vigorously restating their unequivocal opposition to any change in American policy.

Nor was the attitude of Congress the only indication of the political hazards this issue presented. Both Arthur Schlesinger, Jr., in *A Thousand Days* and John Kenneth Galbraith in *Ambassador's Journal* have related that at a meeting between Kennedy and Eisenhower just before the inauguration, the outgoing President warned his successor against any new moves. According to these accounts Eisenhower told Kennedy that while he hoped to be able to support the new administration on all foreign policy matters, he would not do so should it favor Peking's recognition or admission to the United Nations. In such an event, Eisenhower let it be known, he would feel compelled to return to public life to make his objections known.

In these circumstances President Kennedy felt confirmed in his view that this was no time to take any new initiatives in the United Nations. He had no doubt in 1961, Schlesinger has written, "that the international gains (if any) of [Communist China's] admission would be far outweighed by the uproar at home." Having made his decision, he took the occasion of a meeting with Vice-President Chen Cheng of the Nationalist government, who was briefly visiting Washington in early August, to publicly pledge American support for the Nationalists and continued opposition to the Communists.

The question still remained as to the most effective strategy to follow when the issue came up in the Assembly. The old technique of annually postponing any action, which Secretary Rusk proudly recalled he had a part in inventing while serving as Assistant Secretary of State in the Truman Administration, appeared to be wearing thin. Moreover, the situation was very involved in 1961, with other applications for UN membership affecting the conflicting interests of the Western-oriented states, the neutralists, and the Soviet bloc.

Trying to thread its way through these difficulties and prevent any further erosion of support for our traditional position, the administration decided to allow a direct vote on the expected Soviet resolution to expel the Nationalists and admit the Communists. With some judicious hints about the interrelationship between support for our position and the allocation of foreign aid funds, Washington felt reasonably certain it could win this vote. Then to assure the future, the American delegate would introduce a further resolution making any change in China's representation "an important question" that henceforth could be effected only through a two-thirds majority.

The task of implementing this revised policy fell on Stevenson's shoulders. In another passage in *A Thousand Days*, Kennedy is quoted as expressing his sympathy for his UN ambassador. "You have the hardest thing in the world to sell," he told Stevenson, "it really doesn't make any sense—the idea that Taiwan represents China. But, if we lose this fight, if Red China comes into the UN during our first year, your first year and mine, they'll run us both out. We have to lick them this year.

We'll take our chances next year. . . . So far as this year is concerned, you must do everything you can to keep them out. Whatever is required is OK by me."

Lick them—that is, the proponents of Communist China's admission—the United States did. Having accepted, however reluctantly, the responsibility of upholding official American policy, Stevenson argued his case energetically when the Assembly took up the Russian resolution. He denounced the Chinese Communists—these "latter-day empire builders"—for their aggression in Korea and Tibet, in Laos and Vietnam, and declared that only their renunciation of the use of force as an instrument of national policy would make them eligible for any sort of consideration as members of a world organization devoted to peace. When Peking promptly rejoined, "Listen, Stevenson: it is the right of 650,000,000 Chinese people to recover China's legitimate seat," the American delegate as quickly returned to the attack. "The root of the problem," he stated, "lies . . . in the hostile, callous, and seemingly intractable minds of the Chinese Communist rulers."

The test came on December 15. The Assembly defeated the Russian resolution to change China's UN representation—the vote was 48 to 37, with nineteen abstentions—and then accepted the American proposal making future consideration of the issue an "important question" by a commanding majority of 61 to 34, with seven abstentions. The United States had carried the day.

Over and beyond this ancient question, the Kennedy Administration found itself immediately on coming into office dealing with a new, explosive, and far more acute issue that might easily have led to direct conflict with Communist China. This was the status of Laos. That little country appeared to be on the eve of a takeover by Communist forces, and Washington feared a breakthrough in our containment policy threatening the security of all Southeast Asia. Vietnam, where the new administration was prepared to continue the support its predecessor had given the embattled regime of Ngo Dinh Diem, was still a baffling problem, but at the opening of 1961 Laos appeared to be the crisis point.

The sovereignty and freedom of Laos were guaranteed by the agreements reached at the Geneva Conference in 1954, and the gentle, peace-loving Laotians asked no more than that they be let alone. The geographic position of their country, however, made them unhappy pawns in the Cold War. Both Soviet Russia and Communist China (as well as North Vietnam) were actively supporting the local Communist-led insurgents—the Pathet Lao—in their campaign to set up their control over all Laos. To counter these moves the United States had been encouraging and backing the pro-Western, anti-Communist forces within the country.

Torn between these outside influences and the opposing domestic factions representing neutralism, westernism, and Communism, Laos was undergoing an unceasing civil war. Three rival princes, with such improbable names as Souvanna Phouma, Boun Oum, and Souphanouvong, were in the field. Their intrigues and conspiracies, the successive governmental crises and indecisive coups d'état, the advances and retreats on a shifting military front, appeared to the Americans as having all the features (except for a romantic heroine) of a Ruritanian musical comedy. It was hard to take it all seriously. Yet behind the intriguing façade of princely rivalries the critical situation now developing was highly dangerous.

After some shifting about in its approach, the Eisenhower Administration had finally thrown its full support to the rightists under Prince Oum and his strong man, General Phoumi Nosavan, in order to break away from an immoral neutralism. Our goal, Secretary Dulles proclaimed, was to make Laos a "bastion of freedom." Yet in spite of the millions of dollars poured into the effort to establish this pro-Western regime on a firm basis, the results were proving to be disastrous. Its reactionary political policies drove the neutralists into the Communist camp, and on the battlefield the Royal Laotian Army, under General Phoumi Nosavan's command, was completely incapable of effective fighting. The Pathet Lao, with increasing outside aid, expanded the territory under its control. As 1960 gave way to 1961, the Communists seemed to have complete victory within their militant grasp.

"Whatever's going to happen in Laos, in an American invasion, a Communist victory or whatever, I wish it would happen before we take over and get blamed for it," Theodore Sorensen has quoted the President-elect as telling him, reported in his book, *Kennedy*. But things did not get this far before inauguration day. The President consequently faced the intricate and involved problem (on which he was to spend more time in his first two months of office, Sorensen tells us, than on any other subject) of what the United States should do in Laos.

Kennedy's dilemma was a very real one. Subscribing as he did to the falling-domino theory—that if one Indochinese state fell under Communist domination the others could hardly escape a like fate—he was convinced that the United States should protect Laos from further aggression by "externally supported Communists." On the other hand, he believed that any direct action to meet this threat through military intervention ran the grave risk of a direct confrontation with Communist China and a spreading war throughout Southeast Asia.

The decision the President reached was to avoid intervention and yet hopefully block Communism by encouraging a new program for the neutralization of Laos. He would reverse the Eisenhower-Dulles policy of trying to make the little country an outpost of the free world; instead, he would seek the cooperation of the other interested powers in removing Laos from the context of the Cold War under new international guarantees. To implement this program Kennedy first insisted on a cease-fire to which all three princely contenders, representing the right-wing, neutralist, and Communist factions, would agree. The Geneva Conference would then be reconvened under the co-chairmanship of Great Britain and Soviet Russia to work out the new rules of neutrality for a coalition government. The goal of the United States, President Kennedy announced at a press conference, would be the establishment of a peaceful Laos, "an independent country not dominated by either side."

At the same time, the President undertook to make very clear, so informing the Chinese Communists through the medium of the ambassadorial contacts in Warsaw, that the alternative to acceptance of the neutralization of Laos would in all probability be American military intervention. When the Pathet Lao launched a new offensive in spite of the proposed cease-fire, he publicly warned of the dangers in this situation and declared that the United States "strongly and unreservedly" supported a truly neutral Laos.

The negotiations among the United States, Great Britain, and Soviet Russia, and the on-again, off-again parleys among the competing factions in Laos itself, were very involved, and constantly threatened to break down altogether. The President was under heavy pressure from his military advisers to intervene with force. The Joint Chiefs of Staff were apparently ready to land United States troops in Laos, Vietnam, and Thailand to bring things under control, and if the Chinese then moved in, to bomb their homeland. Kennedy asked them, Sorensen has written, "Is this our best bet for a confrontation with Red China?"

Influenced perhaps by what the military had told him at the time of the Cuban fiasco of the Bay of Pigs, Kennedy was skeptical of their advice and held to his determination to avoid intervention. Then in late April his caution was rewarded. The rival princes reached agreement for a cease-fire, and a new fourteen-nation conference was summoned to negotiate the guarantees that would make Laos both independent and neutral.

The United States thereupon found itself once again going to an international meeting where in spite of its refusal to recognize Communist China, it would be involved in direct negotiations with the Peking government. This was not too happy a prospect, especially when Foreign Minister Chen Yi (who had succeeded Chou En-lai in this office, though the latter remained Premier) took a rather less than friendly stand. He let it be known that his government considered Laos a victim of American imperialism and would never be a party to an agreement providing international control over its neutrality. An affronted State Department, reflecting the spirit that marked our participation in the Geneva Conference of 1954, went so far as to instruct the American representative, Averell Harriman, to have no direct contacts with the Chinese delegation.

According to both Schlesinger and Galbraith, however, Kennedy countermanded these instructions. Indeed Galbraith, who was then our envoy in New Delhi, takes full credit for this move overruling the State Department. "I sent an indignant letter to the President on the subject," he has written, "and this ridiculous bar was removed." Whether or not this is the whole story, Kennedy gave Harriman full rein to do whatever he thought necessary and steadfastly upheld the latter's patient, skillful efforts to win Peking's adherence to an agreement which would have been meaningless without its participation.

The conference opened in Geneva on May 14, 1961, and lasted for over a year. The truce in Laos repeatedly broke down, the Pathet Lao renewed its assaults on the government, and the three princes could not agree on the composition of a coalition government. As the negotiations dragged on through the year and into 1962, Kennedy repeated his warnings that a breakdown in Geneva would compel the United States to intervene, and to drive this home he ordered a build-up of United States forces in the general area. He dispatched a carrier task force to the Gulf of Siam and increased the number of American troops already stationed in friendly Thailand to a total of 5,000. These moves led Peking to denounce this country for trying to turn Laos into a base for aggression against China, but the President stood firmly by his policy, following a hair-trigger line between diplomacy and more forcible measures. "It is a very hazardous course," he said at a press conference on May 9, 1962, "but introducing American forces . . . that also is a hazardous course."

At long last the situation seemed to be resolved. Prince Souvanna, the neutralist leader, announced that he had succeeded in forming a coalition government, which he would head, with both the rightist Prince Boum Oum and Prince Souphanouvong of the Pathet Lao as key members. The conference accepted this new government. On July 23, 1962, it issued a formal declaration signed by all the participating nations, including the United States and Communist China, wherein they agreed that they would respect Laos's sovereignty, neutrality, and independence and re-frain from any interference in its internal affairs.

Throughout these negotiations, in spite of the important roles played by Great Britain and Soviet Russia as the co-sponsors of the conference, the real protagonists were the United States and the People's Republic of China. The former was primarily trying to reenforce containment by blocking Communist control of Laos through the Pathet Lao; the latter was seeking to prevent the extension of American influence over Laos in order to maintain its own power and position. The two nations, each anxious to avoid a direct confrontation that might lead to war, accepted a compromise in agreeing to establish Laos as a neutral buffer state.

The Geneva accord in 1962—as in the case of that in 1954—was not the success hopefully envisaged at the time. It was violated in succeeding years, ultimately by both sides, with increasing abandon. The coalition government eventually broke down altogether and left a divided, quar-reling country. The Pathet Lao returned to incessant guerrilla warfare, with overt support from outside Communist sources, and won control of a great part of the north. Possibly the Chinese, as well as the Russians and the North Vietnamese, never had anything else in mind. Far from being settled, the status of Laos remained an acute problem.

Nevertheless, the Geneva Conference averted for the time American military intervention in Laos and any deeper entanglement in its troubled affairs. President Kennedy felt justified in saying with guarded optimism that the conference was "a heartening indication that difficult . . . in-ternational problems can in fact be solved by patient diplomacy."

Nothing in the Geneva accords applied to what was becoming the even more discouraging course of events in Vietnam. Here the Ken-nedy Administration, like its predecessor in Laos, found itself backing a weak, inept, and corrupt government. Nonetheless, continued aid was given President Diem even though his government appeared to be rapidly losing all popular support. Washington felt that in trying to hold the line against Communist expansion in this area, there was no alternative but to support Saigon. The President made no suggestion of Vietnam's possible neutralization or of any sort of accommodation with the Vietcong or Ho Chi Minh.

Asked at a press conference on May 8, 1963, why the United States was willing to commit itself militarily in South Vietnam and not in Laos, Kennedy replied that the two situations were very different. We had found a way whereby it was hoped we could maintain Laotian neutrality, but in the case of South Vietnam we had been committed for a good many years to uphold its political integrity. This still seemed to be the best course to follow. It might prove necessary to seek other remedies, the President concluded, but we had adopted for each country what we regarded as the best strategy and "we will have to wait and see what happens."

The political breakdown in Vietnam, the governmental crisis that led to President Diem's assassination, the increased military aid given to the successor government in a desperate effort to rally continued resistance to the Communists—all this lay just over the horizon. Kennedy was to bequeath to his successor even graver problems in Vietnam than Eisenhower had left him in Laos.

While the agreement on Laos was still in the making, the underlying relations between the United States and Communist China underwent a further strain. For a third time the irrepressible issue of Formosa flared up portentously. Quemoy was once again the focal point. Put to the test was President Kennedy's campaign pledge that he did not intend to let either the Chinese Communists or the Chinese Nationalists decide for the United States whether it should fight over the offshore islands.

In the Chinese calendar, 1962 was the "Year of the Tiger," and it seemed to inspire a certain restlessness on both sides of the Formosan Straits. Ignoring his promises in 1958 to seek liberation of the mainland only through peaceful measures, Chiang Kai-shek was once more talking of an invasion, in a renewed belief that Communist China's internal problems, now accentuated by serious food shortages, meant that his hour was at hand. "There is no doubt," he proclaimed with his usual assurance, "that we can annihilate the Communists, reunify our country, and restore freedom to the people of the mainland in the nearest future." At the same time Peking was once again belligerently stating its firm intent to liberate Formosa and unite all China under Communist rule. Warning off the United States, the Communists began to concentrate military forces, including aircraft, in neighboring Fukien.

As this situation grew more threatening in late June, American policy makers, in the phrase of one State Department official, were "on tenterhooks." It was the old dilemma. Conforming to past patterns, opinion was divided between those who felt that the United States should give Chiang Kai-shek active support in invading the mainland, even at the risk of war, and those who believed that our policy should be cautious and restrained, with its overriding objective the maintenance of peace.

President Kennedy does not appear to have hesitated over the course he was prepared to follow. In spite of his previous criticism of the Eisenhower-Dulles policy, he immediately stated that the United States would stand on the ground it had consistently maintained since 1954. It was prepared to defend Formosa against a Communist attack, he told a press conference on June 27, and then added, in words that he might have borrowed from his predecessor, that any threat to the offshore islands "must be judged in relation to its wider meaning for the safety of Formosa and the peace of the area."

Thus Kennedy fully accepted the responsibilities that since the Korean war we had taken over as our fixed national policy. For the benefit of both the Communists and the Nationalists, however, he also strongly restated that our commitments under the terms of the Mutual Defense Treaty with the Republic of China did not involve support for any offensive action on the part of the Nationalists. "We are opposed to the use of force in this area," Kennedy said emphatically. "The purposes of the United States . . . are peaceful and defensive."

This forthright statement had an immediate restraining effect on both the Communists and the Nationalists. The confusions and controversy, the alarms and excursions of 1955 and 1958 were avoided. As contrasted with the earlier crises neither side made any further moves to fulfill their respective "sacred missions" to win over all China. The only significance of this brief happening in the summer of 1962 was that it once more showed how intractable was the unsettled issue of Formosa's status.

This flurry of excitement in Sino-American relations, subsiding as quickly as it had arisen, soon gave way to another development on the Asian scene that for a time threatened to have more serious consequences than anything that had happened since the Korean war. The long-simmering dispute over conflicting Chinese and Indian territorial claims along the Tibetan border, which had first surfaced in 1959, led to a brief but threatening Sino-Indian war. The United States was not directly involved. Nonetheless this clash presented in a newly acute form the issue of American responsibilities in aiding China's neighbors to resist Communist aggression.

The fighting broke out in October 1962 near an Indian outpost on the northeastern frontier and also at Ladakh, on the border of Kashmir and Tibet. Prime Minister Nehru announced that he was ordering the Indian army to drive the Chinese out of all disputed territory. The Peking government warned that such action was fanning the flames of war and that India should draw back from the precipice. Tension mounted. Then ten days after this first clash the Chinese launched a major offensive—"naked, large-scale aggression," the Indian defense minister charged—which drove back the defending forces in both sectors in a precipitate retreat. The way was open for a Chinese invasion of the vast Indian plain. An unhappy Nehru, who had clung so persistently to a neutralist, nonaligned role in the East-West conflict, appealed to the United States for arms and equipment.

Expressing its sympathy for India in the face of the "violent and aggressive action" of the Chinese Communists, the United States promptly declared its willingness to meet this request for assistance, and through Ambassador Galbraith immediate arrangements were made to airlift infantry arms and light artillery to the fighting front. Respecting India's wishes, we agreed to take this action with assurances that the United States did not intend to force India into a military alliance. Moreover, we would provide further and heavier arms should they prove to be needed.

This taut situation in Asia with its threat of an escalating war was almost ignored by the American people, for it was overshadowed by a far graver international crisis. On the very day that Prime Minister Nehru called on his countrymen to resist Communist China's attack, on October 22, 1962, the Cuban missile affair came to its climax. Having incontrovertible evidence that the Soviet Union was establishing bases on Cuba with the cooperation of the government of Fidel Castro, President Kennedy dramatically announced that the United States was imposing a quarantine on any further shipment of Russian military equipment and would consider the launching of any missiles from Cuba as a Soviet attack on the United States. As the whole world waited anxiously for Moscow's reaction—peace or nuclear war hanging in the balance—India seemed a remote concern. Even when the Russian ships turned back, Premier Khrushchev accepted American demands, and the danger of war was averted, little attention could be spared for the far-off Sino-Indian hostilities.

Washington nevertheless realized that if the Chinese Communists invaded the Indian plain in force, all Asia might find itself in a war that directly or indirectly would inevitably involve the United States. Theodore Sorensen has written in *Kennedy* that in spite of his preoccupation with Cuba, the President "wondered aloud which crisis would be the more significant in the long run."

The danger in India heightened, then suddenly waned. Writing in *Ambassador's Journal*, Galbraith has quoted his diary entry for November 21, "Yesterday was the day of ultimate panic in New Delhi," and then the entry for November 22, "Yesterday like a thief in the night peace arrived." What happened was that Peking unexpectedly announced that it had ordered a cease-fire, commenced the withdrawal of its troops, and declared its willingness, if India took similar measures, to enter upon negotiations for a settlement of the boundary dispute. Peace was somewhat more difficult to conclude than Galbraith's terse diary entry suggested, but terms were eventually worked out.

In not attempting a deeper invasion of India, the Peking government exercised the careful restraint that so often governed its policy. It had, however, already achieved what were probably its basic aims over and beyond agreement on a disputed boundary. Through their spectacular military success the Chinese Communists had dealt a heavy blow to India's prestige and greatly served to build up the image of the People's Republic as the predominant power in Asia.

The United States welcomed the cessation of hostilities; it also saw in these developments a gain for its own policies. Its faith in nonalignment shattered by China's assault, New Delhi might well be expected to reconsider India's strategic interests and henceforth act in closer accord with the West in resisting any further expansion of Communist power in Asia.

In each of these Asian developments in 1961–62—the Laotian crisis, the Sino-American confrontation in the Formosan Straits, and the clash of Chinese and Indian troops—the United States consistently followed a policy designed to block any expansion of Communist China. The implementation of this policy greatly differed from country to country. We threw our weight behind neutralism in Laos, declared our intent to defend Formosa by force of arms, and gave India military assistance. But the attitude of the Kennedy Administration in each instance (as well as in Vietnam) was definitely based on the underlying principle of containment. In applying this doctrine in Asia, however, there were now new confusions. The rift in Sino-Russian relations raised the question of the continuing validity of a policy first adopted under such different circumstances in 1950.

The United States had initially acted on the assumption that in taking a determined stand against any extension of Chinese power, we were combating a concealed form of Russian imperialism. Our attitude then somewhat shifted, to see in Chinese aggressiveness another manifestation of the worldwide Communist conspiracy directed against the free world—what John Foster Dulles meant when he said that both Soviet Russia and Communist China "were under the domination of what might be called international Communism." However, by the early 1960s the monolithic character of Communism—so far as this had ever existed—was clearly shattered and a policy based on outworn premises was called into question.

Washington still did not know what was really happening. If the actual relationship between Moscow and Peking, beyond their formal treaty of friendship and alliance, had been shrouded in confusion ever since 1949, the mists of uncertainty were now, over a decade later, more impenetrable than ever before. Once again the Kremlinologists and Sinologues, the whole battery of Communist experts in this country, were at odds over how to interpret the significance of the Sino-Russian quarrel and how far it might eventually be carried.

The State Department long remained cautious in attempting to evaluate the situation. In July 1961 Secretary of State Rusk acknowledged there was "solid evidence of some tension between Moscow and Peking," but he quickly added that he did not think the prospects of division "would be a sound basis of policy for the free world." President Kennedy commented at a press conference some months later that it was impossible to talk with any precision on relations between Russia and China—it was a matter of surmise on which experts differed. "I don't feel," he said, "that it is probably useful now for us to attempt to assess it."

Always in the background was the natural rivalry of two strongly nationalistic powers whose conflicting ambitions had in the past led to frequent clashes as the old Chinese empire sought to resist the aggressive designs of Russian imperialism. In its absorption with the menace of a supposedly monolithic Communism, the West disregarded or greatly minimized this built-in conflict between Russia and China along a common border stretching from Manchuria to Sinkiang. However, what was now added to this ancient political rivalry was the embittered polemical dispute over the nature of socialism, and whether Russians or Chinese were proving themselves the more faithful disciples of Marxism-Leninism.

In its fervid militancy Peking was accusing Moscow with increasing shrillness of a heretical revisionism in promoting accommodation with the capitalist world through a policy of peaceful coexistence. Moscow countered with angry charges that those who rejected coexistence accepted an adventurism that had nothing to do with socialist theory. Where the

Chinese called for unrelenting defiance of Western imperialism, which they described as a "paper tiger," the Russians declared that it should be remembered that "the paper tiger has nuclear teeth."

Lengthy and involved disquisitions on what constituted the true Marxist faith, spiced by mutual recriminations of betrayal of the Communist cause, filled the pages of Moscow's *Izvestia* and Peking's *People's Daily*. What has been described as a "bewildering jungle of polemics and vilification" masked an essentially political struggle for dominance in Asia and for paramount influence in the worldwide Communist movement. It had ramifications in eastern Europe, in Cuba, and in the Congo, as well as in the Far East.

An early manifestation of the mutual distrust and suspicion, the incipient conflict dividing Communist China and Soviet Russia had occurred during the Sino-American crisis in the Formosan Straits in 1958. It will be remembered that Premier Khrushchev assured the Peking government that it could count on Moscow's "moral and material aid," and then somewhat later, but only after the real crisis was over, belligerently wrote President Eisenhower that an attack on Communist China would be deemed an attack on the Soviet Union. Peking's leaders bitterly complained that they had been let down when support was really needed and that Khrushchev's delayed note to Eisenhower was no more than a face-saving gesture. In China's book the Soviet Union showed itself willing to abandon its socialist ally because of its abject desire for a rapprochement with America.

The ideological battles and polemical warfare between Peking and Moscow soon had their counterpart in even more concrete evidence—the disarray within Communist ranks. Neither side went so far as to disavow their military alliance, but there was a sharp curtailment in the economic and military support the Soviet Union extended to the Chinese People's Republic. In 1959–60 the Russians scrapped a number of agreements for helping the Chinese equip their military forces, recalled the Russian technologists who were assisting in the creation of China's modern industrial plant (they left, it was said, with their blueprints under their arms), and, even more significantly, refused any further aid in the development of China's nuclear capacity.

In angry reaction to this changed policy, the Peking government became all the more determined to develop its industrial power independently, to strike out on its own in building up a strong military position, and to give a high priority to producing an atom bomb. "It is no new story," a Peking broadcast scornfully declared, "that Soviet leaders, in collusion with American imperialists, plot to bind China hand and foot." Proudly defiant, the Chinese Communists announced that even if they were unable to produce a bomb for one hundred years, "we will neither crawl to the baton of the Soviet leaders, nor kneel before the nuclear blackmail of the U.S. imperialists."

Watching these developments closely, the State Department sought early in 1963 to enlighten the American public as best it could in a nationwide television broadcast titled "Red China and the U.S.S.R." Averell Harriman, now Undersecretary of State, and Roger Hilsman, the new Assistant Secretary of State for Far Eastern Affairs, reviewed the ideological aspects of the Sino-Russian rift, recounted the incidents that had occurred along the border between the two countries, and discussed the basic differences in Peking's and Moscow's approach, the former preaching the inevitability of war between capitalism and socialism, and the latter declaring the possibility of coexistence. But while they agreed that it was difficult to see how the Sino-Soviet bloc could ever recover its former unity, they cautioned that so long as the military alliance remained operative, no irreparable break could be taken for granted.

Dean Rusk about this same time repeated that it was too early to assume that the basic unity of the Communist world could not be easily reestablished in the event of a direct conflict with the free world. And President Kennedy in his turn stated his belief that the differences between the Soviet Union and Communist China were not over ultimate goals but only over the best means to attain them. "A dispute over how to bury the West," he said, "is no grounds for Western rejoicing."

In short, the differences developing between Communist China and Soviet Russia did not appear to Washington to make the threat of Communism any less menacing because its disciples were "no longer a single flock of sheep following blindly behind one leader." Breaking away from Soviet leadership and making itself the great champion of Marxism-Leninism, an aggressive, determined China could deepen rather than lessen the dangers of Communist expansion in Asia. Fearing as he did that a situation might develop more dangerous than any the United States had faced since World War II, President Kennedy saw no reason to abandon the basic tenets of containment.

The new trends in Chinese policy certainly afforded little comfort for those who hoped that the Sino-Russian break might induce Peking's leaders to adopt a more conciliatory attitude in world affairs. Even though they exercised a measure of restraint in accepting the neutralization of

Laos, the status quo in the Formosan Straits, and a reasonable settlement in India, they were soon attacking both capitalistic America and socialistic Russia with an almost hysterical vehemence. As the only true heirs of Marxism-Leninism, the Chinese Communists bitterly assailed what they considered to be a Russo-American alliance aimed at China. Peking's virulent propaganda termed the settlement of the Cuban missile crisis a pusillanimous Russian surrender to American pressure. Hoping to supplant both American and Russian influence in the underdeveloped countries of the world, the Peking government gave increased support to revolutionary uprisings throughout Latin America and Africa. It sent arms and military advisers to Communist cadres that followed its leadership in promoting Maoism in the Congo, Somalia, and Tanzania.

The Chinese also refused to participate in any disarmament talks or in the negotiations paving the way for the test ban treaty that was finally signed in August 1963. The *People's Daily* declared that Russian participation in the talks was a capitulation to imperialist blackmail which only consolidated the "nuclear monopoly." It then scornfully characterized the treaty itself as no more than an American-Russian conspiracy to try to block China's development of its own nuclear power.

In singling out the United States with wearing repetitiousness as "the most ferocious enemy of world peace," the Chinese redoubled their attacks on American policy as seeking to ring their country with military bases in order to prevent China from realizing its historic destiny as a nation supreme in all Asia. Striking out at the imperialistic reactionaries who sought to isolate the Peking government from the world community, Premier Chou En-lai declared their attempt was wholly futile for it was "they themselves who have become more isolated."

On another occasion, in June 1962, Peng Chen, the mayor of Peking and a leading polemicist in attacking both American imperialism and Russian revisionism (he was to be purged in 1966), succinctly outlined just what the United States would have to do if peace were to be assured. "The U.S. imperialists," he said, "must get out of Korea, get out of Taiwan, get out of South Vietnam, get out of Laos," and then added for good measure, "get out of the whole area of Asia, Africa, and Latin America."

This rage of propaganda was often little more than just that—self-assertive appeals to the nationalistic ambitions of the Chinese people. It often seemed to mask a sense of insecurity and even fear. Certainly Communist China's bark was always fiercer than its bite. Knowing their country's own inner weaknesses, the Communist leaders in Peking well knew

China was as yet in no position to fulfill its wide-ranging ambitions for international power.

While official Washington nonetheless appeared to find confirmation of its fears of Chinese aggression in these propagandistic outbursts, the question was again being raised by 1962, both within and without the administration, whether our traditional policy in seeking the political, economic, and cultural isolation of the Chinese People's Republic was not helping to create the very thing we feared. Those who had long been critical of our hard line suggested that the United States was itself fostering Communist China's extreme chauvinism and its ethnocentric defiance of the rest of the world.

They pointed out that the policy of nonrecognition, the prohibition of trade and cultural exchanges, had done nothing to achieve their original purpose of hastening the passing of Communism in China. On the contrary, such policies continued to justify Peking's ever more persuasive appeals to the nationalist sentiments of the Chinese people to support a government against which almost every other nation—now including Soviet Russia—had set its hand.

That something seemed to be very wrong with our China policy was tacitly acknowledged at least within the lower echelons of the State Department and by a number of ambassadors in Asian posts. Reporting on a meeting of the latter at Baguio, in the Philippines, in March 1962, Chester Bowles, who had now become a special adviser to the President, stated that the conferees were agreed that the time had come "for more solid thought and fewer slogans" in dealing with China. It was imperative in their opinion, Bowles went on to say, that the United States consider more realistically the new pressures being generated on the Asian mainland. Ambassador Galbraith also reported some five months later that at a comparable meeting in New Delhi, not one of those present objected to the admission of Communist China to the United Nations.

In March 1963, when Averell Harriman relinquished his post as Assistant Secretary for Far Eastern Affairs to Roger Hilsman, he gave his successor some interesting advice, according to the latter's account in *To Move a Nation*. Hilsman reports Harriman telling him he should immediately begin "to think about laying the groundwork for what the President might do about China policy in his second administration."

That Kennedy himself was hoping to make a new approach is also suggested from various sources. In spite of his continued acceptance of the need to contain any further Communist expansion in Asia and his political caution in sustaining the basic Eisenhower-Dulles policies, he clearly wanted to break new ground in our approach to Communist China. Schlesinger implies this in *A Thousand Days*, and Sorensen does so even more explicitly in *Kennedy*.

At his last press conference, on November 11, 1963, the President expressed a point of view significantly differing from that of his predecessors in the 1950s. Asked about various proposals that were being advanced for a possible resumption of trade with Communist China, he said that in view of the policy China was currently pursuing no such step was being planned. However, he then went on to say: "If the Red Chinese indicate a desire to live at peace with the United States, with other countries surrounding it, then quite obviously the United States would reappraise its policies. We are not wedded to a policy of hostility to Red China."

A month later—after the President's death—Assistant Secretary Hilsman made an important speech seeming to reflect the advice Harriman had given him in respect to laying the groundwork for a new policy toward China. He did not call for any abrupt or immediate changes. He scored the aggressive attitude that Peking was exhibiting and what he called its paranoid view of the world. He declared that the United States had a responsibility to prevent the Chinese Communists from attacking or subverting their neighbors, and he reaffirmed our commitment to defend Formosa. But he then went on to say, in repudiation of the old doctrine of John Foster Dulles, that we had no good reason to believe that the Communist regime in China was a passing phase. The hope for the future, Hilsman declared, lay in the gradual evolution of more moderate forces within the existing government; the United States should seek to encourage rather than block their growth.

"We pursue toward Communist China," he said, trying to give a new perspective to our attitude by paraphrasing a classic canon of the past, "a policy of the open door; we are determined to keep the door open to the possibility of change and not to slam it shut against any development which might advance our national good, serve the free world, and benefit the people of China."

Hilsman's speech attracted nationwide attention. The Committee of One Million, reflecting all the old prejudices, promptly attacked it as marking out a road that could only lead to appeasement. At the other extreme, some liberals criticized it as not actually promising anything new. More generally, however, editorial writers and other commentators were highly approving of this effort to substitute rationality for emotion in an attempt to break through the walls of suspicion and mistrust that so completely separated Communist China and the United States. They praised Hilsman's speech for its plea for a dispassionate stocktaking in our approach to the most vital problem standing in the way of Far Eastern peace and stability.

Before this talk was given, during an earlier White House discussion over a possible shift in our China policy, President Kennedy made a comment, as recorded by Theodore Sorensen, which in retrospect has a special poignancy. " 'And let's face it,' he said to me half in humor and half in despair," Sorensen writes, " 'that's a subject for the second term.' "

Neither his second term nor his reappraisal of China policy was to materialize. As a consequence of his assassination on November 22, 1963, only eleven days after his press conference statement that we were not wedded to a policy of hostility toward Red China, Kennedy was to have no chance to implement the more conciliatory approach he envisaged.

13

Behind Vietnam

DURING THE WHOLE of President Johnson's term of office, from his succession to Kennedy to his withdrawal as a candidate for reelection in 1968, Far Eastern developments bulked larger in the American consciousness than at any time since the Korean war. Vietnam was of course the agonizing issue that absorbed national attention, that so cruelly divided the country and had such tragic consequences at home and abroad. But behind Vietnam was Communist China.

Ever since Dean Acheson declared in 1949 that "the United States does not intend to permit further expansion of Communist domination on the continent of Asia or in the Southeast Asia area," China had loomed in the background. For whatever might be said of the imperialist ambitions of Soviet Russia or of any more generalized international conspiracy, Communism in Asia was primarily the People's Republic of China. This was the actuality in eastern Asia when Acheson had initially set forth China policy. Now in the late 1960s, as a consequence of the containment policy, American planes were flying bombing missions over North Vietnam and American combat forces were fighting desperately in South Vietnam's jungles and paddy fields.

The United States was still acting on the assumptions of the Cold War. Little consideration was given to the fragmentation of the Communist world or the attitudes of a restless Asia still in the grip of a new age's revolutionary forces. "It is of the greatest significance," Townsend Hoopes has written in his penetrating study *The Limits of Intervention*, "that the new perspectives did not materially alter the judgments of the men closest to President Johnson. The tenets of the Cold War were bred in the bone." Secretary Rusk, whose ideas and convictions were so firmly rooted in the Stalinist era, accepted unquestioningly the principles that had governed Secretary Acheson's stand in 1949. "It is just as essential," he stated in 1966, "to 'contain' Communist aggression in Asia as it was, and is, to 'contain' Communist aggression in Europe."

Ever since the Chinese revolution our Far Eastern policy had been directed toward this goal. The United States reacted decisively to the Communist assault in Korea; through the intervention of the Seventh Fleet it pledged its military strength to prevent a Communist takeover of Formosa; it promptly extended aid to India when the Chinese attacked on the Tibetan border; and it had provided military assistance first to the French, and then to independent Cambodia, Laos, and South Vietnam, to combat the forces of Communism in Southeast Asia. We had also taken the lead in creating SEATO as an anti-Communist alliance to forestall what Secretary Dulles called the twin dangers of the Peking government's open military aggression and its fomentation of subversive activities in neighboring countries.

All of this has been recapitulated to stress the fact that the People's Republic of China as the embodiment of the Communist menace, whether Peking was believed to be acting independently or at the beck of Moscow, has in effect determined the course of American policy in the Far East for the past two decades. Instead of charting our own course, with positive affirmation, we have reacted almost automatically along predetermined lines to every move China has made, or seemingly threatened to make, in challenging our interests in Asia.

"We are in Vietnam," as John Fairbank has most concisely stated, "because of the Chinese Communist revolution."

As we have seen, President Kennedy consistently carried forward the basic Eisenhower-Dulles containment policy even though he may have privately believed it had become too negative and rigid. He modified it somewhat in promoting the neutralization of Laos rather than trying to maintain that unhappy country as a bastion of freedom, but he was as determined as his predecessor to hold the line in Vietnam, with little concern whether the forces operative there were those of Communist conquest or revolutionary nationalism. "China is so large, looms so high just beyond the frontier," he said in easy assumption of the menace from the north. Kennedy saw a resurgent, aggressive China that, might well, unless it were rigorously held in check, upset the entire balance of power in eastern Asia.

So too President Johnson. In 1964 he repeatedly affirmed that the United States had to support South Vietnam because in the interest of the free world, it was committed to helping our Asian friends resist an ambitious China. True enough, he also said this same year that "we are not about to send American boys nine or ten thousand miles away from home to do what Asian boys ought to be doing themselves." But this was during a presidential election; politics demanded that he mask what he was already planning. His underlying attitude found more forthright expression in the unequivocal statement that "we will not permit the independent nations of the East to be swallowed by Communist conquest."

After his election for a second term, Johnson elaborated on this theme. "Over this war—and all Asia—is another reality: the deepening shadow of Communist China," he said on April 7, 1965. "The rulers in Hanoi are urged on by Peking. . . . The contest in Vietnam is part of a wider pattern of aggressive purpose." A month later he reverted to the idea that the real target of Communist China was "not merely South Vietnam; it is Asia." Stating that Peking's leaders hoped to discredit America's ability to thwart their goal of supremacy in Asia, Johnson asserted that "in this domination they shall never succeed." Other administration officials were of a like mind. Vice-President Hubert Humphrey said the threat to world peace was a militant aggressive Asian Communism, with its headquarters in Peking. Secretary of Defense Robert McNamara declared that if the United States and its free-world allies failed to meet this challenge in Southeast Asia, "we will inevitably have to confront it later under even more disadvantageous conditions."

Even more pronounced were the views, as a private citizen, of Richard Nixon. He declared on March 15, 1965, that the Vietnam war was not one between the North and South, or between the United States and North Vietnam, but a war between the United States and Communist China. "A United States defeat in Vietnam," Nixon said, "means a Chinese Communist victory."

This emphasis on China as fundamentally accounting for American intervention in Vietnam was carried to its utmost extreme in a news conference Secretary Rusk held on October 12, 1967. To explain why our security was endangered, he raised the frightening specter that within a decade or two there could be a billion Chinese on the mainland, armed with nuclear weapons—and no certainty about what their attitude toward the rest of Asia might be. American interests, and ultimately our national security, he warned, would be gravely jeopardized should China succeed in establishing Communist control over those areas in Southeast Asia that the United States was endeavoring to protect by its stand in Vietnam.

"These are vitally important matters to us, who are both a Pacific and an Atlantic power," Rusk said. "So we have a tremendous stake in the ability of the free nations of Asia to live in peace. . . . That does not mean that we ourselves have nominated ourselves to be the policemen of all Asia. . . . But we have a part; we have accepted a share, and we have accepted that share as part of the vital national interest of the United States."

This was a startling statement. It implied that in Rusk's view everything else was subordinate to our protection of the stakes of American power. They were threatened by Communist China; the urgent, inescapable point of defense was Vietnam. By the curious process of asserting and reasserting the importance of our "share" in maintaining Far Eastern security, it had become a matter of vital national interest for which we should be ready to go to war.

In his critical account of Vietnam, *The Abuse of Power*, Theodore Draper has written that there is something "hallucinatory about the theory that Communist China is the real enemy in Vietnam." Many other academic authorities and government experts feel very much the same way. They see little reason to believe that either currently or in the near future Communist China could actually command the power that would make it the menace Rusk conjured up so fearfully.

Whatever the reality of either Chinese intentions or Chinese power, American policy in Southeast Asia grew out of a conviction that China was the real enemy. Sometimes greater stress has been placed on the aid Soviet Russia has given North Vietnam, sometimes on vague suspicions of world Communism's support for Hanoi, but official attitudes have been more concretely fashioned by fears of the imperialist ambitions of the Chinese People's Republic.

Peking's aid and assistance to Ho Chi Minh's regime, to the Vietminh and then to the Vietcong, has been consistent and unwavering since 1949. China has just as regularly assailed the United States for interfering in Vietnam's internal affairs and warned that there are limits to Chinese restraint. "China and the Democratic Republic of Vietnam," an article in the *Peking Review* stated on August 10, 1964, "are fraternal neighbors closely related like the lips and the teeth. The Chinese people cannot be expected to look on with folded arms in the face of any aggression against the Democratic Republic of Vietnam." After United States planes commenced their bombing raids on the North, Premier Chou En-lai repeated these warnings and Foreign Minister Chen Yi stated categorically that should American combat forces attack North Vietnam, China would be driven to fight. "We have made all the preparations," Chen Yi declared. "We do not want to send troops into Southeast Asia beyond our frontiers. . . . But if the countries which are our friends ask for help, we will not fail to do it."

Nevertheless, Communist China did not intervene in Vietnam. Apart from labor battalions, it sent no troops or "volunteers" across the frontier. Its military assistance has perhaps in the long run been more important than that of Russia; its political influence in Hanoi has certainly been very great. But unlike its course in Korea, Peking has stood carefully apart from more active participation in the war.

This restraint cast a shadow over the Johnson Administration's contention that the United States had no alternative to fighting in Vietnam to protect vital national interests threatened by the aggressive Chinese Communists. Washington found it increasingly difficult to explain our policy when Peking so studiously refrained from hostilities. To sustain an action that originally grew out of a pragmatic political decision that the United States must at all costs contain Chinese Communist expansion in Southeast Asia as a threat to national security, administration spokesmen now felt compelled to cast about for additional explanations to bolster the case for continuing the Vietnam war. These new explanations constituted what a skeptical English observer has called President Johnson's "thundering moralisms."

The thesis now emphasized was that the United States had to keep faith with its obligations under the Southeast Asia Collective Defense Treaty and could not honorably retreat from the responsibility it had assumed to defend Vietnamese freedom and democracy. We had accepted a binding moral commitment to safeguard the lives and safety of the people from their Communist enemies; we were in Vietnam because we had promises to keep. Having once undertaken to protect Vietnam, and pledged our prestige and honor to this undertaking, the United States, whatever its own interests, could not honorably draw back. "We will not retreat from the obligations of freedom and security in Asia," President Johnson sonorously declared on August 12, 1966.

Rusk advanced all possible arguments for staying the course. Asked on one occasion by a group of British editors whether the United States was fighting in Vietnam to contain Communist aggression or to defend that country's independence, the Secretary of State sought the best of both worlds by indicating that these goals were but different sides of the same coin. "I don't know," he said, "that there is a choice between these objectives."

There were appeals to patriotism. Senator Richard B. Russell, chairman of the Senate Armed Services Committee, admitted that intervention in Vietnam had been a grave political mistake and had no strategic justification whatsoever in terms of national security. But that did not mean we should back down. "The United States does have a commitment in South Vietnam," he said in June 1965. "The flag is there, United States honor and prestige are there. And, most important of all, United States soldiers are there."

Needless to say, as more and more people, in Congress and without, questioned the original reasons for intervention and grew increasingly skeptical of these moral justifications, the public became greatly confused over what the United States was really doing in Vietnam. If national security was not actually endangered under the looming shadow of Communist China, could our professed ends possibly justify the means we were employing for their attainment?

In Vietnam itself during this period which led to the disillusionment of the Johnson days, events proceeded along that fateful course that, beginning with President Eisenhower's conditional promise of aid to Ngo Dinh Diem's regime in October 1954, had resulted a decade later in full-scale military intervention. The gradual increase in economic and military support during the Kennedy years, with establishment of a military mission that grew from 800 to 16,000 men; the decision of President Johnson to bomb the North and send combat troops to South Vietnam; and the consequent escalation of the war until half a million American troops were fighting South Vietnam's battles—all this is a familiar though still confused story.

So too is that of the growth of popular opposition to the war, which the shifting and sometimes contradictory statements coming from Washington could never satisfactorily explain. A steadily increasing segment of the public finally came to regard our intervention as politically and strategically unwarranted, totally unjustified from the point of view of the national interest, and above all, morally indefensible. Never before in all their history had the American people endured such a frustrating experience. As the military victory so confidently proclaimed on innumerable occasions eluded their grasp, the United States forces found themselves ever more deeply mired in the Vietnam morass.

With so much of the countryside laid waste by our bombing attacks, an incalculable loss of life among the innocent and longsuffering Vietnamese people, and our own casualties steadily mounting, the war became in Senator Ernest Gruening of Alaska's telling phrase, "no more than a bloody and wanton stalemate." Nor were the frustrations ended for a divided people here at home when in 1968 President Johnson finally acknowledged that a military victory was impossible and began his desperate efforts to extricate the American forces. It was no easy task to reverse the train of events and discover an "honorable" path to peace.

Vietnam has inspired a vast literature of defense, explication, and condemnation. Our involvement will long remain a matter of embittered controversy. But whatever may be said of the "interlocking" of Vietnam and the multifaceted problem of China, this narrative in following its own course must necessarily keep its focus on Sino-American relations in and of themselves. These remained highly strained against the background of war in Vietnam. And this in turn suggests that entirely apart from what might immediately happen in Southeast Asia, failure to resolve the deep tensions between the United States and Communist China might lead to further Vietnams, if not a direct clash between the two rival powers.

Although the Johnson Administration at least initially maintained that the threat of Communist China was primarily responsible for our intervention in Vietnam, no apparent efforts were made, so far as this was indeed the case, to get at the heart of the matter. Our established policy of avoiding all contacts with the Peking government that might suggest diplomatic recognition of it blocked any direct approaches to seek out a path to peace in Southeast Asia. We might try to talk with the Soviet Union, also so busily supporting North Vietnam with arms and ammunition, but not with the Chinese People's Republic.

Peking's warnings against our advancing into North Vietnam were simply met by counterwarnings. In reply to the statements of Chou En-lai and Chen Yi, the President's Special Assistant on National Security Affairs, McGeorge Bundy, stated on television that Communist China would be making a bad mistake if it became involved in the Vietnam war, for it would find that unlike the situation that had prevailed in Korea, Chinese planes or other military forces would not enjoy a "privileged sanctuary." On at least two subsequent occasions Secretary of State Rusk reenforced this warning. While, on the other hand, assurances may have been conveyed to Peking through the ambassadors' meeting in Warsaw that we had no designs on China itself, the United States did not go beyond this in any direct discussions or negotiations.

Asked at a news conference on June 23, 1964, whether any attempt had been made to talk with the Chinese about the broader dangers inherent in the Vietnam conflict, President Johnson said only that "they are aware of our attitude and they have no doubt of our policy or our position."

Two years later, when the United States was so much more deeply involved in Vietnam, the question came up again. Senator Mike Mansfield, who had earlier stated that he did not believe Hanoi would be able to negotiate a settlement without at least the tacit consent of China, suggested on June 16, 1966, that the United States initiate direct negotiations with Peking on the foreign minister level to consider the problem of peace in Southeast Asia. His proposal awoke no response in the State Department. It perhaps shared the views of Senator Everett Dirksen. In reply to Mansfield the Republican minority leader stated that for the United States to initiate a conference "with the sinner" would be a "humiliating experience." Convinced that only a military victory in Vietnam would contain China's ambitions, the Johnson Administration apparently saw little value—and little likelihood of success—in trying to talk with its militant government.

To a considerable extent this unwillingness to make any direct approaches to Communist China would appear to have been owing to the intransigent attitude of Secretary of State Rusk. In so strongly maintaining that our commitment to defend Vietnam was vital to our national security, he apparently did not believe that our stand should be affected by the risk it might entail of a broader conflict. If the United States allowed its anxiety over how Peking might react to govern its policy, Rusk said on one occasion, we would soon find "a Red China much more voracious and much more dangerous." He was asked at a Senate hearing on February 18, 1966, for his views on the menace of China as compared with that of prewar Nazi Germany. Acknowledging that there were differences in the current situation in Asia and the threat once posed by Hitler, Rusk nevertheless stated that he also saw "enormous similarities."

He airily dismissed the idea that self-defense could anywhere enter into Peking's calculations. Premier Chou En-lai had complained to Edgar Snow that the presence of American troops in Korea, the Formosan Straits, and Vietnam was a direct threat to China's security. But the Secretary of State could not see any possible justification for Peking's being fearful of American policy. He was so certain—in undoubted sincerity—that our assistance to the anti-Communist countries on China's periphery was solely in the interest of peace that it was impossible for him to conceive how the Chinese could otherwise interpret our actions. Rusk could not envisage the possibility that the United States might have taken actions that to the Chinese appeared to be imperialistic; he saw only what he considered Peking's insatiable ambition to drive the Americans out of eastern Asia in order to establish their own dominant rule.

He stood steadfastly by the policies he had advocated as Assistant Secretary of State during the 1950s, that is, unrelenting opposition to the Chinese People's Republic and unwavering support for the Republic of China on Taiwan. In explaining his position early in January 1965, Rusk employed words that could hardly have paralleled more closely those used by John Foster Dulles eight years earlier. "We think," he said in reference to the Chinese Communists, "that anything in terms of trade expansion, or recognition or admission to the United Nations that tends to encourage them that their policy is paying dividends is not in the interest of getting peace established in the Pacific."

As for Nationalist China, Rusk still accepted Chiang Kai-shek's government as rightfully that of all China, and declared that the United States would never abandon its people to "Communist tyranny." "We recognize the Republic of China," he said decisively on June 27, 1966, "as the Government of China with all the implications that go with it." Visiting Taipei shortly afterward, he reassured the generalissimo that "we are constant in our relations and in our alliance to the Republic of China."

While President Johnson fully backed his Secretary of State, Rusk's insistence on maintaining an attitude carried over from the Stalinist era did not command universal support within the State Department. "Mr. Rusk has inexplicably clung to views of the Chinese Communists that seem to be those of a zealot," James C. Thomson, Jr., who had recently resigned as assistant to the Assistant Secretary for Far Eastern Affairs, wrote in the *Atlantic Monthly* in October 1967. "He has singlehandedly obstructed recurrent attempts within the Administration to bring about a modification of our rigidity on China."

The one exception to the lack of communications between Washington and Peking was the ambassadorial meetings at Warsaw. They did continue, subject to frequent adjournments, and provided Secretary Rusk with an answer to those critics who deplored his resistance to more direct contacts. He often referred to these talks—"Here let me clear away a myth," was his usual opening—in defending himself against the charge of being wholly unwilling to talk with the Chinese Communists. The ambassadors had met no less than 120 times, he said in April 1966, and made the claim that through these meetings the United States "has perhaps had more discussions on serious matters with Peiping than any government having diplomatic relations . . . with the possible exception of Soviet Russia."

The talks in Warsaw, generally held in a hunting lodge provided by the Polish government, were conducted in virtual secrecy and under the most formal conditions. It was customary for the American and Chinese delegates to enter the building through separate entrances, escorted by Polish protocol officers, and carefully avoid any but the necessary official contacts. From all accounts, the atmosphere was invariably one of frozen suspicion and mutual hostility.

For several years every attempt to break through this wall of distrust and make some headway had invariably foundered, as had the original talks in 1955, on the problem of the status of Formosa. The two sides' opposing views on this issue seemed an insuperable obstacle to any progress toward accommodation along other lines. Then, by the early 1960s, an interesting reversal in their respective approaches had taken place. Peking had originally expressed a willingness to explore other issues without imposing as a precondition American withdrawal from Formosa, and Washington had insisted that China renounce the use of force in that area as an essential prerequisite to taking up any other questions. Now, a decade later, the United States was willing to bypass the Formosa problem in an effort to come to agreement on such peripheral issues as the cultural exchanges it had formerly rejected, but Communist China demanded American "surrender" of Formosa before its envoy would talk of anything else.

Peking made known its new stance in a statement issued as early as 1961. "It is better to keep Sino-American relations frozen and stalemated for many years," this document read. "All differences must be settled at the same time if a settlement is expected; that is, the U.S. withdrawal from Taiwan, formal recognition of the new China, the exchange of reporters, and so on, must be settled together." In supporting this approach, Communist propaganda declared that America's imperialist ambitions gave "the lie to its own professions of willingness to better relations with China." An article in the *Peking Review* stressed not only our stand in defending Formosa but our support for Chiang Kai-shek in his aim "to harass the mainland and even prepare for 'an invasion.' "

The United States for its part naturally held Communist China wholly responsible for the lack of any progress. Whatever our ambassador brought up, Secretary Rusk said in April 1964, the Chinese envoy brushed it aside with the reiterated demand that the United States hand over the Formosan people to Communist control. We rejected this demand on the twofold ground, the Secretary of State continued, that in the first place they were not ours to surrender, and in the second, because we didn't think anyone could accept it. "At that point," he concluded, "the conversation then goes into the record-playing business."

For all their apparent futility, the Warsaw meetings at times served a useful purpose. In utilizing them in 1962 to let the Chinese Communists know directly where the United States stood on the neutralization of Laos, to inform them during the Formosan crisis that same year that we had no intention of backing Chiang Kai-shek in any attack on the mainland, and later in trying to reassure them that our intervention in Vietnam in no way threatened China, Presidents Kennedy and Johnson were able to make their views more authoritatively known in Peking than might otherwise have been possible. In these three instances the ambassadorial contacts may well have been instrumental in preventing Peking from making dangerous miscalculations.

But, in what one commentator described as their "ritualistic sterility," the negotiations did not dig any deeper. They did not come to grips with the basic problems of the Sino-American rivalry behind the Vietnam war.

14

The Close
of the Johnson Administration

ON OCTOBER 16, 1964, a new element was introduced into the balance of power in the Far East: on that day the Chinese Communists successfully detonated an atomic bomb.

This dramatic event was not entirely unexpected. The Peking government had refused to sign the test ban treaty and was known to be concentrating on the development of a nuclear capacity. Toward the close of September, Secretary of State Rusk had warned that a first nuclear explosion would probably occur in the near future. Nevertheless, the actuality of the bomb could hardly fail to have a great impact on China's Asian neighbors and on the whole Western world.

In a press conference following announcement of the bomb test, President Johnson greeted the news calmly. He said that it was no surprise, and while it constituted a great tragedy for the Chinese people and did not serve the cause of peace, he did not see any need to alter American policy.

A few extremists felt differently. In an article in the *Saturday Evening Post* the columnist Stewart Alsop called for prompt military action in attacking the Chinese bomb sites. Somewhat later Representative L. Mendel Rivers, chairman of the House Armed Services Committee, declared that the United States should take the risk of an air strike to destroy China's nuclear capacity before it was too late. However, neither the administration, the Congress, nor the American public showed the slightest indication of favoring what would have been a preventive war.

The Peking government confidently boasted of its bomb, and was especially proud that it was produced in spite of the withdrawal of all Russian aid. "This is a major achievement of the Chinese people in their struggle to increase the national defense capability and oppose the United States policy of nuclear blackmail and nuclear threats," the official announcement stated. But in the light of so many earlier statements that the atomic bomb was actually a paper tiger, an editorial in the *People's Daily* repeated that the real safeguard for China's security was not the bomb but still remained the "ever-victorious thinking" of Mao Tse-tung and the leadership of "the glorious, great, and correct Communist Party." "To tell you the truth, Mr. Johnson," this editorial continued, "China was never cowed by your threats when it had no nuclear weapons."

Simultaneously with announcement of the bomb Premier Chou En-lai issued another statement. His government, he said, "solemnly declares that at no time and in no circumstances will China be the first to use nuclear weapons." Going further, he proposed that with China now a member of the nuclear club, the powers should hold a summit conference to consider the complete prohibition and destruction of all nuclear weapons. Somewhat later, he made the suggestion that the United States and Communist China should themselves conclude a formal agreement that neither power would be the first to use atomic bombs against the other.

The United States showed no interest in these proposals. Dean Rusk promptly characterized them as no more than propaganda and a smokescreen to cover the Peking government's refusal to sign the test ban treaty. Other official announcements stressed that without adequate safeguards and controls, China's proposed approach to arms limitation was meaningless. President Johnson was even more scornful of what he interpreted as an effort on Peking's part to promote its own aggressive ambitions. It fools no one, he said decisively, "when it offers to trade away its first small accumulation of nuclear power against the mighty arsenals of those who limit Communist China's ambitions." The logic in rejecting any negotiations with Peking in existing circumstances may have appeared irrefutable, but the question was left open of how, without such talks, any effective halt could be brought to the still further proliferation of atomic weapons.

For all the relative calm that greeted China's first step toward becoming a nuclear power, the American people could not entirely escape a new sense of foreboding as they accepted the cold harsh fact that their Asian rival could actually produce an atomic bomb. They had long since realized that the Chinese Communists had built up a powerful fighting force on the mainland. They could not forget Korea. Yet they had felt secure in their belief that China could not wage war overseas and could not itself directly threaten America. The bomb changed all this. Moreover, in spite of limited resources, the Chinese Communists gave every evidence of a determination to build up an effective nuclear striking power as rapidly as possible. In succeeding years they carried out further bomb tests at a far more rapid pace than the Western nations had anticipated. The United States realized that it would have to take this new development into consideration in further strengthening its own security system. The danger of a Chinese nuclear attack seemed wholly hypothetical on many counts—nuclear power has its own built-in limitations, as postwar history has indicated—but here was a new factor in Sino-American relations that would have been unimaginable only a few years earlier.

The potential danger in Communist China's possession of the bomb was in no way lessened in Washington's eyes by new signs of its grandiose ambitions. Wholly apart from continued aid to North Vietnam (even though it refrained from active intervention), Peking was again trumpeting its determination to support revolutionary wars of liberation wherever they might break out in resistance to the world imperialistic forces headed by the United States. One demonstration of this belligerent attitude was the widely publicized manifesto issued by Defense Minister Lin Piao on September 3, 1965.

Entitled "Long Live the Victory of the People's War," this inflammatory document was an all-embracing declaration of Chinese Communist philosophy—which the more fearful compared with Hitler's Mein Kampf. Lin Piao advanced the theory that the depressed rural areas of the world—Asia, Africa, and Latin America—were in revolt against the cities, as represented by Europe and North America. Here was an irrepressible conflict. The submerged people were fighting from their revolutionary bases against the monopolistic power of capitalist imperialism. Lin saw the United States as the leader of the world's reactionary forces, having stepped into the shoes of German, Italian, and Japanese Fascism, and all those engaged in wars for freedom and independence should direct the spearhead of their struggle against America.

"The United States imperialist policy of seeking world dominion," he declared, "makes it possible for people throughout the world to unite all the forces that can be united and form the broadest possible united front for a converging attack on U.S. imperialism." And further in this striking manifesto Lin confidently predicted that "U.S. imperialism, like a mad bull dashing from place to place, will finally be burned to ashes in the blazing fires of the people's wars it has provoked by its own actions."

Later in this same month of September 1965, Foreign Minister Chen Yi directly charged the United States with threatening China itself with war. But his country was fully prepared. "If the U.S. imperialists are determined to launch a war of aggression against us," he said at a news conference in Peking, "they are welcome to come sooner, to come as early as tomorrow."

In the face of these bellicose statements the policy makers in the Johnson Administration, as previously those in the Kennedy Administration, were confirmed in their view that there should be no softening in the American attitude toward the Chinese Communists. "We should not encourage them," to quote a further statement by Dean Rusk that was once again so much in the tradition of John Foster Dulles, "by rewarding them for a policy which is contrary to the prospects of peace."

One battlefield for implementing our policy, as it had been for so many years, was the United Nations. The technique President Kennedy had adopted to keep out Communist China remained in force, but by 1965 the situation was considerably changed from that of earlier years. The general alignments were the same. Great Britain, France, and India were still the leading non-Communist nations supporting the admission of the Chinese People's Republic. Secretary General U Thant also favored it. The United States, as always, headed the opposition, and it was prepared to exercise all possible pressure on its client states to maintain the status quo. What was now different was that Communist China had taken the stand that it was interested in membership only if the United Nations was completely reformed.

Early in 1965 an article in the *Peking Review* suggested this new attitude in commenting on Indonesia's recent withdrawal from the UN. The world organization was revealed as no longer "sacred and inviolable," this article said. "President Sukarno has kicked the backside of this tiger." Some months later Foreign Minister Chen Yi took it upon himself to outline the conditions under which his government would accept membership. The United Nations should not only oust "the Chiang Kai-shek clique," he asserted, but it should cancel its earlier resolutions condemning

China and North Korea as aggressors and in their stead adopt one condemning America for its aggressions in Taiwan.

The Assembly paid little attention to such diatribes from Peking. When the customary resolution for admitting the Chinese Communists and expelling the Nationalists was submitted (since 1963 Albania rather than Soviet Russia had become its sponsor), the issue was debated with customary acerbity. The newly appointed American delegate, Arthur J. Goldberg, was, as Stevenson had been, a rather reluctant proponent of our official policy, but he nevertheless took the offensive in declaring that Communist China's belligerency was the antithesis of everything the United Nations stood for. Singling out what he called Lin Piao's "incredible manifesto," he cited it as evidence of Peking's underlying attitude and declared that the Assembly could not forsake its responsibility to demonstrate "to those who use violence that violence does not pay."

The Assembly voted on November 17. It first adopted a resolution that the representation issue was an "important question" requiring a two-thirds majority. The count was 56 to 49, with eleven abstentions. Then taking up the Albanian resolution for substituting the Communists for the Nationalists, it duly rejected it—but by what was actually a tie vote of 47 to 47, with twenty abstentions. This was by far the closest vote since the issue had arisen fifteen years earlier and revealed a startling erosion in the American position.

The Chinese Communists hailed the "humiliating setback" for the United States in the narrow margin of its victory but at the same time stated that the vote revealed once again that the United Nations was an imperialist-dominated organization. The United States might succeed in keeping out the Chinese People's Republic for 1,000 years or 10,000 years, the *People's Daily* declared defiantly, "without harming China one iota."

While the Johnson Administration was winning this somewhat dubious victory in the United Nations, criticism of the inflexibility of American policy toward China began to come more out in the open than ever before. The political climate of the mid-1960s, as first shown in 1963, differed markedly from that of earlier years. The old China bloc had disintegrated. As the moderator of one roundtable meeting put it, China had for sixteen years been a taboo topic under the continuing influence of McCarthyism (the public, Russell Baker wrote in the *New York Times*, "loyally refused to think about the place"), but it could now be discussed with a freedom heretofore impossible.

The American people, their attention fastened on Vietnam, were very confused over what was happening in Communist China. The Great Proletarian Cultural Revolution whereby Mao Tse-tung sought to revive the militant spirit of Communism was already beginning to create havoc on the mainland. The activities of China's missions abroad in fomenting revolution in Africa and Latin America also raised new and disturbing questions. Public opinion surveys published in 1966 as a result of extensive studies for the Council on Foreign Relations reflected many cross currents. They revealed that among those persons interviewed who knew at least something of Chinese affairs, a majority still opposed either recognition of the Peking government or its admission to the United Nations, but most of them favored Sino-American negotiations that might ease the tensions exacerbated by the Vietnam war.

Sentiment was growing in business circles for some modification of the trade embargo. The increasing commerce between Communist China and such nations as Great Britain, Canada, France, and Japan awoke all the old ideas of the potentialities of the China market and renewed previously expressed disappointment that the United States was excluded from this trade while our rivals were making the most of it. The San Francisco Area World Trade Association forwarded a report to Congress in January 1965 urging a change in official policy. The existing attitude toward Communist China was unrealistic, this report stated, and new contacts should be made that might lead to a "normalization" of commercial relations.

Impatience with our negative policy also found expression in a growing number of newspaper editorials and magazine articles. They called for a reappraisal of Far Eastern objectives and of our methods of achieving them. Occasionally, as in one article in the *Reader's Digest* with the inflammatory title "We Must Stop Red China Now!" the demand was voiced for a more assertive stand, but generally these articles reflected the concept of the "open door" in our relations with China to which Roger Hilsman had given new currency in his talk in 1963. Among other periodicals, the *Nation*, the *New Republic*, and the *Christian Century* favored closer contacts with Peking, but this approach was by no means limited to the liberal press. Several articles in the *Saturday Evening Post*, including one by Arnold Toynbee entitled "Speaking Out: We Must Woo Red China," took much the same line in criticizing current policy and urging a more conciliatory stand on the United Nations issue, trade, and cultural relations.

Many of these critics expressed the view that in its obsession with Communism born of the Cold War pressures of the 1950s the United

States was overlooking the changing political structure in eastern Asia. Walter Lippmann wrote that the old concepts of spheres of influence represented the only pragmatic approach in world affairs. The Johnson-Rusk policy ignored "the cataclysmic consequences of the collapse of empires" in his opinion, and the United States should be prepared to acknowledge, as it had in the case of Soviet Russia, that Communist China also had a legitimate right to a sphere of influence.

The political scientist Hans Morgenthau emphasized the confusion in our policy resulting from equating the power of the new China with Communism. The fundamental fact, he said, "is not that China has a Communist Government but that she has resurrected her traditional role as the predominant power in Asia." Donald S. Zagoria, then of the Research Institute on Communist Affairs at Columbia University, said in the *New York Times Magazine* that without condoning violence, the United States should accept Communist China as a great power and adapt itself to "a reasonable amount of Chinese influence in Asia."

Other writers revived the question of whether our program of military containment and political isolation was the real answer to preventing the further spread of the influence of Communist China. In contradiction of the conventional wisdom, some suggested that an independent Vietnam, even though controlled by the Communist forces of Ho Chi Minh, might prove to be a more effective protection for American interests in Southeast Asia than a client state that could not command popular support among the Vietnamese people.

A general underlying theme in these articles was that the United States should follow a more moderate and pragmatic course. Rather than continuing to maintain the political isolation of the Peking government, we should make every effort to bring it back into the mainstream of world affairs. Accepting Communist China for what it is, ran the new arguments, our policy should be directed toward trying to strengthen the forces of moderation within that country as the most promising means of persuading Peking to forswear force as an instrument of foreign policy.

More important than these articles were a number of speeches on the floor of the Senate. Fulbright notably set the tone for a new approach to the Far East in an address as early as March 25, 1964, which was subsequently published in paperback and attained a wide circulation under the title *Old Myths and New Realities*. He covered the whole range of foreign affairs, but in relating Vietnam to the basic problem of our relations with Communist China he specifically called for a complete reorientation in our thinking.

"We are committed with respect to China and other areas in Asia to inflexible policies of long standing from which we hesitate to depart because of the attribution.to these policies of an aura of mystical sanctity," Fulbright declared. While their reexamination had long been prevented by the fear of government officials that such a review would arouse a vehement public outcry, he now felt that the time had come to take these risks. It would be extremely useful, he said, "if we could introduce an element of flexibility, or, more precisely of the capacity to be flexible, into our relations with Communist China." He stated that under existing circumstances he did not favor any immediate change in respect either to recognition or representation in the United Nations, but believed that efforts should be made to draw the Peking government into new East-West agreements on trade, cultural exchanges, and the limitation of arms.

Reminiscent of the situation in the 1950s when the Republican opposition to any concessions in dealing with the Chinese Communists helped to freeze our policy into such a rigid mold, the more conservative members of that party currently in Congress again took a strong stand against any shift in policy. But, somewhat ironically, they were now not only supporting a Democratic administration, but one that was under attack by the liberal members of its own constituency. More royalist than the king, the Republicans were ready to uphold President Johnson in maintaining an unyielding stand against any moves that might suggest appeasement.

Prominent among them was Richard Nixon, who in April 1964 had just returned from a Far Eastern tour made in the interests of the Pepsi Cola Company. He advocated strengthening our policy toward Communist activities in Asia, and applying this doctrine to Vietnam, strongly urged that the United States should encourage the South Vietnamese forces, regardless of the risks entailed, to follow enemy troops in "hot pursuit" into North Vietnam and Laos. Nixon was upheld in this position by a Republican leader in the House, Melvin Laird, who at the time was chairman of the House Republican Conference. The Johnson Administration, the future Republican President's future Secretary of Defense said emphatically, would come perilously close to losing all G.O.P. support if it did not make clear that its policy was directed toward a complete victory over Communist insurgency in Southeast Asia.

The attacks on the Johnson-Rusk policies, not only in relation to Vietnam but also Communist China, gathered increasing headway. Among those liberal Democratic senators who by 1966 were calling for a new approach to Sino-American relations were, in addition to Fulbright, such party leaders as Mike Mansfield, Hubert Humphrey, and Robert Kennedy. Also, less well known at the time, Senator Eugene McCarthy of Minnesota and Senator George McGovern of South Dakota became outspoken advocates of closer relations with Peking. "We must be prepared for rebuffs, insults, and misinterpretation," McGovern realistically said in one speech. "But with enough patience, an imaginative policy aimed at drawing China into the family of nations should bear more fruit than a policy designed to isolate, antagonize and hamper her development."

The most thorough airing of over-all Far Eastern policy took place in a series of public hearings held by the Senate Foreign Relations Committee in March 1966. Against the background of what Senator Fulbright declared to be the danger that "China and America may be heading toward war with each other," these hearings had the primary purpose of educating the public. The committee invited a broad array of Far Eastern experts as witnesses, ranging widely from "hard liners" to "soft liners." However, a decisive majority, while still believing that the United States should maintain a resolute stand against aggression, were also convinced that we should seek to develop closer relations with the Chinese Communists. As Professor A. Doak Barnett of the East Asia Institute at Columbia University tellingly phrased it, American policy should be "containment without isolation."

The most forceful opponent of any change in our attitude was former Representative Walter Judd, whose views had not altered since he played such an influential role as one of the leaders of the congressional China bloc in the 1950s. The United States should make no concessions whatever, he declared, for they would only encourage Peking's aggressiveness. He ended his testimony: "Keep Red China on first base." Upholding Judd's intractable position, the conservative *National Review* demonstrated that in some quarters the spirit of McCarthyism still lingered on. It declared that the proponents of change were spokesmen of the Red China lobby and that the concept of containment without isolation was no more than "the now fashionable euphemism for appeasement."

Among the several experts who favored a new approach, John Fairbank was one of the most persuasive witnesses. Reviewing the long course of China's history, he heavily stressed the strength of those traditional forces that lay behind its people's ambition to attain a wholly independent world position. He dwelt on the natural craving of the new Peking government to attain the recognition that would balance a century of national humiliation. The whole thrust of his argument was that the United States should recognize the legitimacy of Chinese aspirations and invite China's participation in world affairs in a spirit of greater understanding. He recognized that "the Chinese are no more amenable to sweetness and light than other revolutionaries," and in encouraging them to join the United Nations, our attitude should still remain one of firmness against unreasonable concessions. But containment alone was a blind alley, in his view, unless it was allied with more constructive policies.

"In short," Fairbank stated, "my reading of history is that Peking's rulers shout aggressively out of manifold frustrations, that isolation intensifies their ailment and makes it self-perpetuating, and that we need to encourage international contact with China on many fronts."

Neither Johnson nor Rusk appeared to be overly impressed by this critical testimony before the Senate committee. The President reiterated his familiar thesis that Communist China and not the United States was responsible for the strained relations between the two countries. We were very anxious to have closer contacts, he said, but whenever this country made any such suggestion, Peking "hangs up the phone." He added that until there was some change in China's attitude, he doubted "if these academic discussions will do much more than satisfy a yearning for information."

The Secretary of State took much the same line. He emphasized that Washington was "in touch with Peiping all the time" and, as he had on previous occasions, complained somewhat plaintively that "unless you are prepared to surrender Formosa, there is nothing to talk about."

The administration could not, however, entirely ignore the attacks on its inflexibility. Before the year was over Rusk was to appoint a new advisory committee of China experts, some of whom had appeared at the Senate hearings. More important, the State Department moved cautiously to encourage Sino-American cultural exchanges. In addition to the news correspondents first accredited in 1957 (some of whom were still waiting in Hong Kong for Chinese visas), it was now ready to broaden the category of those eligible for travel in China to include scientists, physicians, scholars, and members of Congress whose visits might be considered in the public interest. On September 16, 1966, Rusk actually went so far as to say that a current goal of American policy was an exchange of visitors between China and the United States to help break through "the walls of isolation that Peking has built around itself."

Except for a scornful characterization of these overtures as "an indirect revelation of the U.S. as a paper tiger," Communist China made no response to them. Since our rejection of the initial invitation to American correspondents a decade earlier, Peking had barred all Americans from visiting China and withheld foreign travel permits from its own citizens. This time it was wholly by China's choice that the bamboo curtain remained lowered, with all cultural exchanges still rigidly barred.

In spite of this rebuff, the rhetoric of official statements relating to China reflected a less antagonistic attitude than in previous years. President Kennedy had set a new tone when he said on the eve of his assassination that the United States was not wedded to a policy of hostility. In spite of Vietnam, President Johnson was now to emphasize in his turn that "we do not believe in eternal enmity." On separate occasions he stated that the United States had no intention of denying China's legitimate needs for national security; that only through the free flow of ideas and people could China's isolation be ended and suspicion give way to mutual trust; that a misguided China should be encouraged toward a better understanding of the outside world; and that he hoped time would eventually permit a Sino-American reconciliation.

Although nothing was done to give concrete effect to these broad statements, the Johnson Administration was clearly following its predecessor's lead in abandoning the ancient thesis that Communism in China was only a passing phase. In facing the reality of the Peking government's strong hold on power, Washington appeared to be trying to encourage the more moderate elements within China to bring their country back into a rational relationship with the West.

Even Dean Rusk seemed to be bending somewhat before the winds of change. At a press conference he expressed the hope that the blunting of revolutionary militancy in China might some day make possible an era of good relations, but then he quickly drew back. "I don't want to speculate on that unduly," he said in answer to a further question, "because we see no indications from Peiping that they are prepared to be an active and a loyal member of the world community."

Communist China sometimes appeared to be speaking with two voices. Premier Chou En-lai was quoted as saying that America's pursuit of its imperialist ambitions was making war inevitable, and at the same time as asserting that peaceful coexistence was a realizable goal toward which China was working. In the *People's Daily* belligerent outbursts were followed by cautious hints of possible accommodation. But if China's attitude seemed to be uncertain, confused, and often contradictory in 1966, this had a very natural cause. In starting the Great Proletarian Cultural Revolution, Mao Tse-tung had set in motion forces that for a time looked as though they were getting beyond control.

The outside world watched with amazed incredulity as China found itself convulsed by the inexplicable events of these days. The intraparty strife and political turmoil, the rampaging attacks of the youthful Red Guards who were called upon to suppress bourgeois revisionism, the fierce battles of the wall posters, the demonstrations and counter-demonstrations among rival factions, the denunciations of veteran Communist leaders and the violent purging of many of them, the hysterical emphasis on the "Thought of Mao Tse-tung," the moving in of the army when the Red Guards got so completely out of hand—all combined to create a shifting, kaleidoscopic scene that was incomprehensible to the West.

Nor were the Chinese Communists' foreign policies any easier to understand than domestic developments as they waged their fierce polemical war against both the United States and Soviet Russia and appeared to glory in their isolation from the rest of the world. Moreover, their avowed campaign to stir up revolution among the underdeveloped nations was hardly as successful as they had hoped. In their fervor the Chinese agitators had sown the seeds of distrust. There were quarrels with Cuba, setbacks in Algeria, growing distrust in Ceylon. With their faith in Maoism shaken by the tactics that Communist China was pursuing both at home and abroad, a number of other Afro-Asia states turned away to follow a more independent course in their struggles against colonialism. A harassed Peking government recalled many of its ambassadors from their foreign posts.

When the question of Chinese representation in the United Nations came up once again in 1966, Secretary General U Thant declared that Communist China appeared to be suffering a "nervous breakdown." But he was still sympathetic. China, he said, had been treated "as an outcast, as an outlaw and as a culprit"; the duty of the international community was to nurse it back to health. But the United Nations remained skeptical of this prescription. The previous trend in favor of the Peking government was reversed when a majority of 57 to 46, with seventeen abstentions, voted against its admission.

"In just a year," correspondent Max Frankel wrote in the New York Times on November 3, 1966, "the upheavals inside China have changed its reputation from that of a formidable challenger of the United States throughout Asia and of the Soviet Union inside the Communist world to that of a hobbled giant riddled by dissent and thus incapable of sustained growth and self-assertion."

In these circumstances, so largely accounting for China's paranoiac mood, little opportunity existed for any constructive action looking toward the improvement of relations between Peking and Washington. The rhetoric of conciliation found no further practical expression after the rebuff of our unilateral suggestions for cultural exchange. In January 1968 even the Warsaw ambassadorial talks were indefinitely adjourned.

During the final days of the Johnson Administration, our continued involvement in the long and bloody war in Vietnam so absorbed the country that very little active consideration was given to relations with Communist China. They were pushed far into the background; popular discussion of the need to reappraise our policies faded away. The immediate urgency of discovering a way to end the war in Vietnam eclipsed everything else.

With mounting evidence that more and more people throughout the country were convinced that a military victory was impossible and that intervention had been a tragic mistake, Johnson was finally forced to act. On March 31, 1968, he dramatically announced that he was curtailing the bombing in North Vietnam and inviting Ho Chi Minh to the conference table. This policy shift, given even greater impact by the President's withdrawal as a candidate for reelection, riveted popular attention on the prospective negotiations. Their outcome would crucially affect every aspect of the political structure in eastern Asia.

15

The Continuing Impasse

IN THAT MOST REMARKABLE of political years, 1968, which found
the Republicans coming back into power with Richard Nixon's defeat
of Hubert Humphrey in the presidential campaign, Vietnam remained
the pervasive, inescapable, seemingly insoluble issue that almost completely
dominated the national scene. The pressure upon the outgoing Johnson
Administration to bring the conflict to an end was mounting week
by week. Protests and demonstrations throughout the country, especially
on the part of young people, reflected the rapidly spreading belief that
our continued involvement in Vietnam was not only a colossal error in
and of itself but was blocking effective action in meeting such grave
domestic problems as race relations, the crisis in the cities, and the war
against poverty.

The peace talks that commenced in Paris during May made no appre-
ciable progress; even when Johnson called a complete bombing halt at the
close of October, the deadlock continued. The new President would face
the imperative challenge of getting the negotiations moving or finding
some other way to meet the popular demand for the withdrawal from
Vietnam of our military forces.

Apart from the immediacy of this compelling issue, a revived interest
could also be discerned—though somewhat dimly—in 1968, and then more
clearly in 1969, in the need for that thorough reappraisal of our Far
Eastern policy that had been agitated in 1966 and then virtually dropped.

More than ever it was felt that something must be wrong with attitudes that had led the United States into such an impossible situation as a deadly war in Vietnam. Those who condemned our whole course in Southeast Asia were with near unanimity equally critical of our policy toward Communist China. Many observers were convinced that whatever might happen in Vietnam, the United States could not afford to lose more time in coming to grips with the continuing danger inherent in the hostile character of Sino-American relations.

"There is a flood of debate over every possible conceivable move, military or political, which might help bring the Vietnam war to an end, but little serious thought is being devoted to the broader problems of our relationship with Asia that underlie the Vietnam fiasco," Edwin O. Reischauer, former ambassador to Japan, wrote in 1968 in his penetrating study *Beyond Vietnam.* He felt that the idea that first things come first— that until the outcome in Vietnam was settled it was neither necessary nor desirable to rethink broader policies—was tragically wrong. The risk, Reischauer said, was that "American policy may be left to drift toward new disasters."

The country generally had come to accept a more objective view of the situation in eastern Asia. The public as well as official Washington realized that the one-time monolithic character of Communism was shattered and that the Chinese People's Republic was following a wholly independent course in defiance of the Soviet Union as well as of the West. No longer was any credence given to the wishful idea that Communist rule in China would eventually collapse if the Peking regime was effectively ostracized. The underlying strength of nationalism not only in China but in the other nations of Asia was accepted as it had not been in the past.

This more pragmatic attitude, however, did not free the United States from the legacy of the 1950s. It was still bound by that network of security treaties that John Foster Dulles had concluded with Japan, South Korea, the Philippine Republic, Australia, and New Zealand; by the obligations embodied in the Southeast Asia Collective Defense Treaty; and especially by the binding commitments for the defense of Taiwan and support for Chiang Kai-shek written into the Mutual Defense Treaty concluded with the Republic of China.

We had been persuaded in the 1950s of the need to surround China with this ring of military alliances as part of our defensive strategy against Communist aggression in the Pacific. Now under quite different circumstances we still found ourselves, as former Undersecretary of State George Ball has written in *The Discipline of Power,* "dug . . . into a series of hard and fast commitments that deprived us of all flexibility in dealing with the vast China mainland." Our attitude toward the Peking government was gradually changing. Nevertheless, a policy that originally owed so much to the idea that Communism in China was a temporary phase whose passing could be hastened by politically isolating the Peking regime was hardly conducive to the normalization of relations.

Moreover, the dangers inherent in Sino-American rivalry were heightened in the late 1960s by Communist China's continued development of nuclear weapons. On June 27, 1967, Peking triumphantly announced the production of a hydrogen bomb ("A fresh victory for Mao Tse-tung's thought!"), and in this country the Congressional Atomic Energy Committee warned that by the early 1970s the Chinese might well have the ability to launch intercontinental missiles across the Pacific. A more clear and present danger was that Peking might attempt to blackmail its Asian neighbors, but even the seemingly remote possibility of a Chinese attack on American cities became a matter of very real concern to the Johnson Administration.

"There is evidence," Secretary of Defense McNamara said on September 18, 1967, "that the Chinese are devoting substantial resources to the velopment of both nuclear warheads and missile delivery systems . . . one can conceive conditions under which China might miscalculate."

This contingency entered into debate over the development within the United States of an antiballistic missile system. We had heretofore been exclusively concerned with the dangers of a possible Russian attack, but this new threat from the Far East suggested the need for an immediate defense program against the small-scale assault that Communist China might conceivably be able to launch. To what extent this danger from China was the really determining factor in administration policy or was used as an excuse for starting construction of a protective system that could later be expanded may be open to question. However, McNamara has reported that "we decided in late 1967 to go forward with this Chinese-oriented ABM deployment."

In its further development, which became with the advent of the Nixon Administration such a hotly disputed political issue, a limited ABM system was again defended on the ground that it was a military necessity because of Peking's developing nuclear capacity. American diplomacy in the Pacific would not be credible, President Nixon said at a press conference on April 18, 1969, "unless we could protect our country against a Chinese attack aimed at our cities. The ABM will do that and the ABM Safeguard System therefore has been adopted for that reason."

A direct clash between the United States and Communist China involving nuclear weapons was unimaginable to most Americans. Nevertheless, these new developments in both countries gave an added dimension to the twenty-year-old Sino-American conflict. For all its absorption in the renewed efforts to find a way out of Vietnam, the Nixon Administration would be constrained to heed the warnings that relations with Communist China could not be neglected.

Nixon's record before becoming President in 1969, as has been brought out so repeatedly in this narrative, singled him out as one of the most belligerent of hawks on Far Eastern issues. His anti-Communist attitude was born of the McCarthy era, and he was invariably in the vanguard of Cold War warriors. In 1954 he had been willing to take all the risks of "putting our boys in" to support French resistance to Communist expansion in Indochina. He had taken an adamant stand, unwilling to concede an inch of territory, in respect to the offshore islands during the Formosan crises of 1955 and 1958. Since 1965 he had been in the forefront of those political leaders supporting the escalation of the war in Vietnam. Formerly closely associated with the old China bloc, he had through the years consistently opposed any move toward accommodation with Communist China. No one had ever accused Richard Nixon of being soft on Communism.

Prior to the election he set forth his views on Far Eastern policy at some length in an article entitled "Asia After Viet Nam," published in *Foreign Affairs* in October 1967. It ranged broadly over the whole Pacific landscape, with predictable emphasis on the necessity for maintaining a strong military stand against any threatened Communist expansion. More specifically, Nixon declared that American policy "must come urgently to grips with the reality of China." By this he did not mean, as he phrased it in sharp reaction to a number of current proposals, "rushing off to grant recognition to Peking, to admit it to the United Nations and to ply it with offers of trade." On the contrary, Nixon declared, the United States should recognize the menace to American interests in Communist China's growing power and do everything possible to check it. He stressed the importance of our containment policy but, foreshadowing in some measure his later ideas, also proposed that the non-Communist Asian states should assume greater responsibility for their own defense. With

SEATO becoming little more than an "anachronistic relic," Nixon said, these nations should develop their own regional military alliance to forestall the Chinese threat.

Nixon recognized that in the long run, whatever immediate measures might be adopted, Communist China should be brought back into the family of nations. But there was no suggestion that the United States might be itself blocking this through helping to incite Peking's chauvinistic anti-Westernism. He believed with President Johnson that any accommodation was dependent on China's altering its attitude, and our policy should be to induce it to do so. "The way to do this," he said succinctly, "is to persuade China that it *must* change: that it cannot satisfy its imperialistic ambitions." In concluding his article Nixon revealed his affinity with the Asia Firsters of an earlier day. "Without turning our backs on Europe," he wrote, "we have now to reach out westward to the East, and to fashion the sinews of a Pacific community."

There was little here to suggest the emergence of a new Nixon who in dealing with the problems of the Far East would encourage a fresh approach or be more conciliatory in his attitude toward Communist China. Nor at his first press conference as President did he give any evidence of having modified past opinions. He was asked about possible plans for trying to improve Sino-American relations. Rather than offering any suggestions along this line, he turned his answer into a strong affirmation that his administration would continue to oppose Communist China's entry into the United Nations. The Peking government, Nixon said, had neither indicated any desire to join the world organization nor shown any intent to abide by the principles of the UN charter, and in these circumstances "it would be a mistake for the United States to change its policy."

Yet in spite of his negative reaction to this question and his reassertion of our traditional stand on the UN issue, Nixon was soon to demonstrate that he did not in fact intend to maintain the tough and rigid position expected from his past record. This first Republican administration since that of President Eisenhower, whose policies had been so strongly directed against any association whatsoever with Communist China, was ironically enough to prove more receptive to new ideas in trying to break through existing barriers than either of the intervening Democratic administrations.

A first sign of this more open-minded approach was Washington's attitude toward the ambassadorial talks in Warsaw. In November, after Nixon's election, the Chinese proposed to resume the negotiations and set the date of February 20, 1969. Moreover, they revived the old idea, first brought up following the Bandung Conference in 1955, of exploring the possibilities of a Sino-American agreement for peaceful coexistence. On coming into office, Nixon strongly welcomed this proposal. While, in line with his earlier statements, he intimated that only if the Chinese showed a different attitude on major substantive issues could there be much hope of progress in the renewal of the ambassadorial talks, he nonetheless said he looked forward to them. As later revealed, the American ambassador in Warsaw was instructed to work toward an agreement on peaceful coexistence as well as opening up the old question of cultural exchanges.

Any expectations of progress in Warsaw were shortlived. On February 18, 1969, just three weeks after President Nixon's first press conference, the Peking government abruptly canceled the ambassadorial talks with only forty-eight hours' notice. The nominal excuse was that the United States had granted political asylum to a defecting Chinese diplomat and thus demonstrated, in Peking's words, that the new administration in Washington had "inherited the mantle of the preceding United States Government in flagrantly making itself the enemy of the 700 million Chinese people." A more probable interpretation of Peking's move was that political pressures arising from the power struggles of the Great Proletarian Cultural Revolution forced the ruling clique to renew the traditional attacks on the United States.

In spite of this blunt cancellation of the Warsaw talks and Peking's revived anti-Western campaign, the United States did not respond in kind. It refrained from the polemical counterattacks that might have strained Sino-American relations still further. The State Department declared that we stood ready to participate in the ambassadorial meetings whenever the Chinese changed their minds and were themselves ready to do so.

Secretary of State William Rogers, acting obviously with the President's approval, was the spokesman for our more conciliatory attitude. He had had little or no practical experience with the Far East; he had given no previous indication of what his ideas might be. But he proved in many ways to have a quite different attitude toward China than any of his predecessors in the State Department since 1949. Acting quietly in the background and never seeking the center of the stage, Rogers appeared to be free of the obsessive convictions or engrained prejudices that had in the past so often marked the State Department's approach to Asian affairs.

He set forth his views in a significant policy statement on April 21, 1969. The United States, Rogers said, accepts the existence of a Communist China on the mainland and a Nationalist China on Taiwan as "facts of life" that cannot be ignored. He spoke of our treaty relations with the latter regime, a political entity but not representative of all China, and expressed the hope that the problems to which these relations gave rise could be peacefully settled. As to the Communist regime in Peking, he said that it was currently in deep trouble and displayed a hostile attitude to the United States. However, he believed that conditions on the mainland and also Peking's outlook on the West would in time change. "Meanwhile," Rogers declared, "we shall take the initiative to reestablish more normal relations with Communist China and shall remain responsive to any indications of less hostile attitudes from their side."

This was hardly the voice of Dean Rusk, let alone John Foster Dulles. Where Rogers differed most from them was in his willingness to try to move ahead without expecting any immediate response from Peking. He was ready to take the initiative without demanding a quid pro quo and to look toward the long future in trying to ease Sino-American tensions. In subsequent talks he repeatedly said that while the United States regretted that Communist China had not as yet made any response to our overtures, we would not give up the hope of more cordial relations.

Those members of Congress and other public figures who were interested in China applauded the stand the Nixon Administration was taking; they urged still further efforts along these lines. As we have seen, public opinion had greatly changed since the days when statements such as those made by Secretary Rogers would have been promptly condemned as appeasement. Moreover, with the Republicans in control, as had been the case with the ending of the war in Korea, Washington was far more free to follow a conciliatory approach in dealing with the Chinese Communists than it would have been with the Democrats still in office.

The experts who had in 1966 testified before the Senate Foreign Relations Committee on the need to come to terms with China held to the views they had then set forth. They believed that the United States should "deter, restrain, and counterbalance Chinese power," as the statement of one group expressed it, but should also keep its options open to take advantage of any changes that "may emerge in the context of Chinese political evolution." Somewhat more simply, this meant flexibility rather than rigidity, containment without isolation. More forthrightly, a new body, the Committee for the Reappraisal of Far Eastern Policy, called for immediate consideration of both American recognition of the People's Republic of China and its admission to the United Nations.

John Fairbank once again took the lead. In a number of magazine articles he stated his belief that the United States should recognize that its involvement in eastern Asia was a natural consequence of its status as a great power, be more responsible in playing this inescapable role, and try to develop a policy that would look constructively toward accommodation rather than conflict with mainland China. Writing in *Foreign Affairs* in April 1969, he emphasized as he had previously the difficulties posed by China's "implacable self-esteem." He felt, however, that the United States by its own "over-fearful and over-active" policies was helping to stimulate an aggressive, expansionist Chinese policy. In the quaking belief, as he phrased it on another occasion, that the Chinese had suddenly become ten feet tall, the United States was overreacting and we should "cut our fear of China down to realistic size."

Another contributor to popular discussion, previously on record for criticism of past policies derived from his own experience in the State Department, was James C. Thomson, Jr. Writing in the *New Republic* of May 1, 1969, he proposed a fresh approach to the problem of Formosa (by now commonly referred to as Taiwan) in order to break down the greatest single obstacle to any Sino-American accord. Peking, he suggested, should accept the autonomy of Taiwan, and Washington should acknowledge Communist China's residual sovereignty. Something of this sort, Thomson urged, was the only alternative to a return to "grim Ruskean inaction."

The *New York Times* called for continued efforts to search out a path to Sino-American accommodation in spite of Peking's cancellation of the Warsaw talks. One editorial specifically proposed lifting the embargo on trade, ceasing our opposition to Communist China's representation in the United Nations, and exploring the *de facto* demilitarization of Formosa.

The very fact that such broad concessions could be publicly discussed without raising McCarthyist outcries again underscored the changes taking place in public sentiment. This new mood was further illustrated at a conference sponsored by the National Committee on United States–China Relations, held in New York on March 21–22, 1969, which drew an audience of some 2,500 persons for a frank, outspoken review of our China policy.

Among the speakers some few condemned what they considered "irresponsible and uninformed denunciation" of our earlier actions and also refurbished the old arguments for the Peking government's containment and isolation. The great majority, however, were insistent on the need for a reconsideration of our objectives. Among the participants such important figures as Theodore Sorensen, Arthur Goldberg, Senator Jacob Javits, and Senator Edward Kennedy were agreed that the passions of the past should be discarded and our attitude toward China readjusted in terms of Far Eastern realities.

Breaking through the barriers that only a few years earlier would have made such candor politically suicidal, Senator Kennedy made a series of specific recommendations. Where Robert Kennedy as a critic of China policy had gone no further just the year before than to assail an attitude "founded upon fear and passion and wishful hopes," his younger brother now called for ending the trade embargo, reopening American consular offices on the mainland, supporting Peking's representation in the United Nations, and extending diplomatic recognition. Edward Kennedy also believed that while we should continue to recognize and support against attack the Nationalist regime on Taiwan, we should withdraw our token military presence.

One more straw in the wind. About this same time the League of Women Voters, which for three years had been conducting an intensive study of the China problem, reported a consensus among its nationwide chapters in favor of opening negotiations for recognition of the Chinese People's Republic, supporting its admission to the UN, and abolishing the trade embargo.

The Nixon Administration was not yet ready to adopt any such radical measures, but it was nonetheless alert to the demand for more liberal policies and on its own account anxious to take whatever forward steps were politically feasible. At the close of July the State Department announced two moves. It stated with considerable public fanfare that passports for travel in Communist China would henceforth be automatically validated for journalists, teachers, students, scientists, doctors, and members of Congress, and declared that the existing trade embargo would be modified to allow American citizens traveling abroad to bring home Chinese goods up to a value of $100.

These steps were in one sense minuscule, and Harrison Salisbury of the *New York Times* reported that their effect "probably will be nil." The travel authorizations actually went little further than the shift in the State Department's attitude a few years earlier; permission to buy $100 worth of Chinese goods benefited only a handful of tourists and Hong Kong's avid curio dealers. Not unexpectedly, the Peking government paid no attention to the State Department's announcements.

Nevertheless, these steps were significant; they had broken through the patterns of the past. Asked shortly afterward whether this meant a shift in American policy, Secretary of State Rogers replied that it was a "very minor change" but could be interpreted as symbolic of the American wish for peace. As President Nixon was later to say, the United States had avoided any dramatic gesture that might have invited a dramatic rebuff, but it had underlined its willingness to work toward a more normal Sino-American relationship.

About this same time President Nixon, on a journey to Asia and then on around the world, took the occasion of a stopover at Guam on July 25, 1969, to outline his general views on Far Eastern policy at an informal press conference. He did not permit direct quotation, and as reported by the press, what he said was vague and somewhat contradictory. The emphases in his discussion, however, broke fresh ground and promptly led the newspapers to announce a "Nixon doctrine."

The President's principal concern was Vietnam. He had announced his plans for a gradual withdrawal of American troops and thereby succeeded to a remarkable extent in defusing the violent controversy over American policy. Through his emphasis on the "Vietnamization" of the war, he appeared to be acting on the assumption, however problematic, that this program would provide the means for our disengagement from a hopeless struggle and an end to the Vietnam problem. However, in his meeting with reporters at Guam, the President also dealt more generally with the lessons of Vietnam and how he felt our Far Eastern policy should be directed in the future.

He stressed the importance of America's historic stake in eastern Asia and acknowledged the serious threat to our interests from Communist China. But, he said, in his opinion this threat was much less dangerous than it had been five or even ten years ago, and he cited the minimal role China seemed to be playing in Vietnam as compared with that of Soviet Russia. Henceforth the United States, while maintaining its established position in confronting China, must avoid the military entanglements that could lead to future Vietnams.

What then emerged was the Nixon doctrine. While studiously fulfilling all our treaty commitments in Asia, the President believed we should strongly emphasize economic rather than military aid to our non-Communist Asian friends and, most important, insist that they do more to help themselves. Except in the case of a nuclear threat, Nixon said, we had a right to expect these nations to handle the problem of their own national security.

The President was to develop his ideas more formally in later speeches, and the question could well be raised whether this Nixon doctrine was really new or a return to an earlier position on Far Eastern policy. In January 1950 Secretary of State Acheson had declared that in the event of an attack on any country beyond our defensive perimeter in the Western Pacific, "the initial reliance must be placed upon the people attacked to resist it." President Nixon was saying nearly two decades later that the United States looked to any Asian nation threatened by aggression "to assume the primary responsibility of providing the man-power for its defense." However, there was this interesting and significant difference, reflecting the international changes of twenty years, in how the two men elaborated on what might be the further reaction to trouble in Asia: Acheson had said that behind the first steps to repel aggression "stood the commitments of the entire civilized world under the charter of the United Nations"; Nixon declared without mention of the UN that the United States would "provide a shield if a nuclear power threatens the freedom of a nation allied with us or of a nation whose survival we consider vital to our security."

The Nixon doctrine was at the time generally accepted as expressing the President's intent to limit our commitments in the Far East by transferring to the Asian nations themselves greater responsibility for the containment of Communism. But his continued emphasis on the great importance of our historic stake in Asia and on our vital interests there did not suggest that he was contemplating any real retreat.

The different interpretations that could be given to the doctrine were illustrated by the initial reactions in Taipei and Peking to the reports of the press conference at Guam. The Chinese Nationalists were concerned that the emphasis upon the Asian nations helping themselves meant that the United States was backing away from its pledged military assistance to Chiang Kai-shek. The Communists found the most significant aspect of the President's remarks his reassertion that the United States was committed to playing a major role in Asia.

It remained to be seen whether the Nixon doctrine would be imple-mented in any significant way. This largely depended on the course of events in Vietnam, and in the meantime, the further evolution of policy toward Communist China itself appeared to be following an erratic and rather contradictory course.

The deepening cleavage between the Chinese People's Republic and Soviet Russia, which led in 1969 to a series of border clashes and even talk of possible war, raised the question whether the United States could promote its own interests by taking sides with either power. Washington rejected any such policy; we would remain completely neutral. Moreover, a State Department spokesman said, the United States would not allow Peking's invective to stand in the way of our seeking a closer accord with Soviet Russia or Moscow's apprehensions to prevent us from attempting to bring China "out of its angry, alienated shell."

In sharp contrast with its professed commitment to this latter objective, however, the Nixon Administration was standing firmly on the past in respect to Chinese representation in the United Nations. As the President had earlier stated, there would be no change in our traditional stand against Communist China's possible admission. The *New York Times* complained that we seemed to be following a two-headed policy that was both "sterile and contradictory" in urging Peking to cooperate with the international community and at the same time exerting our influence to keep the door closed to its entry into the world peace organization.

In any event the United States delegate to the UN Assembly, Representative Irving Whalley, was instructed to oppose the annual resolution for expelling the Chinese Nationalists and admitting the Communists. Great Britain, France, and the Scandinavian countries were among those who voted in its favor; Canada, Italy, Belgium, and the Netherlands abstained; among our European allies only Greece and Turkey followed our lead. But for the twentieth time American policy prevailed. After agreeing that the representation issue was an "important question," the Assembly rejected the key resolution on Peking's entry by a vote of 56 to 48, with twenty-one abstentions.

The debate differed greatly, however, from that of earlier years. The Soviet representative took no part in it, those of other countries showed little interest, and the United States delegate spoke without rancor. In declaring his position Whalley stressed the Republic of China's right to maintain a membership that went back to the founding of the United Nations and the Peking government's apparent lack of interest in joining the UN. Far from resorting to the vilification of Communist China as an outlaw nation so customary in the past, Whalley described American efforts to break down the walls of isolation surrounding Peking. He repeated the assurances of both President Nixon and Secretary Rogers that in spite of Communist China's negative reaction to our conciliatory overtures, "the United States intends to persevere."

During this same period faint signs appeared—barely discernible signals —that the United States might possibly be getting through to Peking in making known its desire for less antagonistic relations. Chinese propaganda softened, with at least some toning down of the usual attacks on American imperialism. As the country began to recover from the ravages of the Great Proletarian Cultural Revolution and restore political and social stability, its leaders seemed willing to modify their frenzied hostility to the United States. They perhaps felt they had to weigh in the scales the possible consequences for China of a further deterioration in Sino-American relations at a time when the border clashes with Soviet Russia were becoming more threatening.

Even though what might actually be taking place in the councils of the Communist high command remained, as always, an impenetrable secret, the eager China-watchers in both Hong Kong and Washington were encouraged to believe that a shift in policy was in the air. Reports from visitors attending the twentieth anniversary of the establishment of the People's Republic of China on October 1, 1969, suggested that Peking might be ready to sound out the prospects for a direct Sino-American dialogue.

The first break came in early December. The Chinese chargé d'affaires in Warsaw, Lei Yang, meeting the American ambassador to Poland, Walter J. Stoessel, Jr., at a diplomatic reception, somewhat casually proposed a resumption of the ambassadorial talks, which had now been suspended for almost two years. Stoessel quickly agreed. After some further informal discussion, the two envoys met at the Chinese embassy on January 20, 1970, to resume the talks officially.

This was the 135th of these off-again, on-again ambassadorial meetings that since 1955 had constituted the only link between Washington and Peking. In conformity with a long tradition of complete secrecy, nothing more was announced concerning this conference between Stoessel and Lei Yang than that their talk had been "useful and businesslike."

This meant little or nothing. Any immediate progress on issues that their predecessors had been discussing for fifteen years could hardly be expected. The one hope was that the completely deadlocked problem of the status of Taiwan could be placed in deep freeze while the two envoys considered other questions on which some give-and-take might be possible.

In the meantime—following the agreement to resume the talks but prior to their official commencement—the Nixon Administration gave a further and quite unprecedented indication of its conciliatory attitude. The State Department announced that through a policy decision approved by the President, subsidiaries or affiliates of American corporations operating abroad would be permitted to sell nonstrategic goods to Communist China and to buy Chinese products for resale in foreign markets, and that the $100 ceiling on tourist purchases of Chinese goods was being lifted.

These moves constituted a really substantial modification in the twenty-year-old trade embargo; they could pave the way toward a full resumption of commercial relations. And once again the United States had acted independently, without asking agreement or concessions from the Peking government.

It might again be pointed out that this was a Republican administration, headed by a one-time implacable foe of any concessions to Communist China, that was taking these steps in trying to shatter the rigid mold of Sino-American relations. President Nixon was approaching the China problem more realistically than any of his predecessors since the Korean war, and he was doing so not only in words but in deeds.

"If the day ever comes when we enjoy anything like a 'normalization' of relations with the People's Republic of China," Richard Rovere wrote in the *New Yorker* on January 17, 1970, "he [Nixon] will probably be an ex-President; nevertheless, if it happens, a large share of the credit will be his, for he, once regarded as an ally, if not the instrument, of the 'China Lobby,' has taken the first real initiative in that direction in almost a quarter of a century, and has taken the risks that go with it."

Nixon's fresh approach to relations with Communist China was soon afterward further stressed in his broad-ranging report to Congress on "United States Foreign Policy for the 1970s." In dealing with Asia he did not dispel the ambiguities in the new Nixon doctrine, but he stated forthrightly that it was greatly in the interest of the United States to take whatever steps were possible to improve our "practical relations" with Peking. We intended to uphold our treaty commitments for the defense of the Republic of China and would not ignore any hostile acts on the part of the Chinese Communists, Nixon stated, but at the same time we would seek to promote understanding and create "a new pattern of mutually beneficial actions."

After proudly listing the steps his administration had already taken to encourage trade and cultural relations, the President expressed the view that the renewal of the ambassadorial talks in Warsaw might indicate that our new approach was proving useful. In concluding this section of his message, he again stressed that the United States was not seeking to exploit the clash between Communist China and the Soviet Union but desired improved Sino-American relations because peace was impossible "so long as some nations consider themselves the permanent enemies of others."

As the 1970s opened, the prospects of any closer accord between the United States and the People's Republic of China were nevertheless not too encouraging. The rivalry that had characterized their relations ever since the Communist victory in 1949 showed few real signs of abatement. While the ideological aspects of Sino-American rivalry, born of the suspicious days of the Cold War, were substantially moderated, none of the basic issues stemming from this conflict was settled. Recognition of the Peking government, its representation in the United Nations, the normalization of trade and cultural relations—these questions had received no final answers. Nor had those involving China's neighbors. Acting under the aegis of the UN, the United States had succeeded in halting Communist aggression in Korea, but only an uncertain truce prevailed along the Thirty-eighth Parallel. No progress whatsoever had been made in resolving the direct Sino-American confrontation over the status of Taiwan. The war in Vietnam dragged on. While the United States had lowered its voice, there was no idea of renouncing what President Nixon called its "national destiny" to protect peace and freedom in eastern Asia in opposing Communist China's ambition to set up an exclusive sphere of interest for a revived Middle Kingdom.

The resumption of the Warsaw talks suggested that both nations were aware of the gravity of this political conflict and of the danger that it might lead to war. Yet there was no assurance that either the United States or Communist China was ready to make the concessions that could lead to a successful breakthrough in the continuing impasse. No real rapprochement, no prospective settlement, was in sight. Against the frightening background of both nations' expanding military power and nuclear armaments, the awesome challenge of the 1970s was whether in spite of these disheartening conditions a way could be discovered to provide lasting security in the Pacific world.

Bibliographical Notes

General Sources

I

THE OFFICIAL UNITED STATES RECORD of Sino-American relations
is available in papers and publications of the State Department. They
include *United States Relations with China, With Special Reference to
the Period 1944–1949*, 1949, generally known as *The China White Paper*
and reissued under that title, 2 vols., Stanford, Calif., 1968; the series
American Foreign Policy, 1950–55, Basic Documents, 2 vols., 1957, thereafter, beginning with 1956, published annually as *American Foreign
Policy, Current Documents*, 1959–69; and the monthly *State Department
Bulletin*, 1949–69.

In some instances even more helpful are the records of congressional
investigations and hearings. The more important in terms of this narrative
are *Military Situation in the Far East, Hearings Before the Armed Forces
and Foreign Relations Committees*, Senate, 82nd Cong., 1st Sess., 5 parts,
1951; *Hearings on the Institute of Pacific Relations, Internal Security
Subcommittee of the Committee on the Judiciary*, Senate, 82nd Cong.,
1st Sess., 15 parts, 1951, 1952; *Nomination of Philip C. Jessup, Hearings
Before a Subcommittee of the Committee on Foreign Relations*, Senate,
82nd Cong., 1st Sess., 1951; *U.S. Policy with Respect to Mainland China,
Hearings Before the Committee on Foreign Relations*, Senate, 89th Cong.,
2nd Sess., 1966. The material in the latter hearings has been brought
together in Akira Iriye, *U.S. Policy Toward China* (paperback), Boston,
1968. See also annual volumes of the *United Nations Yearbook*.

II

Primary source material in memoirs or journals is quite extensive. For the years of the Truman Administration there are the *Memoirs* of Harry S. Truman: *Year of Decisions*, Garden City, N.Y., 1955, and *Years of Trial and Hope*, Garden City, N.Y., 1956. In addition to several volumes of his speeches, most notably McGeorge Bundy, ed., *The Pattern of Responsibility*, Boston, 1952, is Dean Acheson's brilliant account of his years at the State Department, *Present at the Creation*, New York, 1969.

For the 1950s Dwight Eisenhower has left a two-volume record: *Mandate for Change, 1953-56*, New York, 1963, and *Waging Peace, 1956-61*, New York, 1965. There is no comparable material for John Foster Dulles and while a number of biographies have been published (to be noted under Chapters 9–11), no effective use has yet been made of his private papers. A further primary source on the Eisenhower Administration is Sherman Adams, *First-Hand Report*, New York, 1961, but it has very little on China policy.

Although President Kennedy left no memoirs and Secretary of State Rusk is still to do so, the two important inside books on this administration, Arthur M. Schlesinger, Jr., *A Thousand Days*, Boston, 1965, and Theodore Sorensen, *Kennedy*, New York, 1965, are invaluable. Some material bearing on China may also be found in John K. Galbraith, *Ambassador's Journal*, New York, 1969.

The troubles of President Johnson with Far Eastern policy, especially of course Vietnam, have led to the publication of several important books by involved members of his administration. Roger Hilsman, a former Assistant Secretary of State for Far Eastern Affairs, has written *To Move a Nation*, New York, 1967; George W. Ball, former Undersecretary of State, is author of *The Discipline of Power*, Boston, 1968; and a former undersecretary of the Air Force, Townsend Hoopes, has written *The Limits of Intervention*, New York, 1969.

Further memoirs will be noted under the appropriate chapter headings.

III

For such a recent period of history, newspaper and magazines are indispensable. I have relied heavily on *The New York Times* and if justification for its use as a source were necessary, I might cite Arthur M. Schlesinger, Jr., who on the basis of his own Washington experience in reading foreign cables and official dispatches has written (*Saturday*

Review, May 3, 1969) that "95 percent of the information essential for intelligent judgment is available to any careful reader of *The New York Times.*"

For both information and especially interpretive comment, such magazines as *Foreign Affairs, U.S. News and World Report, The Reporter, New York Review, Christian Century, New Republic, Orbis, Far Eastern Survey, Asian Survey,* and *China Quarterly* have been particularly rewarding.

IV

Important but unofficial sources with much documentary material are the annual volumes *United States in World Affairs,* prepared by Richard P. Stebbins (except 1955, when prepared by Hollis W. Barber) and the companion *Documents on American Foreign Relations,* which are published annually under the auspices of the Council on Foreign Relations, New York, 1949–67. Especially valuable, with its chronological record of developments both in this country and in the Far East affecting Sino-American relations, is *China and U.S. Far East Policy, 1945–1967,* published by the Congressional Quarterly Service, Washington, D.C., 1967.

V

For Chinese material I have had to rely on translated excerpts from documents, speeches, and newspaper articles. A great mass of material is available through the American Consulate General in Hong Kong (distributed without charge until the end of 1969; now for a moderate fee) in *Survey of the China Mainland Press* and *Current Background—Selections from China Mainland Magazines.* Also, in English, is the *Peking Review.* Its translations of official documents and articles from the *Jen-min Jih-pao* (*People's Daily*) and other Chinese sources regularly present the Communist propaganda line from Peking. A short cut to much of this material, and one that I have used extensively, is the chronological record appearing in *China and U.S. Far East Policy.*

VI

Among secondary sources, apart from the more specialized studies to be noted under separate chapter headings, a few stand out with special prominence. The background leading up to the period covered in this narrative has been treated with unusual skill and careful documentation by Herbert Feis in his appropriately named *The China Tangle: The American Effort in China from Pearl Harbor to the Marshall Mission*, Princeton, N.J., 1953, while Tang Tsou, in another well-named book, *America's Failure in China, 1941–50*, Chicago, 1963, has very ably brought the story through the Chinese revolution. In my opening chapters I have drawn extensively from these books. A special debt should also be acknowledged to John K. Fairbank for his various writings on Sino-American relations, especially *The United States and China*, New York, 1948, rev. ed., 1958, and the collection of essays *China—The People's Middle Kingdom*, Cambridge, 1967. I have also relied in many instances on O. Edmund Clubb, *Twentieth Century China*, New York, 1964.

The Council on Foreign Relations has sponsored a series of studies under the general title *The United States and China in World Affairs*. The volumes that have proved most useful are Robert Blum, *The United States and China in World Affairs*, New York, 1966; A. T. Steele, *The American People and China*, New York, 1966; and Kenneth T. Young, *Negotiating with the Chinese Communists: The American Experience, 1953–67*, New York, 1968. For an account of this series see James C. Thomson, Jr., "Dragon Under Glass," *Atlantic Monthly*, October 1967.

A useful collection of readings is Franz Schurman and Orville Schell, eds., *The China Reader*, Vol. III, *Communist China*, New York, 1967. Also useful is the symposium of articles edited by Tang Tsou, *China in Crisis*, Vol. II, *China's Policies in Asia and America's Alternatives*, Chicago, 1968. A recent broad survey is Akira Iriye, *Across the Pacific—An Inner History of America–East Asia Relations*, New York, 1957.

Among general studies of postwar American foreign policy with interesting material on China may be noted John Spanier, *American Foreign Policy Since World War II*, New York, rev. ed., 1962; Louis J. Halle, *The Cold War as History*, New York, 1967; and Ronald Steele, *Pax Americana*, New York, 1967.

Books dealing specifically with Communist China are legion. The most valuable in relating its policies to this country is A. Doak Barnett, *Communist China and Asia—A Challenge to American Policy*, New York, 1960. The same author has written *Communist China: The Early Years, 1949–55*, New York, 1954, and *China After Mao*, Princeton, N.J., 1957. Other titles are R. G. Boyd, *Communist China's Foreign Policy*, New York, 1962; Alice Langley Hsieh, *Communist China's Strategy in the Nuclear Age*, Englewood Cliffs, N.J., 1962; Charles P. Fitzgerald, *The Chinese View of Their Place in the World*, Oxford, 1964; Guy Wint,

Communist China's Crusade, London, 1965; and Harold C. Hinton, *Communist China in World Politics*, Boston, 1966.

Two books whose titles suggest their subject matter are Stuart Schram, *Mao Tse-tung*, New York, 1966, and Robert Payne, *Mao Tse-tung*, New York, 1969.

CHAPTER SOURCES

Chapter 1

THE SKETCH OF BACKGROUND EVENTS in this chapter is based on contemporary reports in the *New York Times* supplemented by material from Tang Tsou's *America's Failure in China* and Clubb's *Twentieth Century China*. The Kennedy quotations are from the *Congressional Record*, House of Representatives, 81st Cong., 2nd Sess., Appendix A, 993.

Two highly interesting accounts of the China scene by Americans there during the revolution are John F. Melby, *The Mandate of Heaven: Record of a Civil War, China 1945–49*, Buffalo, 1969, and Derk Bodde, *Peking Diary, 1948–49*, New York, 1947.

Chapter 2

My own previous book, *China and America—The Story of Their Relations Since 1784*, Princeton, N.J., 1946, is the general source for the historical background and most of the quotations in this chapter. I have supplemented it with some material from later books, most importantly Paul Varg, *Missionaries, Chinese and Diplomats*, Princeton, N.J., 1958, and Harold R. Isaacs, *Scratches on Our Mind: American Images of China and India*, New York, 1958, reprinted as *Images of Asia: American Views of China and India*, New York, 1962.

The opening quotation from John Foster Dulles is found in the *State Department Bulletin*, December 18, 1950. Chiang Kai-shek's *China's Destiny* was published in New York in 1947.

Chapters 3 to 5

The treatment in these chapters of the Communist revolution and American policy in 1949–50 has been largely based on the *China White Paper*, the *State Department Bulletin*, various Senate hearings including

Military Situation in the Far East, the *Memoirs* of President Truman, news stories in the *New York Times*, and articles or editorials in a number of current magazines. I have also drawn on miscellaneous material in the Truman Library, for the most part letters to the White House, and contemporary newspaper files.

Apart from his own *Present at the Creation*, interesting accounts of the policies of Dean Acheson, who has as yet no formal biographer, are the chapter on his role as Secretary of State by Hans Morgenthau in Norman Graebner, ed., *An Uncertain Tradition*, New York, 1961; David S. McLellan, "The Role of Political Style: A Study of Dean Acheson," in Roger Hilsman and Robert C. Good, eds., *Foreign Policy in the Sixties*, Baltimore, 1965; and Cabell Phillips, "Dean Acheson Ten Years Later," *New York Times Magazine*, Jan. 18, 1959.

Memoirs for these years include those of our last ambassador to mainland China, John Leighton Stuart, *Fifty Years in China*, New York, 1954, and of the Secretary General of the United Nations, Trygve Lie, *In the Cause of Peace, Seven Years with the United Nations*, New York, 1954. Also Arthur H. Vandenberg, Jr., *The Private Papers of Senator Vandenberg*, Boston, 1952, and Albert C. Wedemeyer, *Wedemeyer Reports!*, New Haven, Conn., 1958.

In addition to the more general books already noted, a few studies helpful for this period are H. Bradford Westerfield, *Foreign Policy and Party Politics*, New Haven, Conn., 1955; Joseph Barber, ed., *American Policy Toward China: A Report on the Views of Leading Citizens in Twenty-three Cities*, New York, 1950; Robert P. Neuman, *Recognition of Communist China? A Study in Argument*, New York, 1961; Joseph W. Ballantine, *Formosa: A Problem for United States Foreign Policy*, Washington, D.C., 1952; and Quincy Wright, "The Chinese Recognition Problem," *American Journal of International Law*, July 1955. See also William Reitzel, *et al.*, *United States Foreign Policy, 1945–55*, Washington, D.C., 1956.

For extreme right-wing interpretations of events in China, see Freda Utley, *The China Story*, Chicago, 1951; Anthony Kubek, *How the Far East Was Lost: American Policy and the Creation of Communist China, 1941–49*, Chicago, 1963; and John Flynn, *While You Slept*, New York, 1951.

Chapter 6

The influence of the Asia Firsters, McCarthyism, and the China lobby in policy making has a literature of its own which I have drawn upon over and beyond the primary sources already cited for the preceding chapters. Arthur M. Schlesinger, Jr., initially took up what he called the "new isolationism" in an article in the *Atlantic Monthly* in May 1952, and this topic was further developed in Norman Graebner, *The New Isolationism, A Study in Politics and Foreign Policy Since 1950*, New York, 1956. For the ideas of one of the isolationists' spokesmen, see Robert A. Taft, *A Foreign Policy for Americans*, New York, 1951, and on their early influence, Blair Bolles, "Asia Policy and the Election," *Far Eastern Survey*, Dec. 6, 1950.

For Senator McCarthy, see *Major Speeches and Debates of Senator Joe McCarthy, 1950–51—Unabridged from the Congressional Record*, and among biographical studies, Jack Anderson and Ronald W. May, *McCarthy—The Man, the Senator, the 'Ism,'* Boston, 1952; Richard W. Rovere, *Senator Joe McCarthy*, New York, 1959; and Earl Latham, *The Communist Conspiracy in Washington*, Cambridge, Mass., 1966. There is also some interesting material in Eric F. Goldman, *The Crucial Decade— And After: America 1945–1960*, New York, 1961. See also Owen Lattimore, *Ordeal by Slander*, New York, 1950.

On the topic of its title, *The China Lobby in American Politics*, the book by Ross Y. Koen, published New York, 1960, is not readily available as noted in the text. More reliable in any event are the articles by Max Ascoli, Charles Wertenbaker, and Philip Horton in *The Reporter*, April 15 and April 29, 1952. They have been reprinted in Max Ascoli, ed., *Our Times, The Best from the Reporter*, New York, 1960.

On the Committee of One Million, see especially "The Lobby of a Million Ghosts," the *Nation*, January 23, 1960.

Chapters 7 and 8

The close interrelationship between the Korean war and China policy is obvious, but no attempt is made here to cite the war's bibliography in any detail. A first official record is Department of State, *Policy in the Korean Crisis*, 1950, and among other accounts I have found useful are Glenn D. Paige, *The Korean Decision, June 24–30, 1950*, Chicago, 1968; Robert Leckie, *Conflict: The History of the Korean War*, New York, 1962; and David Rees, *Korea: The Limited War*, New York, 1964. Most valuable for this study is Allen S. Whiting, *China Crosses the Yalu: The Decision to Enter the Korean War*, New York, 1960.

On the MacArthur-Truman controversy, see Truman's *Years of Hope and Trial*, Acheson's *Present at the Creation*, and Douglas MacArthur,

Reminiscences, New York, 1965. Among the books the controversy has inspired are John W. Spanier, *The Truman-MacArthur Controversy and the Korean War*, Cambridge, Mass., 1959, and Richard H. Rovere and Arthur M. Schlesinger, Jr., *The General and the President*, New York, 1951.

Other general studies relating to the Korean war from special angles include Mark W. Clark, *From the Danube to the Yalu*, New York, 1954; Courtney Whitney, *MacArthur: His Rendezvous with History*, New York, 1956; Ross N. Berkes and Mohindar S. Bedi, *The Diplomacy of India*, Stanford, Calif., 1958; and Alexander L. George, "American Policy-Making and the North Korean Aggression," in *World Politics*, January 1955.

Also important for this chapter are the annual volumes of the *United Nations Yearbook*.

Chapters 9 to 11

Such primary sources for earlier chapters as the State Department's *American Foreign Policy, 1950–55, Basic Documents*, the *State Department Bulletin*, the *New York Times*, etc., are supplemented for the Eisenhower years by the President's *Memoirs;* Anthony Eden's *Full Circle*, Boston, 1960; Matthew B. Ridgway's *Soldier*, New York, 1956; and the recollections of our ambassador to the Republic of China, Karl Lott Rankin's *China Assignment*, Seattle, 1964.

Apart from speeches and other material available in the *State Department Bulletin*, two important contemporary articles by John Foster Dulles may be singled out: "A Policy of Boldness," *Life*, May 19, 1952, and "Policy for Security and Peace," *Foreign Affairs*, April 1954. Among the biographies of the Secretary of State are John A. Beale, *John Foster Dulles*, New York, 1959; Richard Goold-Adams, *John Foster Dulles—A Reappraisal*, New York, 1962; Eleanor Lansing Dulles, *John Foster Dulles —The Last Year*, New York, 1963; and Andrew H. Berding, *Dulles on Diplomacy*, Princeton, N.J., 1965.

Other books dealing with the Eisenhower Administration that I have consulted, even though their material on China policy is limited, are Robert J. Donovan, *Eisenhower—The Inside Story*, New York, 1956; Richard H. Rovere, *Affairs of State: The Eisenhower Years*, New York, 1956; and Arthur Larson, *Eisenhower, The President Nobody Knew*, New York, 1968.

Contemporary articles of very real importance include James Shepley, "How Dulles Averted War," *Life*, Jan. 16, 1956; Chalmers W. Roberts, "The Day We Didn't Go to War," the *Reporter*, Sept. 11, 1954; Stewart Alsop, "The Story Behind Quemoy," *Saturday Evening Post*, Dec. 13, 1958; Arthur Dean, "United States Foreign Policy and Formosa," *Foreign Affairs*, April 1955; John F. Kennedy, "A Democrat Looks at Foreign Policy," *Foreign Affairs*, October 1957; Allen S. Whiting, "The Logic of Communist China's Policy: The First Decade," *Yale Review*, September 1960; and Stanley K. Hornbeck, "Which China?" *Foreign Affairs*, October 1955.

For a firsthand account of contemporary China by an American, see Edgar Snow, "Report from Red China," *Look*, Jan. 31, 1961; his book *The Other Side of the River*, New York, 1962, and, somewhat later, "Interview with Mao," *New Republic*, Feb. 27, 1965.

Also in the area of contemporary books: American Assembly, *The United States and the Far East*, New York, 1956; E. O. Reischauer, *Wanted: An Asian Policy*, New York, 1955; Roscoe Drummond and Gaston Coblentz, *Duel at the Brink*, New York, 1960; and Sheldon Appleton, *The Eternal Triangle: Communist China, the United States and the United Nations*, East Lansing, Mich., 1961.

Chapter 12

Arthur Schlesinger's *A Thousand Days* and Theodore Sorensen's *Kennedy*, as already noted, add significantly to our knowledge of China policy during the Kennedy Administration. Other primary source material is largely limited to official documents, the speeches of the President and Secretary Rusk, and the *New York Times*. Rusk's early speeches have been collected by E. K. Lindley, *Winds of Freedom*, Boston, 1963, and there is a revealing article by Rusk before becoming Secretary of State, entitled "The President," *Foreign Affairs*, April 1960. For a later character sketch, see Milton Viorst, "Incidentally, Who *Is* Dean Rusk," *Esquire*, April 1968.

Books I have used on relations between Communist China and Soviet Russia during this period are Klaus Mehnert, *Peking and Moscow*, New York, 1963; Donald S. Zagoria, *The Sino-Soviet Conflict, 1956–61*, Princeton, N.J., 1962; William E. Griffith, *The Sino-Soviet Rift*, Cambridge, Mass., 1964; and Oliver E. Clubb, Jr., *The United States and the Sino-Soviet Bloc in Southeast Asia*, Washington, D.C., 1963.

Interesting articles are Byron S. Weng, "Communist China's Changing Attitudes Toward the United Nations," *International Organization*, Autumn 1966; Lincoln P. Bloomfield, "China, the United States and the United Nations," *International Organization*, Autumn 1966; and O. Edmund Clubb, "China's Position in Asia," *Journal of International Affairs*, No. 2, 1963.

Chapters 13 and 14

The growing volume of literature concerned with the United States deepening involvement in Vietnam during the Johnson Administration is quite beyond the province of these bibliographical notes. I will only mention such books especially useful for this narrative: Russell H. Fifield, *Southeast Asia in United States Policy*, New York, 1963; Marcus G. Raskin and Bernard B. Fall, *The Viet-Nam Reader*, New York, 1965; Theodore Draper, *Abuse of Power*, New York, 1967; Bernard B. Fall, *Anatomy of a Crisis*, Garden City, N.Y., 1969; and David Schoenbrun, *Viet Nam—How We Got In—How to Get Out*, New York, 1969.

A more general and sketchy account of foreign policies in this period is Philip L. Geyelin, *Lyndon B. Johnson and the World*, New York, 1966.

Contemporary articles illustrating both increasing interest in eastern Asia and the greater depth of China studies, factual and interpretive, cover a broad range of topics. A highly selective list would include John P. Roche, "Containing China: A Round-Table Discussion," *Commentary*, May 1966; John K. Fairbank, "The Great Wall," *New York Review*, March 28, 1968; Peter P. C. Cheng, "The Formosan Tangle: A Formosan's View," *Asian Survey*, November 1967; Tang Tsou, "Mao Tse-tung and Peaceful Coexistence," *Orbis*, Spring 1964; Samuel B. Griffith II, "Communist China's Capacity to Make War," *Foreign Affairs*, January 1965; Ralph L. Powell, "China's Bomb: Exploitation and Reaction," *Foreign Affairs*, July 1965; Melvin Gurtov, "Recent Developments on Formosa," *China Quarterly*, July-September 1967; Hugo Portisch, "Red China's Two Voices," *Atlas*, October 1964; and Chalmers Johnson, "China: The Cultural Revolution in Structural Perspective," *Asian Survey*, January 1968.

Interesting in their varied approaches are such books as George F. Kennan, *On Dealing with the Communist World*, New York, 1964; American Friends Service Committee, *A New China Policy—Some Quaker Proposals*, New Haven, Conn., 1965; Morton H. Halperin, *China and the Bomb*, New York, 1965; Harlan Cleveland, *The Obligations of Power*,

New York, 1966; J. W. Fulbright, *Old Myths and New Realities,* New York, 1964; and Edwin O. Reischauer, *Beyond Vietnam: The United States and Asia,* New York, 1967.

Chapter 15

The *State Department Bulletin* and the *New York Times,* supplemented by occasional articles in current periodicals, provide the material for the commencement of the Nixon Administration. The President's informal news conference at Guam was reported in full in the *Times* on July 26, 1969, and his report to Congress, "United States Foreign Policy for the 1970s: A New Strategy for Peace," is in that newspaper's issue of February 19, 1970.

Index